METHODISM AND THE WORKING-CLASS MOVEMENTS OF ENGLAND
1800–1850

By the Same Author

METHODISM AND THE COMMON PEOPLE OF THE EIGHTEENTH CENTURY

METHODISM
AND THE
WORKING-CLASS MOVEMENTS OF ENGLAND
1800-1850

By

ROBERT F. WEARMOUTH,

M.A., B.Sc., Ph.D.

THE EPWORTH PRESS
(EDGAR C. BARTON)
25-35 CITY ROAD, LONDON, E.C.1

First published in 1937
Reprinted 1947

To

MY WIFE AND SON

This book is produced in complete conformity with the Authorised Economy Standards

MADE AND PRINTED IN GREAT BRITAIN BY PURNELL AND SONS, LTD., PAULTON (SOMERSET) AND LONDON

CONTENTS

PART II

METHODISM AND THE POLITICAL SOCIETIES OF 1816–1850

PREFACE

THE subject of this book was first suggested to me by Mr. H. L. Beales, M.A., Reader at the London School of Economics and Political Science, through a conversation I had with him one day on the influence of the secular writers upon the early nineteenth-century reform movements. As the appointed adviser of my research studies for four years, he rendered invaluable help by his timely suggestions, his untiring patience when consulting him, and his lively interest in the work at all times. Due acknowledgement is here made to my wife and son for their ungrudging assistance in the preparation of the typescript. While preparing for the press, Mr. Sidney Walton, M.A., B.Litt., afforded useful aid in various ways. Last, but not least, I acknowledge a sense of everlasting gratitude to the Rev. John Clennell, who, as my first tutor, infected the mind with a passion for study, and thus made possible whatever scholastic achievements were afterwards attained. My eleven years' experience of work in a Durham coal mine, beginning at the age of twelve, has enabled me to understand more easily the working-class conditions and ambitions of a hundred years ago.

Much valuable help has also been rendered by the kindly officials of the Reading Room at the London School of Economics, at the British Museum Manuscript Department and General Reading Room, in the Newspaper Repository at Hendon, and at the Public Record Office in Chancery Lane.

ROBERT F. WEARMOUTH.

The publication of this work has been aided by a grant from the Publication Fund of the University of London.

PREFACE

THE subject of this book was first suggested to me by Mr. H. L. Beales, M.A., Reader at the London School of Economics and Political Science, through a conversation I had with him one day on the influence of the secular writers upon the early nineteenth-century reform movements. As the appointed adviser to my research studies for four years, he rendered invaluable help by his timely suggestions, his untiring patience when consulting him, and his lively interest in the work at all times. Due acknowledgement is here made to my [illegible] for [illegible] during the preparation of the typescript. While preparing for the press Mr. Simon [illegible], M.A., B.Litt., afforded useful aid in various ways. Last, but not least, I acknowledge a sense of everlasting gratitude to the Rev. John Clennell, who many years ago inflamed the mind with a passion for facts and thus made possible whatever [illegible] have since been attained. My eleven years' experience of work in a Durham coal mine, beginning at the age of twelve, has enabled me to understand more easily the working-class conditions and ambitions of a hundred years ago.

Much valuable help has also been rendered by the courteous officials of the Reading Room at the London School of Economics, the British Museum Manuscript Department and General Reading Room, the Newspaper Repository at Hendon, and at the Public Record Office in Chancery Lane.

ROBERT F. WEARMOUTH.

The publication of this work has been assisted by a grant from the Publication Fund of the University of London.

PREFACE TO SECOND EDITION

No change in the general plan or in the subject matter has been necessary for the publication of this new edition. A few mistakes in the spelling of names and places have been detected by friends and duly corrected. In this connection special thanks is given to the Rev. F. F. Bretherton, B.A., President and General Secretary of the Wesley Historical Society.

ROBERT F. WEARMOUTH.

May, 1946.

INTRODUCTION

THE PROGRESS, POLITY AND PRACTICE OF METHODISM

METHODISM, on the human side, can be regarded as the child of the Industrial Revolution. Its formative period belongs to the days when silent preparation was being made for revolutionary changes in productive activity. Its growth was slow in the decades when industrial endeavour was still sleepy and sluggish. Its expansion increased as the use of machinery extended. Its success was greatest where new manufactories created additional towns and populous districts. It began to slacken its pace after industry had reached its highest development.

The relation can be put in another way. Would Methodism have been possible had no Industrial Revolution taken place? Could it have been established if populations and districts had remained static? What might have been the confines of this religious revival without the improvement of roads, the introduction of gas-light, and the advent of railways? What sort of meeting-house would have been built minus the increase of capital and bereft of 'the captains of industry'? Think of it how we may, Methodism has always been inexplicably associated with the rise and fall of commercial prosperity. While it may be true to say that Methodism was the child of the Industrial Revolution and was as a consequence greatly affected thereby, it is equally true to say that Methodism aided the progress of industrial activity. The agents of the one were influenced by the agents of the other. Sometimes the agents were the same people, who, operating with similar vehicles, became important in each of the spheres of communal undertaking.

When John Wesley died in 1791, about 80,000 persons were attached to the societies which had been under his care. During his lifetime the Methodist movement had been entirely homogeneous. Immediately after his death the heterogeneous elements began to express themselves. The first division occurred when the New Connexion was formally instituted. Alexander Kilham, one of John Wesley's preachers, and one who was somewhat influenced by the spirit of the age, became the leading religious revolutionary. His rebellious activities were soon terminated by his early decease, due no doubt to overwork and anxiety. The work, however, was continued by others, but progress was exceedingly slow for several decades.

During the years 1807 and 1812 another democratic element was thrown off by the parent body. The Primitive Methodist Connexion, the most successful of all the Methodist offshoots, was established in 1812. This had been made inevitable by the official ban on religious camp meetings.[1] Hugh Bourne, William Clowes, and James Steele, the exponents of this new type of open-air service, were expelled from the Wesleyan Connexion for their disobedience to the Conference command. Their expulsion gave them more freedom to organize camp meeting supporters, who also devoted their talents to the advance of the new cause.

In 1815, William O'Bryan, another Methodist rebel, who refused to be confined within official limits, was instrumental in forming an additional sect called the Bible Christians. Further trouble ensued in 1826 when the Protestant Methodists were established through a dispute over the introduction of an organ in Leeds. A more disastrous dispute occurred nine years later on account of the divided opinion on the administration of the first theological college. After a costly lawsuit between the two contending parties, Dr. Warren, the leader of the rebels against officialism, formed his supporters into a separate religious community and called them the Wesleyan Central Association. The most bitter conflict of Methodist history began in 1849. Influenced by democratic ideas a number of laymen and ministers demanded a greater share in the administration of the laws of the Connexion. This was refused and the ministers were expelled. The final result was the loss of more than 100,000 members and the formation of another Methodist cause.

Although the first half of the nineteenth century can be regarded as the most turbulent in the history of the Methodist Church, yet strange to say it has been the most successful.

[1] The Wesleyan Conference declared 'that even supposing such meetings be allowable in America, they are highly improper in England, and are likely to be productive of considerable mischief. And we disclaim all connexion with them'.—Conference Minutes, 1807.

Throughout the whole of this time, with only one or two exceptions, a continual advance was registered. It was evidently a case of multiplication by division. Methodism developed more rapidly after the death of John Wesley than it did during his lifetime.

The Wesleyan Methodists began the nineteenth century with 90,000 members enrolled in their societies. Apart from two or three exceptions, they yearly increased their numbers until 1850. The first relapse occurred in the turbulent year of 1819. At the Conference of 1820, 5,388 fewer members were reported. A slight decrease, chiefly due to the Warrenite dispute, took place in 1835. Further decreases, mainly caused by the economic depression in the periods concerned, were recorded in 1837, 1842, 1847, and 1848. An additional reason for the relapse of 1842 was the industrial dispute which affected all the Methodist denominations. Yet in spite of these reactions, the numbers reported for 1850 amounted to 358,277 in Great Britain alone, representing an increase during fifty years of over 260,000.[1]

Although the New Connexion Methodists possessed a more democratic constitution than the Wesleyans, their progress was nevertheless slow. In 1849 they counted 17,656 members.[2] The Primitive Methodists, more democratic still in their principles and practice, made substantial progress. Starting with 200 members in 1812, they reached a total of 104,762 by the year 1850.[3] The Bible Christian Methodists counted 10,146 members in 1852, while the Wesleyan Methodist Association, which comprised the Protestant Methodists, the Arminian Methodists, and the Central Association, reported 19,411.[4]

Altogether, the total number of Methodists (apart from the Calvinistic Methodists and the Countess of Huntingdon's Connexion) enrolled as members in 1850 represented one in every thirty-four of the whole nation. But in order to estimate more correctly the proportion some account must be taken of the large number of people that attended Methodist services as adherents. This number has been variously estimated. Some historians believe that the adherents were five times greater than the registered members. Horace Mann, in his census report for

[1] Wesleyan Conference Minutes, 1820–50.
[2] Methodist New Connexion Minutes, 1849.
[3] Primitive Methodist Conference Minutes, 1850.
[4] Census of Religious Worship, *Parliamentary Papers*, 1852–3, Vol. lxxxix, pp. 89, 91.

1851 (*Parliamentary Papers*, 1852–3, Vol. LXXXIX, p. 82), expressed the opinion 'that the number of persons attending upon the ministrations of the Wesleyan societies' was 'about three times the number of communicants'. On this reckoning the grand total under direct Methodist influence in 1850 would approximate to at least two million people.

In some districts the percentage was greater. The census returns for 1851 show that, out of a population of 1,789,047 in the three Ridings of Yorkshire, 329,572 persons attended the Methodist evening service on census Sunday. This represented one-sixth of the whole population. In Cornwall the percentage was higher. 126,401 people attended the Methodist chapels out of a population of 355,558 approximately one-third. In the area comprising Durham, Northumberland, Cumberland, and Westmorland, 132,622 attended the Methodist meeting-houses out of a population of 969,126, roughly one-seventh. In Lancashire and Cheshire the proportion was less. The number of people attending the evening service out of a population of 2,490,827 amounted to 215,273, about one-twelfth. If any account be taken of the numbers which attended morning and evening services, then the percentage must be considerably higher. While great caution must be exercised when using these figures, they undoubtedly harmonize with facts obtained from other sources.

During this period of progress, the number of Methodist places opened for public worship constantly increased. In 1801 the total number of Methodist meeting-houses was reported to be 825, which provided 165,000 seats. Fifty years later, there were 11,000, with sittings for 2,194,298 people or about one-eighth of the entire population.

Another portion of the population that came under Methodist influence and that cannot be correctly estimated, but must have been considerable, has been usually ignored. Every year a large number of Methodists were taken off the membership roll book for one reason or another. Many of these were called 'backsliders'. Some of these folk, although they had left the Methodist Church, still retained in various degrees, the effect of the Methodist teaching. Others had gone to the Established Church or associated with the older Nonconformist bodies.

If any explanation of this rapid advance is desired, then some account of the circumstances of the time must be given. One factor in the situation was the vast increase in the population that constantly took place. In 1769 the number of inhabitants was not more than eight and a half millions.[1] At the first census of 1801, returns for Great Britain revealed a population of 8,892,536. In 1831 it had passed thirteen millions. By 1851 over seventeen millions are reported. Another factor in the circumstances was the failure of the Established Church to provide for the needs of the new districts. The machinery for creating additional parishes was old and cumbersome. Consequently the building of new churches did not keep pace with the increase of population. Practically nothing was done in this direction until 1817–19, when a million pounds were granted by Parliament for the erection of new places of worship. Nevertheless, progress was still slow and there was always a surplus of population that could not find access to the parish church had they wished. In the parish of Marylebone for the year 1811, there were 60,000 inhabitants while the seating capacity of the local church was only 900. That of St. Pancras was in the same predicament.[2] In 1,047 selected parishes, each containing more than 1,000 persons, there was a total population of 3,460,560, yet the seating accommodation in the parish churches for the same areas was approximately 1,054,231.[3] Earl Stanhope about the same time estimated that 4,000,000 people in England 'had not the means of attending Church'.[4]

There was still a big deficiency of churches in 1824. Manchester had a population of 187,000 and the seating capacity of the Established Church was 22,468. Birmingham had a population of 100,000 and church accommodation for 16,000. Leeds had 84,000 and the Church provided seats for 10,000.[5]

The situation was no better in 1831, although more than a million pounds had been granted by the Government for the building of new churches. Cheshire had on an average one church for every 2,355 inhabitants of the county; Lancashire one for 4,578; Middlesex one for 5,522; Surrey one for 3,059, and the West Riding of Yorkshire one for 3,431.

[1] *Economic Organization of England*, by Sir William Ashley, p .119.
[2] *Quarterly Review*, 1811. Vol. v, p. 365.
[3] *ibid.*, 1813. Vol. x, p. 56.
[4] *Parliamentary Debates*, July 3, 1812. Vol. xxiii, p. 888.
[5] *ibid.*, April 9, 1824. Vol. xi, pp. 344–5.

An improvement had been made by 1851. Cheshire had one church for every 1,868 of the population; Lancashire one for 3,899; Middlesex one for 4,658; Surrey one for 2,743, and West Riding one for 2,384. The total provision by the Establishment, in the rural parishes amounted to only 66 per cent of the population. In the urban parishes it was even less, being only 46 per cent. The county of Lancashire suffered the most in this respect, 40.3 per cent of the inhabitants having seating accommodation. In Durham it was 46.7 per cent. In Northumberland the percentage amounted to 48.8.[1]

Another factor that must not be ignored was the disfavour in which the Established Church seemed to be held by a large section of the working-class community. In all the Radical movements of the first half of the nineteenth century, the Church was held up to ridicule. The high stipends obtained by the bishops and the anti-democratic attitude of most of the clerical magistrates were causes of constant complaint.

All these circumstances gave opportunity to the Methodists to plant their societies. In this matter they were not slow to act. Their agents were always on the lookout to establish new branches. In fact everybody was exhorted to be a missionary and a propagandist. Enthusiasm in this direction was considered an important virtue.

But if a fuller explanation for the progress of the movement be desired, some recognition must be given to the polity adopted by the various sects. Methodism was really republican in Government. At the head of each denomination there existed with limited powers a president. In each case he was elected for twelve months. Re-election was possible, but this occurred only at rare intervals. Absolute control was vested in the Annual Assembly called the Conference. Legislation and administration for the whole body rested entirely with this assembly. Between the periods of its sittings, administration was relegated to an executive committee elected by the Conference or to the district and local courts.

Among the Wesleyans the Annual Assembly was composed entirely of itinerant preachers until 1878, when the laity were first admitted. The constitution of the Conference has exposed

[1] Census of Religious Worship. *Parliamentary Papers*, 1852–3. Vol. lxxxix, pp. 43–131.

the Mother Church of Methodism to very severe criticism, but it must be remembered that among the Methodist societies the itinerant preacher is not far removed from his fellow Methodists. He does not claim any special ecclesiastical unction. The only difference between him and the local preacher is that the latter is a part-time and he is a full-time agent. By virtue of that fact he is more able to devote himself to the work of the Connexion. Moreover, every itinerant must first of all be a member, then a local preacher, unless received as a minister direct from other religious bodies. So there was not the gulf between the Methodist preacher and his flock as some critics seem to assume.

It must also be remembered that the Methodist fellowship was a voluntary one. No one was compelled to be associated with it. Anyone who disagreed with its method of control could at any moment withdraw.

The Primitive Methodist section went to the other extreme in their form of government. Breathing the spirit of the age (which was definitely anti-clerical) and being comprised mostly of the poorer portions of the community, they protected their organization against ecclesiastical predominance. It was arranged that in every Church court from the Conference to the Quarterly Meeting there should be two lay representatives to every minister. That indeed was a sample of democratic authority in 'Church government'.

The other Methodist sections steered a middle course and gave equal administrative and legislative powers to ministers and laymen alike. Needless to say, the arrangement has always worked amicably and successfully.

An important phase of Methodist history is connected with the practical side. Not all the members and adherents were interested, or cared to be interested in, the polity and doctrines of their Church. Most of them, however, were concerned about the exercise of their religious principles. There must have been something attractive in the appeal of Methodism. The response given to it by the working classes was indeed extraordinary. That response was not impulsive or intermittent. It was rather enthusiastic and continuous. What is the explanation? Are the democratic practices or the fundamental doctrines a sufficient explanation? One thing can be said with certainty. Methodism attracted men because it gave them opportunity to exercise their mental and moral powers. It gave them something to do, and thus made them feel they had a share in, and a responsibility for, the success of the movement. It utilized in a remarkable way the talents of the laymen. This employment of the laity represents a new feature in English religious history. In the Methodist society working men, and even women, were often authorized to exercise their talents by doing evangelistic work on behalf of their Church. The seal of authority was placed upon them by making them into class leaders, local preachers, exhorters, and prayer leaders. It was not an uncommon experience for a man of enthusiasm to be requested to form a class with only his own name on the roll book. In a case like this, the ways and means were usually left to his own initiative. He had practically a free hand in the matter. Henceforth his chief concern was to win recruits for his class, and, having enrolled them as members, to watch over their spiritual interests. Sometimes a local preacher or prayer leader might be asked to visit a new district and engage in missionary enterprise in the name of Methodism. In these and other ways the gifts and enthusiasm of a large number of earnest people were enlisted in the Methodist cause. The art of propaganda was one of the most used arts among these religious folk. It was always being exploited by them. The erection of a chapel, the building of a school, the formation of a small society, the beginning of a new class, and even the revival of an old cause, were often dependent upon a plan proposed and carried through by a single individual or a group of people.

Hugh Bourne, a humble carpenter, William Clowes, a working potter, and others of similar position, were responsible for the origin and the organization of the Primitive Methodist Church. When formulating their principles and making their rules, they had help from no one above their own station in life. Nevertheless, the plan which they made has remained in operation for more than a century. William O'Bryan, a farmer's son, by his initiative and persistency was mainly responsible for the formation of the Bible Christian Connexion.

A Methodist class meeting appeared to have a special attraction for working-class people. Every society in the Connexion had its class meetings. These consisted of small groups of Christians who met regularly together for mutual help and fellowship.

Their meeting place was sometimes a private house or a room in the local chapel. A roll of members was carefully kept, and membership tickets were issued quarterly. Every registered member was expected to contribute one penny a week towards the general funds of the society, and something extra when he received his class ticket. Membership of the class always carried with it membership of the Methodist Society. The weekly meeting was somewhat like a family gathering. There was usually a free and easy atmosphere about the place. Each person who attended was expected to take some part in the devotions. He might read the lesson, offer an extempore prayer, or relate his Christian experience. In most cases the leader of the class presided at the meeting, or he might relegate the duty occasionally to the assistant leader. The appointment of class leaders belonged to the Circuit Quarterly Meeting, though nominations might be made by Leaders' Meetings or individual classes.[1] These class meetings provided the life-blood for the Methodist Connexion. Without them Methodism could not have built up such a vigorous constitution. Horace Mann in 1851 (Census of Religious Worship, *Parliamentary Papers*, 1852–3, Vol. LXXXIX, p. 79) regarded 'the system of class-meetings' as 'the very life of Methodism.'

The class leader occupied a very important position in the life of the local society. He was a kind of spiritual adviser to a number of selected people. He was expected to meet them as a group once a week, give them instruction and advice, and collect their class money. Each individual member was taught to regard him as a friend and a shepherd of souls. If they were sick, he had to visit them. If they were negligent in spiritual matters, he must rebuke or exhort them as occasion demanded. His position as a class leader made him a member of the Leaders' Meeting. This meeting was a kind of presbytery which governed the spiritual concerns of the society. All the class leaders came to this meeting, and once a quarter paid to the financial steward the total subscriptions from the members of his class.

The duty of a steward in the Wesleyan Connexion was mainly financial. Once a quarter he received the class money from the various class leaders. He also took charge of the weekly

[1] In Wesleyan Methodism the Superintendent Minister made the nomination and the Leaders' Meeting the appointment.

collections at the public services. Collections for the poor were usually handed to him. From this various income he paid the ordinary charges against the society and provided for the allowances granted to the travelling preacher. In the other Methodist denominations the duty of the steward is mainly spiritual. He is expected to exercise a general oversight of the spiritual concerns of the society. The only financial task relegated to him is to receive the weekly public collections and pass them on to the circuit steward.

The local preacher was also a very important person in the Methodist denominations. Because of some special feature manifested in his character, experience, or mentality, he was given authority to occupy the pulpit and exercise the gifts of a preacher. In large circuits where there were few travelling preachers, the pulpit work of the societies was always carried on by the local preachers. Many of these men were engaged two and three times every Sunday—oftentimes for long periods together. This constant opportunity for oratorical exercises eventually made most of them into acceptable speakers. It was easy and natural for these men who had cultivated their gifts in this way to use such gifts in the spheres of industrial and civic life. That some of them did so, available evidence clearly demonstrates.

Another distinctive position occupied by laymen was that of trustee. This post was often reserved for the wealthy members of society and for the higher class artisan, though a large number of the lower classes at various times were appointed as trustees. The appointment of trustees largely depended on the local circumstances. If a sufficient number of men from the higher ranks were not available, then candidates for the position had to be found among other classes. Among the younger denominations of Methodism the majority of trustees came from the ranks of working men. Every Methodist building was administered by a body of trustees on behalf of the Methodist Connexion. Their chief duties were financial. They were expected to promote ways and means to pay for the erection of Methodist property and to provide the necessary funds for maintenance of the same in good repair and condition.

The exercise of these various functions by laymen in the Methodist constitution entrusted to them a great deal of power and responsibility. Anyone acquainted with the nature of these functions must eventually conclude that Methodism, both in organization and administration, was not autocratic in practice, but liberal and democratic. When seeking a remedy for the estrangement of the working classes from the Established Church, Horace Mann (Census of Religious Worship, *Parliamentary Papers*, 1852–3, Vol. LXXXIX, pp. 168–9) turns to the methods of Methodism. He suggested the adoption of 'a plan afforded by the Methodist community, in which some ten or fifteen thousand laymen are employed not merely in the work of visitation, but also in that of preaching'. 'Nothing, probably,' he asserts, 'has more contributed than this to their success amongst the working population.'

It is very difficult to estimate the extent of the influence of Methodist laymen during the first fifty years of the nineteenth century, but that influence must have been considerable. If numbers alone were counted their influence must have been extraordinary. In the year 1850, over 20,000 laymen occupied the position of local preacher. The exact number of class leaders cannot be calculated. If there was one class leader to every ten members, then the total number of leaders must have exceeded 50,000. It would be nearer the mark to say that 25,000 had been appointed class leaders. Add to these numbers those who exercised the functions of trustee, steward, exhorter, prayer leader, and Sunday-school teacher, then some conception can be had of laity influence.

Leaving aside theological conceptions of the movement of the spirit in man and democratic ideas of methods of government and administration, the many and various opportunities afforded by Methodism for laymen to exercise their gifts, to assume responsibility, and to occupy official positions, explain to a large extent the success of the movement and its attraction for the working classes.

PART I

METHODISM AND MOB VIOLENCE

CHAPTER I

LUDDISM AND OTHER DISTURBANCES

THE widespread disturbances of 1811–1816, as the Hammonds point out, 'can only rightly be understood in connexion with what comes before and after.'[1] A knowledge of the antecedents helps one more easily to diagnose the nature of the complaint and to ascertain the real cause of the trouble. As early as 1800 the Home Office Papers reveal a growing discontent in almost every part of the country. Without exception the root of the grievances was the high cost of necessities. At Nottingham, in April, the Town Clerk reports a tumult in the market-place because of the exorbitant price of food. Two or three of the rioters were in consequence arrested and imprisoned. Similar news came from other centres. In a message from Lichfield the Home Secretary was informed that the colliers 'would rather die by the point of the sword than be starved to death by the farmers'.[2]

After the suppression of these riots some attempt was made to relieve the situation. The Home Office requested the bishops and clergy to report from their respective vicinities the state of crops and the general level of prices. As a result of their reports a proclamation was made recommending 'the greatest Economy and Frugality in the use of every Species of Grain'.[3]

The ebullitions of 1800 and 1801 had been signs of the coming storm. Though information concerning the state of working-class feeling is rather meagre at the Home Office for the years 1801–1810, indications from other sources reveal a growing discontent. Sir Samuel Romilly, writing to M. Dumont in Paris on August 25, 1807, expressed his alarm when he said, 'What is passing abroad, and what is passing at home, affords us but a melancholy prospect; and a man with but little foresight, and only a slight attention to what he sees, even though he

[1] *The Skilled Labourer*. J. L. & B. Hammond, p. 257.
[2] H.O. 42, 52, 1800.
[3] *ibid.*, 42, 55, 1800.

be not either of a very gloomy or a very timid disposition, must think that this country will be fortunate indeed, if it is not soon involved, and perhaps for a long period, in turbulence and disorder'.[1]

The first signs of the prophesied disorder were seen in Nottingham among the framework knitters in 1811 and 1812. Appeals and protests had been presented to the employers by these workmen against the low price of their product. Some of the more humane masters increased their wages. Others rejected every appeal. As a consequence, in March, 1811, over sixty frames belonging to an obnoxious employer at Arnold were broken by bands of enraged workmen. Later in the year more frames were destroyed at Arnold, Bulwell, Basford, and other villages. At Bulwell one of the rioters was killed. He was a weaver from Arnold. When the funeral took place on the following Thursday, 'the scene was truly awful. The High Sheriff, the Under Sheriff, and about half a dozen Magistrates were on the spot, attended by a posse of Constables, and about thirty mounted dragoons, who all proceeded with the funeral to the churchyard; and before the body was removed the Riot Act was read in several parts of the town'.[2] The day before the funeral, fifty-three frames and a corn mill were destroyed at Sutton in the daytime. Other frames were demolished at Kimberley toward the end of the week. During this outbreak, a number of rioters were arrested, but only four committed. In the following week, twenty frames were broken at Basford and several others at Bulwell. These apparently had been destroyed while being removed into Nottingham for safety, although guarded by the military. Before the end of the year, further frames had been broken at Beeston, New Radford, Basford, Ilkeston, and Heanor. The work of destruction spread into Pentridge, Heage, South Wingfield, and Sheepshed. On December 21, the *Leeds Mercury* correspondent reporting from Nottingham says, 'the Insurrectional state to which this county has been reduced for the last month has no parallel in history, since the troubled days of Charles the First.' 'Day after day have the Magistrates, both of the town and county, used every possible endeavour to restore tranquillity; day after day have they added to the strength

[1] *Life of Sir Samuel Romilly*, by his Sons, Vol. ii, p. 233.
[2] *Leeds Mercury*, Nov. 23, 1811.

and activity of the civil powers and called in additional aid of the military; but hitherto their exertions have been of little avail; a mysterious organization has been brought into existence, which baffles every opportunity to suppress it.' In another report (*Leeds Mercury*, December 14, 1811) the rioters were said to be going about 'in small parties, disguised, with their faces besmeared,' placing 'sentinels at the doors' of the houses where the frames were kept, while they 'accomplished their purpose without the least noise'. 'They communicate with each other by means of a watchword, and the firing of a pistol, or gun, is generally the signal of danger, or retreat.' In less than two months 900 frames had been broken, each of them having originally cost £140. By the aid of a secret committee, with the Nottingham Town Clerk as secretary, strenuous attempts were made to suppress the acts of violence. Although handsome rewards were offered for information that would lead to arrest and conviction, no one appeared willing to take such a course of action. On the other hand, according to the *Leeds Mercury* (December 28, 1811), 'the Luddites retaliated and published a proclamation, offering a reward of £2,300 under a solemn promise of secrecy, to anyone, who would give information of any person having given information to the Secret Committee'.

The local authorities appeared to be almost helpless. They appealed to the military and consulted the Home Office. Troops were sent to quell the disorders, and Parliament amended the law against riotous conduct.[1] That not being sufficient the alarmists in the House of Commons hastily passed the Watch and Ward Act.[2] By the help of soldiers and special constables,

[1] United Kingdom Statutes 52, George III, 1812. Cap. XVI. 'An Act for the more exemplary Punishment of Persons destroying or injuring any Stocking or Lace Frames, or other Machines or Engines used in the Framework Knitting Manufactory of any Articles or Goods in such Frames or Machines.' Passed March 20, 1812. Any persons convicted under the Act had to be 'adjudged guilty of Felony, and Shall suffer Death, as in cases of Felony without Benefit of Clergy', p. 48.

[2] *ibid.*, Cap. XVII. 'An Act for the more effectual Preservation of the Peace, by enforcing the Duties of Watching and Warding, until the First Day of March one thousand eight hundred and fourteen, in Places where Disturbances prevail or are apprehended.' Under this Act every man above the age of seventeen and charged or assessed for poor rate was liable to the 'Duties of Watching by Night, and Warding by Day'. 'The Cristos Rotulorum' or Sheriff, or Five Justices had the power under the Act of calling a Session of Justices to decide 'the Expediency of carrying into effect all or any of the Powers and Provisions of this Act', p. 50. Those appointed to the duty of Watch and Ward were to be called 'special constables' and to be under the control of the chief constable of the hundred. They had to be given payment or compensation for their services, p, 53.

some of the rioters were arrested. They were tried in the following March, when seven of their number were transported for a term of seven to fourteen years.

Quietude reigned for a time, but the cause of the trouble remained. The discontented labourers began to meet in secret again. On November 16, 1813, societies of desperate characters are reported at Nottingham. In the February of 1814, Coldham, the Town Clerk of Nottingham, expresses his concern about these societies and suggests the employment of an informer. At the beginning of April, he reports three frames broken at Kimberley belonging to Messrs. Needham and Nixon, and he adds, 'they have been one of the leading Houses in refusing to advance 2d. a pair to a certain Description of Workmen, who have requested and demanded it of their masters'. A fortnight later, he says, 'the disturbances are spreading.'[1] With the advent of the autumn, conditions did not improve, neither did the activities of Coldham diminish. Having associated himself with the hosiers in refusing a requested advance in wages, he also co-operated with them in trying to suppress the various societies and combinations of the workmen. A further explosion of violence was therefore not surprising. During October, an attack was made at Basford on the house of an informer named Garton, and unfortunately two men were killed. In the summer of 1815, General Ludd is still at work, for Mr. G. Sutton, the editor of the *Nottingham Review*, is threatened with a lawsuit because he published one of the General's letters. Before the spring of 1816, Coldham's activity had ended on account of his decease, and his work on the secret committee at Nottingham, which had for its purpose the inquiry into and the suppression of the Luddite violence, was continued by Enfield, his successor as Town Clerk. On June 11, Enfield informs the Home Office 'that the Luddites have again commenced their lawless outrages'.[2] Nineteen lace frames are broken at New Radford. The factory of Messrs. Heathcote and Bodens at Loughborough is attacked and several frames are destroyed. In the following October, a report to the Home Office says that frame breaking still goes on. At the commencement of the year 1817, Luddism was gradually changing its character. One account says, 'The Luddites are now principally engaged in politics and poaching. They are the principal

[1] H.O. 42. 138, 1814. [2] *ibid.*, 42. 151, 1816.

leaders in the Hampden clubs which are now formed in almost every village in the angle between Leicester, Derby and Newark'.[1]

The outbreak in Lancashire followed closely on the heels of that in Nottingham. Signs of the gathering clouds were reported on February 21, 1811, by Chippendale of Oldham. He tells of two armed meetings at Chadderton. A year later, news comes from the Rev. Prescott of Stockport of threats to break machinery. An April 12, informers report that men are joining General Ludd's army. In the same month, riots break out at Manchester, Ashton, Oldham, Rochdale, and Middleton. Fifty rioters are said to have been killed at Manchester. At Middleton on April 20, an attack is made on Mr. Burton's manufactory, and five of the attackers are killed. Two days later, a second attack was made before military assistance could be procured, and Mr. Burton's house was burnt. On that occasion, four of the attacking party were shot dead, and several wounded. On April 24, the factory at West Houghton was destroyed by fire. By the end of April, most of the disturbances had ceased and many of the rioters were in prison, thirty-eight of whom were awaiting their trial for felony. In addition, forty-four prisoners had been lodged in Chester gaol. Special Commissions were appointed by the Government to try the prisoners. At the Chester trial fourteen received sentence of death, and eight were transported for seven years. Of the fourteen that received sentence of death, five were reserved for execution, but only two were finally hung, Joseph Thompson and John Temples. Baron Thompson presided over the Lancaster Commission. Eight of the prisoners were sentenced to death, and seventeen were transported for seven years.[2]

The Luddite disturbances in Yorkshire commenced about the same time as those in Lancashire. Labour-saving machinery had been introduced into several mills, and it was chiefly against these mills that attacks were made. Indications of violence were given as early as the third week in January, 1812. The magistrates of Leeds, having received notification of the intention to break machinery, made defensive preparations, and the rioters were dispersed without doing any damage. On the following Sunday night, however, 'the Gig Mill of Messrs. Oates, Wood

[1] H.O. 42. 158, 1817.

[2] *Leeds Mercury*, June 13, 1812.

and Smithson, at Oatlands, near Woodhouse-Car, was discovered to be on fire'.[1] A few weeks later, the premises of Mr. Joseph Hirst of Marsh, Huddersfield, were entered and great damage was done. 'With their faces blackened, and their persons in other respects disguised,' a number of men, 'having forcibly obtained admittance into the dressing shops, proceeded to destroy all the machinery used in the dressing of cloth, such as dressing frames, shears, and other implements used in what is commonly called Gig Mills, the whole of which were completely demolished.'[2] On March 15, Joseph Radcliffe reports that eleven houses had already suffered depredation. In Mr. Vickerman's establishment at Taylor Hill, near Huddersfield, ten frames and thirty pairs of shears were broken. A few days later, Messrs. Thompsons' mill at Rawdon, near Leeds, was attacked and the machinery destroyed. About the same time several cloths were cut to pieces at Dickenson's premises in Leeds. During the night of April 9, the mill of Joseph Foster at Horbury was entered and many shears and some machinery were demolished. In the night of April 12, William Cartwright's mill at Rawfolds, near Cleckheaton, was attacked. The attackers were driven off, leaving two of their number mortally wounded. On April 14, a food riot occurred at Sheffield. Four days later, W. Cartwright was fired upon, but escaped injury. On April 28, Mr. William Horsfall of Marsden, a manufacturer who had adopted labour-saving machinery, was waylaid and killed.

In spite of the application of the Watch and Ward Act, the depredations continued. During the month of May, according to the *Leeds Mercury* (May 9 and 16, 1812), gangs of twenty and thirty men roamed the countryside, entering people's houses and demanding arms 'on pain of instant death'. Houses were entered at Almondbury, Wooldale, Farnley, Netherby, Meltham, Honley, and Marsden. About the same time windows were broken at Kirkgate, a thrashing machine and a building burnt at Soothill, a beanstack set on fire at Cawthorne, while eleven pairs of shears belonging to Mr. Cartwright's mill were seized and destroyed. In the month of June firearms were repeatedly taken 'by force and intimidation'. Houses were entered at Norbury, Netherton, Ossett, Lee Fair, Holmfirth, Kirkburton, Lockwood, and Huddersfield. Relief ultimately came in the following months. One

[1] *Leeds Mercury*, Jan. 18 and 25, 1812. [2] *ibid.*, Feb. 29, 1812.

reporter (*Leeds Mercury*, Aug. 22, 1812), with a certain amount of satisfaction, reports that 'General Ludd, it seems, is either dead or in a very sickly state, for he never troubles us now'. Perhaps the reason for this was to be found in the fact that the chief leaders were in prison, and among the rest quite a number were abjuring their Luddite pledge and signing the oath of allegiance. When the Special Commission was opened at York on January 2, 1813, the three murderers of Horsfall were sentenced to death. Eight men were tried for the attack on Cartwright's mill, five of whom were found guilty and afterwards executed. Nine others received the same penalty for taking arms and money. Six were transported for seven years.[1]

In a review of the situation, the Secret Committee Report given to the House of Commons on Wednesday, July 8, 1812, stated 'that alarming disturbances, destructive to property, prevailed in the counties of Lancashire, York, &c., and had continued from the month of March, down to the latest accounts on the 23rd of June'. It was also stated 'that the rioters assembled in the night time, with their faces blackened, armed with the implements of their trades, and other offensive instruments, with which they destroyed the property of those that were obnoxious to them'. 'The first object of these rioters seemed to be the breaking of machinery; but they had in many instances resorted to measures infinitely more alarming, namely, demanding of arms; and even carried them off.' 'Sometimes the rioters were under the control of Leaders; and were distinguished not by names but by numbers; were known to each other by signs and countersigns; and carried on all with the utmost caution. They also took an oath' that 'they would not reveal anything . . . under the penalty of being put out of existence.' 'They adopted and submitted to a military discipline; they had regular muster-rolls.' 'They also had their Committees and Sub-Committees, and countersigns, by which they made their written communication.' 'It further appeared that two-pence a week was appointed to be paid by each member to their respective Delegates.'[2]

[1] *Leeds Mercury*, Jan. 16, 1813. Also *The Skilled Labourer*, J. L. & Barbara Hammond, p. 332. Also Report of Proceedings for the County of York, held at the Castle of York from Jan. 2 to 12, 1813, from the shorthand notes of Mr. Gurney, London.

[2] *Leeds Mercury*, July 11, 1812. For a fuller account of Luddism see *Popular Disturbances and Public Order in Regency England*. F. O. Darvall.

Disturbances also occurred at other places. In the latter part of February, 1815, and the early part of March, mob violence broke out in different parts of London.[1] At the end of March, reports from Worship Street Police Office assert that placards on the walls announce the purpose of the rioters to be 'Blood or bread'. 'Don't press the poor too much', read another declaration. 'We have 200 Billinghams.'[2] About the same time keelmen in Sunderland objected to the introduction of machinery and ordered a cessation of work. During the course of the strike enraged workmen destroyed a bridge and set fire to the works of Mr. Nesham. The trouble spread to South Shields, and Robert Green of that town avows that 'all riots invariably begin here, and remain here longest, as the population is particularly riotous, and disorderly'.[3] Before the end of the year, 'riots and disturbances' had broken out in the neighbourhood of Wolverhampton. Lord Talbot observed in his report to the Home Office that 'the whole of this unpleasant business appears to me to have originated in the determination of the Iron Masters to lower wages'.[4] In the course of the following year, riots were reported from Norfolk, Suffolk, Cambridge, and Huntingdon, those in the Isle of Ely being the most serious.

The Rev. Sir B. Dudley, a local magistrate, was very active in the suppression of the riots at Ely. During his temporary absence from the locality, his fellow magistrates agreed with the demand of the labourers that the farmers should pay them 2s. per day, and that the one who hired them should pay the full wage. The latter agreement eliminated the working of the Speenhamland system. But these concessions were too generous for the minister of the Church, and he repudiates them while complaining to the Home Office concerning the weakness of his brother magistrates. For a time he forgets his pastoral functions as a 'Shepherd of the sheep' and leads the military into action against the rioters. During the affray two desperadoes are killed and eighty-six arrested. Major-General Byng afterwards confessed that it was through the 'prompt and determined measures' taken by the magistrate that the riots were 'so completely put down'. The Bishop of Ely commends his faithful clerygman for the 'firmness', 'decision', 'promptitude', and

[1] H.O. 42. 142 & 143, 1815.
[2] *ibid.* 42. 143, 1815.
[3] *ibid.* 42. 147, 1815.
[4] *ibid.* 42. 147, 1815.

'energy' which he had displayed at Ely. It must have been very encouraging to the shepherd of human souls to hear one of the learned judges declare at the Special Assize that 'former good characters ought to have less weight upon the present occasion', and to know that, although many of the prisoners had 'the best characters', twenty-four of them received the capital sentence.[1]

Other disturbances occurred in the West Riding of Yorkshire during 1817. On the evening of June 8, a number of conspirators, it was said, were engaged in a plan by which 'all the military in every district of the kingdom should be secured in their quarters, their arms seized, and that the magistrates and their civil officers should be arrested and placed in a state of restraint'. To carry out this design they had assembled at a public house in Thornhill Lees[2] where 'they were surrounded by a detachment of Yeomanry Cavalry, and taken into custody'. As they were being removed to Wakefield, the cavalry that escorted them were attacked 'by the populace with stones, brick-bats, &c., thrown with great violence. The prisoners were, however, safely lodged in the House of Correction'.[3]

Another disturbing affair took place at Folly-hall bridge on the night of June 8. 'Two or three hundred persons, it is said many of them boys from fourteen to twenty years, assembled' at this place during the darkness. A man named Taylor 'placed himself at their head, and at 12 o'clock, the moment of commencing operations, this fanatic addressed his followers in these terms: "Now, my lads, all England is in arms—our liberties are secure—the rich will be poor, and the poor will be rich". Six yeomanry came upon the scene, but retired for reinforcements. On their return, the would-be insurgents had dispersed. In the meantime, a sort of under-plot was acting and a number of marauders were passing about the neighbourhood, forcing the peaceable inhabitants to open their doors and surrender their firearms'. At Honley, they broke into the house of Mr. Armitage, and the dwelling of Mrs. Dyson was burgled at the same place.[4] In the course of the night, 'an attempt was made

[1] H.O. 42. 150 & 151, 1816.

[2] According to the Hammonds, Oliver the spy had brought these men together. When arrested with the others, General Byng 'contrived his escape and sent him off by mail . . . for Nottingham and Birmingham'. *The Skilled Labourer*, pp. 358, 363.

[3] *Leeds Mercury*, June 14, 1817.

[4] *ibid.*, July 19, 1817.

. . . to assassinate one of the Yeomanry Cavalry'. The horse belonging to Mr. Alexander of Huddersfield was wounded by a ball. A similar outrage occurred at Ossett, near Dewsbury. Several shots were fired into the house of a yeomanry cavalryman because he refused to surrender his arms. Five persons were arrested in connexion with the shooting of the horse. Altogether about thirty-six persons were taken to gaol, most of them being 'of the lowest class of society, illiterate, and ill-informed, and liable to be the dupes of designing men'.[1]

The insurrection in Derbyshire had more disastrous consequences. On Monday, June 8, a number of men assembled in the darkness and set out from the village of Wingfield to go to Nottingham, where they expected to join in a general rising.[2] They passed through South Wingfield, Butterley, Ripley, and Codnor, increasing in number as they proceeded, and using force in some instances to add to their ranks and to provide themselves arms. Some resistance to their demands was shown at one place and a man was fatally injured. Armed with 'pikes' and 'sticks', they got as far as Eastwood, where they were met by a section of the 15th Light Dragoons. At the sight of the troops 'they fled in all directions dispersing over the fields and throwing away their arms'.[3] Forty-eight of the insurgents were arrested and forty of them suffered indictment. 'Several of the prisoners were extremely young, apparently not above fifteen or sixteen years of age. Two or three are cripples.'[4] Thirty-five of the forty who were indicted had to take their trial. All of them were 'evidently of the lowest and labouring class of the community; many of them appeared in Court in blue smock frocks'.[5] At the end of the trial twenty-three received the death penalty, though only three of them were finally hung and beheaded.

Among the many reports of disaffection that were sent to the Home Secretary during the next two and a half years, the most serious was concerned with the Cato Street Conspiracy. For some considerable time before February, 1820, the movements and speeches of a number of desperate reformers under the

[1] *Leeds Mercury*, June 14, 1817.
[2] For Oliver's part in this affair see *The Skilled Labourer*, pp. 359–60. Also 368–70.
[3] H.O. 42. 166, 1817. Also *Newcastle Chronicle*, June 21, 1817. Taken from *Nottingham Review*.
[4] *Newcastle Chronicle*, Oct. 25, 1817.
[5] *Leeds Mercury*, Oct. 4, 1817.

guidance of a man named Thistlewood had been reported to the police officers in London. From the later reports it appears that plans were being made for an attack on certain parts of the city, and the murder of a number of Cabinet Ministers was even contemplated. On the eve of the intended attack the desperadoes were surprised by the appearance of police officers at their head-quarters in Edgware Road. In the scuffle that ensued one officer was killed, but several of the conspirators were arrested. Thistlewood managed to escape, and after wandering for a few days was eventually caught and imprisoned. As a result of the trial in April, he and his companions suffered the extreme penalty.[1] Attempts were made to connect this plot with the political societies in the provinces, but no definite evidence could be produced to show any kind of complicity in the matter.

Popular agitations took place, however, in the West Riding of Yorkshire in the early part of April. At Sheffield, disorderly persons one night went along Attercliffe Road and came back shouting 'Remember the 14th of April'. Almost simultaneously with this outburst, about two hundred men gathered at Barnsley, and, 'all armed with pikes, or other offensive weapons, began to move by different routes towards Grange Moor, the appointed rendezvous'. Having arrived at Flockton, just before the break of day, and finding no 'companions in arms', they threw away their weapons and dispersed. When the military arrived on the moor, they found 'about 100 pikes, a number of guns, scythe-blades, fixed on the ends of poles'. 'They found the revolutionary standard, and the drum which had accompanied the insurgents on their march.' From information privately received, it appeared 'that the standard of rebellion' had to 'be planted in or near Huddersfield, as well as on the north of Lancashire'.[2] Several men were arrested in connexion with these demonstrations, and at the ensuing trial twenty-two were sentenced to death. But having previously pleaded guilty on the advice of the presiding judge, their lives were mercifully spared.

During the next ten years, except for one brief period, quietude reigned among the lower classes. The peace was broken in the spring of 1826. On April 26, Major Eckersley reports the destruction of several power looms at Accrington. Six rioters

[1] H.O. 44. 6, 1820.

[2] *Leeds Mercury*, April 10, 1820.

were killed and several wounded. About the same time the mills of Messrs. Whitehead, Turner & Kays were attacked at Helmshore, Rawtenstall, and other places. A fortnight later an onslaught was made on a mill at Manchester. At the beginning of July, Fletcher's agent reports a largely attended meeting at Betting's Hill, when 'it was finally and conclusively settled upon that Whitehead's person and property be destroyed, on or before the 16th instant'.[1] This deadly project was several times postponed, and finally abandoned as a dangerous task.

Three years later 'alarming associations' were reported from the counties of Wiltshire, Gloucestershire, and Somerset. E. Edward Shepherd informed the Home Secretary that the members of these associations on initiation took an oath which had in it 'a mixture of religion and mischief', and he adds, 'there is more of hell than heaven in it'.[2] The hell was more clearly seen during the next year at Hampshire, Wiltshire, Kent, Sussex, Berkshire, and Buckinghamshire. The main cause of the trouble in Kent and the neighbouring counties was 'the actual misery so long endured' by the labourers 'and their helpless families'. A correspondent in the *Sunday Times* (Dec. 8, 1830) declared that there were 'tens of thousands of Englishmen, industrious, kind-hearted, but broken-hearted beings, exasperated into madness by insufficient food and clothing—by the utter want of necessaries for themselves and their unfortunate families. There is no complaint anywhere that they will not work, or having undertaken to labour for pay, they break their contract. The complaint is on their side, that they cannot get such wages for their work as will keep them above starvation'. 'Tithes and enclosures, and enormous rents, and corn laws, and grinding taxes' are blamed for their distressed condition. When the labourers complained to the farmers about the low wages, the latter avowed it was impossible to pay more because of the overhead charges. The labourers sympathized with the farmers and both parties united in an endeavour to relieve their mutual distress. Their riotous behaviour was soon checked by the strong hand of the authorities, and large numbers of hitherto respectable characters were arrested and eventually convicted. According to the Hammonds, the following numbers received the sentence of transportation at the respective trials, for Berkshire 44, Buckinghamshire 29,

[1] H.O. 40. 20, 1826. [2] *ibid.*, 40. 23, 1829.

Dorset 13, Essex 23, Kent 22, Gloucester 24, Hampshire 100, Huntingdonshire 5, Norfolk 11, Oxford 11, Suffolk 7, Sussex 17, Wiltshire 151.[1]

Another demonstration of mob violence with a different motive occurred in Bristol toward the end of October, 1831. It coincided with, or was caused by, the public entry into the city of the new recorder. Sir Charles Wetherell had just been appointed to this position, ostensibly as a reward for his political services. During the reform discussions, he had become the acknowledged leader of the reactionary group in the House of Commons. In this capacity he had 'rendered himself odious and obnoxious to the people by his vexatious opposition to the Reform Bill'. His entry into Bristol gave opportunity for a hostile demonstration to be made against him. Determined to show their hatred of him, the crowd lashed their fury against the public buildings. 'Forty-two Dwelling-Houses and Workhouses' were 'completely destroyed', exclusive of the 'Mansion House, Excise-Office, Custom House, the Four Toll-Houses, the three prisons, and the Bishop's Castle'. One reporter observed that it was 'really heartrending to see the destruction of property'.[2] Apparently not satisfied with their devastations, the rioters assembled again on the 31st, but they were charged by the military, and one hundred and twenty were killed and wounded. In a further charge two hundred and fifty were sabred. Altogether more than ninety prisoners were taken, and at their trial five received sentence of death.

This explosion of public feeling in Bristol alarmed the supporters of a reactionary Government, and the alarm was increased by reports from other places. Window-smashing took place at Derby. Houses were burnt at Nottingham, while near by, the Duke of Newcastle's Castle was destroyed by fire.[3]

Many rumours and reports of mob violence were sent to the Home Office during the Chartist agitation of 1836–1850, but the most ominous were those of 1840 and 1842. A kind of guerilla warfare had been waged between the magistrates of Sheffield and the Chartists of that city for several months prior to 1840. The local authorities had banned the Chartist open-air meetings in Paradise Square, and had prevented the Chartists going to the

[1] *The Village Labourer*, J. L. & B. Hammond, p. 308.
[2] H.O. 40. 28, 1831.
[3] Place MSS. 27790, p. 103.

Parish Church. Not to be outdone, the latter had held Chartist Camp Meetings on the moors and had formed themselves into political classes. As the class meetings were confined to members of the class, every opportunity was afforded to voice grievances against the magistrates. Matters came to a head at the beginning of January, 1840. According to reports the members of the various political classes in Sheffield and district decided at their private meetings to attack the town on Saturday evening, January 11, and to capture the Town Hall and the Tontine Hotel. For this purpose 'a body of men armed with guns, pikes, daggers and other weapons had collected on the Manchester Road'. They were intercepted by the magistrates and military, secret information having been forwarded them concerning the plan. Most of the class leaders were arrested, and at the ensuing trial Samuel Thompson, one of the insurgents and a class leader, turned Queen's evidence and gave a full account of the attempted outrage. 'The table of the Court presented an appalling spectacle. It was literally covered with pikes, daggers, firearms, combustibles, and other destructive materials mentioned in the evidence. There were dozens of pikes and daggers.' A similar rising took place at Bradford a fortnight later. The prisoners brought in 'large quantities of bullets, ball cartridge, powder, stone-bottles containing . . . combustible matter, guns and pikes, and a quantity of port fire'.[1]

The year 1842 witnessed a vigorous display of Chartist passion. Violence manifested itself in many places. The second week in August was apparently the critical week. At first it was a miners' question in the Potteries. In the middle of June, Mr. Sparrow of Longton reduced his workmen's wages 7d. a day, with a demand that they should produce an extra yard of coal per day, which was equal to 1s. 2d. as a total reduction.[2] The colliers refused to work at this price. In a short while they were joined by others, Earl Granville having reduced his miners' wages at Shelton. Before the end of July, a general turn-out took place. Hunger immediately began to make itself felt. To satisfy their pressing needs the turn-outs introduced a system of organized begging. The local authorities disliked their procedure and threatened to apply the Vagrant Acts. On Saturday, August 6, three colliers

[1] H.O. 40. 57, 1840.
[2] *North Staffordshire Mercury*, Saturday, June 18, 1842.

were locked up at Burslem for begging with boxes in the streets.[1] Nothing of a suspicious character happened till midnight, when suddenly a crowd of 200 desperadoes came down Sneyd Road and attacked the Town Hall. After releasing the prisoners, they attacked the houses of Superintendent Ryles, Mr. Hulme, G. Alcocks, and Mr. Acton, and also broke the windows of the George Inn. Nine days later a more desperate attack on property took place. On Monday, August 15, a mob of miners went to Shelton and turned out the workers that were still employed. They attacked the police office and the rate collector's office, breaking windows and destroying books. From there they went to Chatterley Bridge and tore up the books of Mr. Hollingbury's library. A similar fate was meted out to the books at the Court of Request. The police office at Stoke was also broken into, and furniture, books and crockery were thrown into the street. At Little Fenton, Squire Allen's house was partly destroyed together with deeds and furniture. The crowd took away his money and ravenously drank his wines. A considerable amount of damage was done to the public hall at Longton, 392 panes of glass being broken and much furniture destroyed. Mr. Rose, an obnoxious magistrate, did not escape the fury of the mob. The windows of his house were broken, and some of the furniture spoiled. The Rev. Dr. Vale was singled out for special attention, his entire furniture, beds and books being thrown into the street. His house was also set on fire. The rioters 'made themselves drunk with the doctor's wines and whisky, and most of the property was pillaged and carried off'.[2] Damage was also done to the police station at Fenton, while Charles Mason's house was pillaged at the same place. The arrival of the military prevented further damage. Hanley did not escape the contagion. Mr. Forrester, the agent of Lord Granville's collieries, had his home pillaged, and his office set on fire. Mr. Parker, the magistrate, experienced a worse fate. His house was ransacked and his furniture burned. The local clergyman, the Rev. Mr. Aitken, had his house plundered, his clothing carried away, and the house and library set on fire. On Tuesday, August 16, the George Inn at Burslem was attacked, but the military having been called out were ready for any eventuality. Before the end

[1] *Staffordshire Advertiser* says four men were locked up. Aug. 13, 1842.
[2] *Staffordshire Examiner*, Aug. 20, 1842.

of the day a procession of miners was fired upon by the troops, one man being killed and others wounded.[1]

Disturbances also broke out in Lancashire, Yorkshire, and Cheshire. The beginning of the trouble in Lancashire was due to the action of Messrs. Bayley in reducing the wages of their workmen at Stalybridge. In a very short while, 23,000 operatives at Ashton and Stalybridge were on strike. A portion of them marched to Manchester, and the 'metropolis of distress' was soon in the throes of a general strike. The contagion spread into Cheshire and Yorkshire, a feature of the trouble being the attacks of the roving mobs which stopped the engines of many factories by withdrawing the plugs. Manchester, being the metropolis of Chartism as well as the metropolis of distress, was responsible for mixing the question of the 'people's charter' with that of wages. Many of the strikers vowed they would never return to work till the 'Charter' was granted. But hunger and imprisonment broke their resolution, and after several weeks' strike the workmen everywhere resumed their work, but not before hundreds of their fellows had been cast into prison.[2]

The real cause of all these troubles was evidently economic and not political.[3] Political theory, philosophical teaching, utilitarian ideas, and revolutionary thoughts had less to do with the disturbances than the distress under which so many people continually suffered. The English working men had no desire for conflict. They possessed no innate tendency toward revolution. While the action of revolutionaries on the Continent was not lost on the subject masses of Great Britain, the majority of workmen were loyalist at heart and lovers of domestic peace. In spite of the influence of Tom Paine and his disciples, only a minority were tainted with the spirit of disaffection. But hunger strictly limits the patience of most men, and distress makes some folk very reckless.

[1] *Staffordshire Examiner*, Aug. 20, 1842. Also *When I Was a Child*, by An Old Potter. The latter was an eye-witness of the shooting.

[2] At the Staffordshire Commission 220 prisoners appeared for trial, 56 of them being transported. See the *North Staffordshire Mercury*, Oct. 22, 1842. Out of 66 charged at the Cheshire Commission 13 were transported. See *Macclesfield, Stockport & Congleton Chronicle*, Oct. 6, 1842. No Commission was appointed for York, but 57 prisoners appeared at the York Assizes in September, 1842. No one received more than 18 months' imprisonment. See *York Herald*, Sept. 10, 1842. *The Bradford Observer* at the end of August puts the number of rioters confined at York somewhere in the region of 172, Aug. 25, 1842. A large number of prisoners were tried at the Lancashire Commission, 11 being transported and 115 imprisoned. See *Liverpool Courier*, Oct. 12 and 19, 1842.

[3] The Bristol Riots may be regarded as an exception.

There can be no doubt about the economic distress during the early years of the nineteenth century. The war with France had many effects. It tremendously increased the national debt. It disturbed the smooth working of the currency. It enhanced the cost of living, and it greatly impoverished the wage-earning classes. Among the worst effects for the poorer folk was the great increase in the price of wheat. From 1797 to 1801, the price of wheat averaged 79.1 shillings a quarter. In that five year period, the highest price reached was in March 1801, when wheat sold at 154.5 shillings. From 1802 to 1807, the average price was 69.9 shillings a quarter. During 1807 to 1811 it averaged 88.5 shillings. In March, 1812, wheat sold at 150.3 shillings.[1] Bread and potatoes being the chief commodities of consumption by the poorer people in those days, one can easily imagine the terrible results. Wages did not increase in proportion to the rise in the cost of food. In some cases wages were lower.

Conditions were not improved by the introduction and the general application of machinery. This aid to manufacture made it more profitable to employ larger quantities of female and child labour. Adult male labour became less necessary and more easily discarded. The hand-loom weaving, for example, a prosperous industry till the end of the eighteenth century, received a heavy blow from the new invention. Unemployment, instead of being uncommon, now became extremely prevalent. Those who had work were often employed only half their available time. While no figures are possible, a review of contemporary writers can leave no doubt about the facts. The only means of amelioration were the dreaded workhouse and the crumbs of private charity. In many families distress and starvation became a daily experience. Even children were sometimes born with the hope fondly embraced by their parents that one day they might help to remove the family burden.

The immediate cause of the trouble in Nottingham was the conduct of 'the Wholesale Hosiers' of the 'Stocking-weaving Establishments' who had been obliged to curtail their hands. 'This produced considerable discontent among the workmen. Their riotous spirit, however, was increased by the trade having brought into use a certain wide frame, which was a considerable

[1] Select Committee Report on Agriculture, 1833. Parliamentary Papers, Vol. v, p. 12.

saving in manual labour, tending still further to the decrease of the hands employed.'[1] The editor of the *Leeds Mercury* (Nov. 23, 1811) ventured the opinion that the rioters had made a mistake in blaming low wages and improved frames for their distressed condition. 'They ought to be informed,' he asserted, 'that the real cause of the evils of which they so loudly and justly complain, is the long continuance of a heart-sickening war, without visible object, and apparently without end.' The Duke of Newcastle, reporting on the riots in Nottingham, avows it to be the frames of the obnoxious in trade that are destroyed. He also expresses the opinion 'that the original cause' of all the violence '*is* the *distress of the workmen* who have unquestionably been most hardly treated by their employers'.[2] An anonymous publication in the name of General Ludd contains a song which gives the Luddite explanation of all the violence.

> Brave Ludd was to measures of violence unused
> Till his sufferings became so severe
> That at last to defend his own interest he rous'd
> And for the great work did prepare.

In another part of the song he describes the object of his anger.

> His wrath is entirely confined to wide frames
> And to those who old prices abate.

The main cause of his anger is expressed in the following lines.

> And foul imposition alone was the cause
> Which produced these unhappy results.[3]

A later communication from General Ludd of Sherwood Camp exclaims, 'I have waited patiently to see if any measures were likely to be adopted by Parliament to alleviate distress in any shape whatever; but their hand of conciliation is shut and my poor suffering country is left without a ray of hope'.[4] On December 28, 1812, a public meeting was held in Nottingham in order 'to petition for peace'. The meeting had been called because of the widespread distress among the inhabitants. In the parish of

[1] *Leeds Mercury*, Nov. 23, 1811.
[2] H.O. 42. 118, 1811.
[3] *ibid.*, 42. 119, 1812.
[4] *ibid.*, 42. 120, 1812.

St. Mary's 'between nine and ten thousand' were 'receiving parish pay'. The number of paupers in the other parishes were in a similar proportion. 'Thus', said the correspondent (*Leeds Mercury*, Jan. 2, 1813), 'more than one-fourth of the population of this once flourishing town is reduced to a state of extreme poverty by the continuance of the ruinous war in which we are engaged.' One of the speakers at the gathering described the difference that was caused by the war. The penny loaf, which in pre-war days had weighed nine ounces, was now reduced to three ounces, 'and the paupers in one parish alone had increased from 200 or 300 to near 9,000'. In a letter sent to the Home Office on the following day, the Town Clerk, referring to the recent frame breaking, says, 'The Trade of this Town is in the most lamentable state and the distresses of the poor and working classes severe beyond description'.[1] On May 16, 1816, the overseers and guardians of Hinckley informed the Home Secretary that 'one half of the framework-knitters and other mechanics are, at this time, out of employment and that, very shortly, the other half will be in the same dreadful situation'.[2]

Concerning the disturbances of Lancashire and Cheshire, a similar explanation can be given, but a contrary opinion was expressed by the 'Secret Committee of the House of Lords on the Disturbed State of certain Counties'. According to this enlightened body, a general rising was intended and expected, but the only rising possible was that engineered in the minds of a few spies and deluded men. As early as February 25, 1811, R. Fletcher speaks of the 'want of employment' among cotton weavers as the means of supplying the Jacobins with 'great opportunities of instilling disaffection into the lower orders'.[3] A few months later, a petition from 8,000 cotton weavers of Stockport reveals 'the most deplorable state of poverty and want'.[4] At a meeting of clergy, manufacturers, and inhabitants of Bolton, held on November 12, a petition is authorized to be sent to the Prince Regent informing him that an 'advance in the price of flour, meal, and potatoes' has taken place, while at the same time 'the wages of the labouring-classes are lower'.[5] In his report on the riots of April, General Maitland of Manchester puts it on

[1] H.O. 42. 130, 1812.
[2] *ibid.*, 42. 150, 1816.
[3] *ibid.*, 42. 114, 1811.
[4] *ibid.*, 42. 115, 1811.
[5] *ibid.*, 42. 117, 1811.

record as his opinion that their real cause was to be found in the high price of provisions, and reduced wages.[1]

The origin of the disturbances in Yorkshire and other places was similar to that in Nottingham and Lancashire. On May 17, 1812, Joseph Wigfull of Sheffield reports 'many hundred thousands of industrious persons nearly in a state of desperation by distress'.[2] Labour-saving machinery was adding to the distress, and many people believed this to be the principal cause of all their troubles. Hence the reason for the attempted destruction of those mills where the obnoxious machinery had been introduced.

In the Northern area, the Rev. Dr. Gray of Sunderland, referring to the disturbances at South Shields, says, 'the man had just grounds of complaint and suspicion'.[3] Major-General Riall of Newcastle informs the Home Office that the shipowners at South Shields 'have tried every measure to deceive the strikers'.[4] A similar charge is laid against the shipowners at Sunderland. He declares that they have 'broken their faith in a very shameful manner'.[5] Unemployment appears to have been extremely prevalent in the North Midland area during 1816. A. B. Haden of Wolverhampton reports 'vast numbers of colliers, forge-men and mechanics' out of work.[6] In the Metropolitan district, most of the trouble was caused through discontent in connexion with the Corn Laws, and the high price of provisions was the chief cause of the disturbances in the agricultural districts of East Anglia.

The distressed condition of the working classes was aggravated by the inability of the central and local authorities to understand the situation. A new economic problem confronted the nation, namely, that of changing economic conditions. Although it might be 'perilous for a nation to sacrifice its agriculture to the development of its industries . . . in the course of the nineteenth century England deliberately made the experiment'.[7] Such a change as this could not adequately be counteracted by the protective measures adopted by the Government in relation to imported commodities, and by a '*laissez faire*' attitude toward wages and working conditions. Consequently, the first effects of the economic revolution on the working classes were disappointing and even injurious. Goodwill between masters and

[1] H.O. 42. 123, 1812.
[2] *ibid.*, 42. 123, 1812.
[3] *ibid.*, 42. 146, 1815.
[4] *ibid.*, 42. 146, 1815.
[5] *ibid.*, 42. 146, 1815.
[6] *ibid.*, 42. 152, 1816.
[7] *History of the English People in* 1815, Elie Halévy, p. 179.

workmen did not keep pace with the application of machinery. Relations between them became very bitter in some localities. Unemployment began to play a very important part in the situation at this time. No attempt was ever made on a national scale to grapple with this problem, and no official endeavour was made to relieve the distress of the unemployed. When the stricken workmen tried to save themselves by Trade Union action, they found the laws against them. Yet all through the years of the Luddite disturbances, a great combination existed against the working classes. The Home Office, with all the power of Government behind it, co-operated with the local magistrates (many of whom were employers themselves), who in turn worked with the employers of labour. The latter by an arbitrary act could always reduce wages or discharge their workmen to meet the changing conditions of trade. If the workers resented this action and tried to prevent reductions of wages, it was a simple and an easy task for the masters to call for the help of the magistrates and the military. Workers' combinations were illegal, and secret meetings looked upon as seditious. The workmen therefore were helpless. Every kind of collective action was regarded as a sign of disaffection toward the Government or conspiracy against the State. Any who offended in these ways were punished accordingly.

The same economic cause was operative in the later disturbances, though it was sometimes mixed up with political consideration, and the same official incapacity to deal adequately with the situation was equally apparent. A due attention to these factors will be given in a later chapter.

CHAPTER II

THE METHODIST LOYALTY

METHODISM has always been a loyalist movement, and therefore hostile to every form of mob violence. Its critics represented it as otherwise. As early as 1792, the *Gentleman's Magazine* (Vol. II, pp. 852–3) described it as a 'system which tended to overthrow Church and State'. About the same time the Mayor of Liverpool reported to the Home Office that in many of the new villages there were 'nothing but Methodist and other Meeting-Houses. . . . Consequently the youth of the county are training up under the instruction of a set of men not only ignorant but of whom I think we have of late too much reason to imagine are inimical to our happy Constitution'.[1] Its agents were later described as 'traitors', and under the influence of 'the Jacobins of this country'. The Bishop of Rochester had the suspicion that 'sedition, and atheism were the real objects of their institutions'.[2] In later years they were charged with 'pilfering all the money of the common people, shutting them from all dances and country wakes', and 'sending them penniless into the fields to gaze upon the clouds and smell the dandelions'.[3]

A Government official at Wolverhampton in 1800, describing the conditions of the colliers round Bilston, reports that the district is free from political meetings except at one place 'where a Cheymist and a Brass-Founder (two inhabitants who are Methodists and politically mad)' are agitating the people. So he informs the Home Secretary of his intention to advise the Rev. Mr. Haden, a local magistrate, 'to give to the Cheymist and the Brass-Founder a hint of the suspension of the Habeas Corpus Act'.[4] The Rev. W. R. Hay of Dukinfield, reporting the activities of the disaffected who were holding district meetings, says, 'a person of the name of Ine Wild always chose the delegates of that district. Wild is a Methodist and has regular Methodist meetings

[1] H.O. 42. 20, 1792.
[2] *Gentleman's Magazine*, 1800, Vol. II, p. 1077.
[3] *ibid.*, 1809, Vol. I, p. 43.
[4] H.O. 42. 55, 1800.

at his house'.[1] Another clerical magistrate, the Rev. J. Bowen of Bath, tells the Home Office 'that the rapid progress which the Methodists are making, must tend to the subversion of order'.[2] Even the *Christian Observer* (1808, p. 37), an evangelical periodical, joins in the general chorus of criticism and regards the sentiments of the Methodists as 'unfavourable to our civil as well as ecclesiastical institutions'.

It is clearly evident from contemporary sources that in the first two decades of the nineteenth century the loyalty of the Methodists was widely suspect. That attitude of mind might explain why one of 'the regularly qualified preachers', Mr. M'Kitrick, when in the act of preaching in a village in the township of Tonge, Lancashire, was arrested and escorted to Bolton by 'horse soldiers with drawn swords as tho' they had under Military Law apprehended some desperate Traitor to his country'. J. Butterworth, M.P. complains strongly to the Home Office concerning this, and mentions the fact that several magistrates in Lancashire and other places refused 'to administer the oaths to Methodist Preachers'.[3] It appears that some Luddites had been arrested in the same village some time prior to this incident, and perhaps the authorities thought there was some connexion between them and the Methodists. Lord Sidmouth must have been influenced by all these reports, for he tried to get through Parliament a Bill by which the Dissenting preachers could be controlled in their activities. He was supported by Lord Grey, who believed it was wise to bring the Methodist teachers under the control of Government. A storm of protests was thereby aroused, and for the first time the Methodists and the Dissenters united in Parliamentary action. Such was the strength of the opposition that the contemplated Bill was withdrawn, and another, which was a kind of charter to the Methodists, took its place.

The charge against the Methodists that they were disloyal can find no support in Methodist literature or practice. There is no evidence whatever in the official records of any disloyalty to the State or any intention to be disloyal. On the other hand, they always advocated loyalty to the Constitution. John Wesley, the father of Methodism, was a Church of England clergyman,

[1] H.O. 42. 62, 1801. [2] *ibid.*, 42. 107, 1810.
[3] *ibid.*, 42. 124, 1812.

who constantly professed his allegiance to both Church and State. On one occasion he offered a supply of 200 volunteers for the defence of his country when threatened by a French invasion.[1] The majority of his followers accepted his teaching and adopted his example. Although they organized themselves on the principle of republicanism, in politics they were wholeheartedly monarchical. Irrespective of the charge that they were 'inimical to the Church and State', their influence constantly remained on the side of loyalty to both. The charge was partly due to the prevalent conception of the relation between Church and State, the Church being regarded as one of the 'Three Estates of the Realm'.[2] To dissent from the Church was reckoned by many as disaffection to the State. William Pitt considered 'the Church of England, as by law established, to be so essential a part of the constitution that whatever endangered it, would necessarily effect the security of the whole'.[3] 'The Church and State were so inseparably blended, that when one weakened, the other was weakened also.' 'They must stand or fall together.'[4]

The fallacy of that reasoning was only gradually recognized. The history of the Methodists showed how it was possible to form a separate religious community and yet to have respect for the Established Church, and at the same time to be loyal to the State. The Wesleyans persistently proclaimed their loyalty and friendship for both. In the Conference Minutes of 1793 the following resolution is found. 'Q.25:—What directions shall be given concerning our conduct to the Civil Government? A.1:—None of us shall either in writing or in conversation speak lightly or irreverently of the Government under which he lives. A.2:—We are to observe that the oracles of God command us to be subject to the higher powers; and that honour to the King is there connected with the fear of God.' The Conference of 1793 publicly professed its respect for the Throne and its 'sincere attachment to the Constitution', and it enjoined the same upon all its members.[5]

According to the *Methodist Magazine* (1800, pp. 479–80), the

[1] *Life and Times of John Wesley*, Tyerman, Vol. II, pp. 234–5.

[2] Perhaps another reason for the charge was the democratic tendencies of Methodism. It was developing among the common people the idea of government for the people and by the people. The authorities were naturally afraid of this.

[3] *Annual Register*, 1790, History of Europe, p. 75.

[4] *Parliamentary Debates for* 1796–1797, Vol. III, p. 557.

[5] *Annual Register*, 1793, Appendix to Chronicle, Vol. XXXV, p. 35.

Conference of 1800 sent to the King an address of loyalty signed by the President of the Connexion, and published in the *London Gazette*. In this address the Methodist preachers express their abhorrence at 'the late atrocious attempt against the life of His Majesty', and also their thankfulness for his providential escape. They likewise testify their 'Sincere Respect for and Attachment to Your Majesty's Person, and Government, and our Detestation of all Sedition upon this occasion. We are determined to obey the sacred Injunctions of the God whom we serve, to pray for Kings and for all that are in authority, to be subject to every ordinance of men for the Lord's sake; to obey magistrates; to be ready for every good work; and to lead a quiet and peaceable life in all Godliness and honesty'. A similar exhortation was given in 1803. The Conference unanimously decided that a prayer meeting should 'be held every Friday evening by every Society, and a fast held every First Friday in the month during the present danger of the nation'. An appeal is made to the Methodist members to comply 'with cheerfulness and alacrity' to the requirements of Government. The hope is expressed that they will reveal 'the true spirit of loyalty', because 'it is a genuine principle' in their souls. They are reminded that they 'are also bound by strong ties of gratitude to our Sovereign and his Government'.[1] At the next Conference, 'the appointment of a Monthly Fast, and a Weekly Prayer Meeting, in behalf of the nation', is authorized to be continued.[2]

One of the reasons given for the resolution against camp meetings passed by the Conference of 1807 was that such meetings were 'likely to be productive of considerable mischief'.[3] The habit of bringing from 10 to 20,000 people together (as camp meetings were doing) in times of distress and discontent, incurred a great political danger. The Conference desired to avoid every peril. Perhaps the real explanation of the expulsion of Hugh Bourne, William Clowes, and James Steele from the Wesleyan Connexion was the fear that their support of camp meetings would eventually lead to disorder.

At the Conference of 1809 it is suggested that prayers and praise should be offered up in all the places of worship, and a sermon preached for the purpose of showing their thankfulness

[1] *Wesleyan Conference Minutes*, 1803. [2] *ibid.*, 1804.
[3] *ibid.*, 1807.

for the fifty years' reign of King George the Third.[1] A few months later, the Rev. John Stephens, the father of the Rev. J. R. Stephens, preached a notable sermon at Rotherham on 'Christian Patriotism'. In this discourse he speaks in eulogistic terms of 'our beloved country'. He extolled 'the excellence of her constitution; the equality of her laws; the purity of her judges; the uprightness of her magistrates; her civil freedom, &c.' No doubt he spoke the sentiments of his brother preachers, for the sermon was published in the *Methodist Magazine*, just about the time of the first Luddite explosion.[2]

The 1812 Conference is held a few weeks after the passing of the Act which legalized the position of the Methodists. With some idea of its significance, the preachers were full of gratitude for the privileges extended to them. In the address authorized to be sent to every circuit, they speak of 'The well-known loyalty of our Societies, their dutiful attachment to their King and Country'. Referring to the disturbances in 'the Northern Counties', they declare their 'utmost horror' of 'the principles which have given birth to this state of things', 'principles which are alike destructive of the happiness of the Poor, and of the Rich'. They feel assured that their 'Societies are uncontaminated with that spirit of insubordination, violence, and cruelty, which had caused so much distress and misery'. But the alarm must be given 'lest any of our dear people should be drawn away by the dissimulation of evil-disposed men. We proclaim loudly and earnestly, "Fear the Lord and the King; and meddle not with them that are given to change". Avoid them, come not near them'.[3]

The same enthusiasm for King and country is manifest in the 1813 Conference address. 'We cannot but feel', it declares, 'a strong attachment to our civil constitution, and a confirmed regard for our rulers, who have on all occasions, discovered a liberal spirit toward us as a people. We are therefore still resolved to recommend both by word and deed, the duty of fearing God and honouring the King.'[4] Similar sentiments are repeated at the following Conference, when an address is sent to the Prince Regent.[5] All the Methodist societies are confidently said to be 'firmly and unalterably attached to the excellent Constitution of

[1] *Methodist Magazine*, 1809, p. 400.
[2] *ibid.*, 1811, p. 897.
[3] *ibid.*, 1812, p. 720.
[4] *ibid.*, 1813, p. 720.
[5] *ibid.*, 1814, p. 716.

our Country'.[1] A correspondent to the *Methodist Magazine*, replying a few months later to a charge of disloyalty made against the Methodists by the *Christian Observer*, calls attention to 'the strong, persistent professions of loyalty made by the Methodists, both from the pulpit and press, from their origin to the present day', and to 'their exemplary civil obedience', which 'will secure them from the imputation of disaffection to the State'.[2]

Succeeding Conferences continued the same attitude, and although other Methodist bodies came into being more democratic than the original body, they too adopted the traditional Methodist loyalty. Their loyalty, however, was never demonstrative. They quietly submitted to the laws of the land, and never permitted their loyalist attitude to mean hatred of political reform. The nearest approach to hostility came in 1843 when the New Connexion Conference, comprising an equal number of ministers and laymen, congratulated its members because they were not associated with the riots of 1842. After referring to the 'political demagogues' and the 'turbulent excitement', together with the 'loss of life and property' connected with these disturbances, the Conference expressed its satisfaction that some of the brethren 'were commendably active in the protection of property, and the restoration of order'. It adds the hope, however, that they will ever be what their history proves they have hitherto been, and which their principles and religion alike require—'faithful to the throne, constitution, and laws of our beloved country, the exemplars of order, loyalty, and patriotism'.[3]

With the Wesleyans the constant profession of loyalty created the doctrines of 'passive obedience' and 'non-resistance', which in turn were transformed into patriotic virtues. Dr. Coke, 'the father of missions', is an example of this. He seems to have been on rather friendly terms with the Duke of Portland. When the Duke was at the Home Office in 1801, Dr. Coke informs him that 'a confidential friend' believed that 'a Grand Association' was 'forming in Lancashire and the North of England similar to that lately carried on by the United Irishmen'. A Mr. Wild, 'a leader of the Methodist Singers at Wesley's Chapel, Sheffield', had told this friend of a story he had heard from somebody else, that 'two thousand in Bolton had been sworn'. In spite of

[1] *Methodist Magazine* 1814, p. 870. [2] *ibid.*, 1815, p. 28.
[3] Conference Minutes, 1843.

the round-about way in which this information had come, Dr. Coke promised his Lordship to inquire into the matter. A second letter came from Manchester two days later. The Methodist preacher feels assured 'that there is a very dangerous association forming in this County at least against the Government'. He hopes to be in Bolton in the course of a week, when he expects to 'obtain some solid information on this subject'. On March 17, he tells the Home Secretary about a seditious meeting held on the night previous, when oaths were administered. Two days later he sends more precise information on the activities of the 'Conspirators'. An oath, based on Ezekiel xxi, verses 25–27, is taken blindfolded by the candidates. A fifth letter is written on March 24 from Macclesfield, and Dr. Coke tells the Duke that the conspiracy has gained ground in the West Riding of Yorkshire, near Huddersfield. On April 4 another letter is sent to the Home Office. This time he forwards a copy of the dreaded oath which is making men into conspirators. Although based on Scripture he regarded it as a serious thing. He informs the Home Office that 'a meeting of these seditious people was lately held in the night in the open air somewhere between Manchester and Oldham'. He fears 'that both Birmingham and Sheffield are greatly infected with this rebellious spirit', while Stockport, Macclesfield, and Congleton 'are entirely free from this plague'. In a footnote he confesses his alarm at the news 'that three Methodists were taken up on suspicion or proof of being engaged in this rebellious business. But on the strictest scrutiny and fullest satisfaction', he proudly asserts, 'I was happy enough to find that those men had been expelled the late Mr. Wesley's Society about five years ago solely for their Democratic sentiments'. A seventh letter is sent on April 7, when Dr. Coke informs the Duke of Portland that 'a meeting of the rebels . . . was held at Royton near Oldham' on the previous Sunday night. He is quite certain that 'there is a Conspiracy against the State now on foot'. A further letter follows on April 18 when he says, 'the Rebels have for some time had regular meetings every Sunday on a large moor near Royton . . . not far from Oldham'. A ninth letter is sent on August 19, just before he sets out for Ireland. He tells the Home Secretary that 'the meetings of the seditious by night are . . . very frequent'. He is afraid that if the French succeed in landing in this country 'the People who now assemble in these parties would become very dangerous indeed, by diverting our forces'. He promises to send information from Ireland if he can be serviceable.[1] As a final note, he makes the suggestion that the Government should spend 'a million of money' annually for some years in order to buy corn. By this means they could thus counter-balance the spirit of monopoly.[2]

Other Methodist preachers in Dr. Coke's time adopted the same loyalist attitude, but they were not so intimate with the Home Secretary. Mr. Isaac, a Methodist preacher stationed at South Shields, discovered in 1810 that a few of his flock had entered into a 'Brotherhood' among the pitmen and had taken an oath of fidelity to each other. He and his fellow preachers 'concerted measures with the preachers in the Newcastle and Sunderland circuits and set to work'. They visited the 'societies, showed them the unlawfulness of the association, warned them that were clear of it to remain so, and insisted that such as had taken the oath should abjure it immediately'. 'Thus the charm of secrecy was dissolved and the brotherhood annihilated. Dr. Taft took a most active part in this business, fearlessly braved the danger of it, and was eminently successful in suppressing it.' As a result of this crusade, some of the preachers 'were waylaid and had to flee for their lives'. 'Mr. Isaac was one of those to whom this happened. One evening on his return to Shields from a country place, several persons armed with bludgeons rushed on him from the left side of the road.' They were determined 'to finish his faculty of breaking up associations', but he ran for his life and escaped from their trap.[3]

During the Luddite disturbances of 1811 and 1812, 'a daring spirit of insubordination and riot manifested itself' in the vicinity of Halifax 'among the workmen connected with machinery. The Methodist preachers were among the first to declaim against such a mischievous feeling being harboured by any of the members in their society; and the superintendent (Mr. Bunting) especially gained the hatred of the hordes of Luddites which abounded in the neighbourhood—a hatred which was considerably increased by the following circumstance. It was intended to bury, at the Methodist chapel in Halifax, a man who had been shot while attempting to break into the mill of Mr. Cartwright, near

[1] H.O. 42. 61, 1801. [2] *ibid.*, 42. 62, 1801.
[3] *Memoirs of Rev. H. Taft, M.D.* pp. 105–6.

Cleckheaton, on Saturday night, April 12, 1812. Vast preparations were made for the funeral, and the corpse was preceded by a procession of his fellow "Luddites", by whom his death was considered in the light of an honourable martyrdom'. Bunting refused to conduct the burial service and relegated the task to the junior preacher. 'Ever after that time the most determined hostility was shown by the working classes against Mr. Bunting, and to such a pitch did their black malignity arrive as to issue the positive threat that his life should be taken.' 'His friends, however, judged it hazardous for him to proceed to his country appointments alone.'[1] In the year 1812 attempts were made near Sowerby Bridge to connect the Methodists with the doings of the misguided Luddites. When some of the rioters were executed, a number of their friends arranged to bring the bodies to the Methodist chapel at Greetland in the Sowerby Bridge Circuit and to deliver addresses from the pulpit. This intention was frustrated by the gates of the chapel being closed against them. Thomas Jackson was stationed in the circuit at this time, and he afterwards said, 'I never hesitated to preach obedience to the laws, according to the precepts of the New Testament, and to warn the people against the dangerous course to which they were incited; yet I was never interrupted in any of my night journeys across the moors, or in lonely roads'.[2]

During the same period at Holmfirth, it was suspected that the roof of the Methodist chapel was used as a depot for stolen property. The place was accordingly searched, but nothing was found. In connexion with this affair the chapel-keeper was questioned, and his replies were so unsatisfactory that he was dismissed. Robert Newton, who was the Methodist preacher at that place, 'bore a faithful testimony against these lawless proceedings and warned the people against them'.[3] He 'did his utmost to allay the Luddite feeling'.[4] 'On this account, as well as on the account of the dismissal of the chapel-keeper, he was understood to be an object of hostility among the adherents of General Ludd, and not a few friends were alarmed for his safety.' 'Two loaded pistols were found secreted in a hedge near his

[1] *History of Wesleyan Methodism in Halifax and its Vicinity*, J. U. Walker, pp. 254–5.
[2] *Recollections of My Own Life and Times*, Thomas Jackson, pp. 136–7.
[3] *Life of the Rev. Robert Newton, D.D.*, Thomas Jackson, p. 73.
[4] *History of Methodism in Huddersfield, Holmfirth, and Denby Dale*, Joel Mallinson, p. 64.

dwelling.'[1] When he finally left the circuit, he 'received a letter of thanks from a magistrate for his efficient help in the preservation of law and order'.[2]

Joseph Butterworth, when protesting to the Home Office against the arrest of a Methodist preacher in Lancashire, reminds the Home Secretary that the Methodists meet together for fellowship, 'and to be instructed in those principles which are the very reverse of everything disloyal, tumultuous, and wicked'. 'Several of our Preachers', he says, 'have been grievously threatened by the Luddites for their loyalty and I think Mr. Robert Newton, a highly respectable Preacher at Huddersfield, had threatening letters put under his door about a month ago—and Mr. Bunting another respectable Preacher at Halifax . . . gave me a fearful account of the disposition of the populous and how unsafe he considered himself.' He also informs the Home Secretary that notices had been read from the Methodist pulpits in Yorkshire, Lancashire, and Nottinghamshire 'to attract the curiosity of the lower orders and counteract the bad spirit among them, and I have had satisfactory accounts of the good impression made on the occasion'.[3] Other prominent preachers revealed the same spirit of loyalty to the Constitution. Richard Watson, in the interval between his leaving the Old Connexion and rejoining again (1801–1812), was for a while a writer on the staff of the *Liverpool Courier*, a constitutional paper and loyal to the Government.[4] Joseph Entwistle was described as a 'Christian patriot', but he never regarded it to be 'his duty to take any prominent part in matters merely political'. He always doubted 'the propriety of the Methodists, as such, embarking in political matters'.[5]

The inculcation of the spirit of loyalty was not lost on the Methodist laymen. Joseph Butterworth may be taken as an example. 'His loyalty . . . was a Christian principle to him.'[6] He exercised a great influence throughout the whole of London, and many of the older men at the Great Queen Street Society were brought up under 'the influence and upon the model of

[1] *Life of the Rev. Robert Newton, D.D.*, Thomas Jackson, p. 73.
[2] *History of Methodism in Huddersfield, Holmfirth, and Denby Dale,* Joel Mallinson, p. 64.
[3] H.O. 42. 124, 1812.
[4] *Richard Watson,* by Edward J. Brailsford, p. 42.
[5] *Memoirs of the Rev. Joseph Entwistle,* p. 435.
[6] *Sermon on the Death of Joseph Butterworth, Late M.P.*, Richard Watson, p. 25.

Joseph Butterworth'.[1] Samuel Hick, 'the Village Blacksmith', may be taken as a type of Methodist in touch with the lower strata of the artisan class. When he first began to preach, he was afraid he would not be able to recollect his text as he could neither read nor write.[2] Although he belonged to Yorkshire his loyalty was unquestionable. On one occasion he saw a regiment of the King's soldiers marching through the village in which he lived. 'He instantly returned to the house, and placed before the men the whole contents of the butlery, pantry, and cellar; bread, cheese, milk, butter, meat and beer went.' He refused every offer of payment. On another occasion he offered to give £600 for the defence of the King.[3]

This Methodist profession of loyalty had a four-fold basis. By harking back to the Bible to justify submission to the State, a theological foundation was provided. Although Methodism sought among other things to establish Scriptural Holiness throughout the land, in its teaching concerning relations to 'the powers that be' it accepted the Pauline conception. Thus to fear God and honour the King were regarded as inseparable duties incumbent upon all Methodists. Obedience to magistrates was equally binding.

Methodist loyalty had an ecclesiastical basis. John Wesley never lost his affection for the Church. His preachers were almost as affectionate. As the Church was considered by them an integral part of the State, love for the one meant affection for the other.

A political basis was supplied through their sense of privileges conferred upon them by the State. In reality the privileges were part of the rights of common citizens. The Dissenters had been fighting for these rights during the most part of a century and a half. As a result of their struggles religious and civil concessions had been won from the State. The Methodists regarded these concessions as a privilege for which they were truly thankful.

That the descendants of John Wesley regarded themselves as privileged people there can be no doubt. The protection of their property, the freedom of their worship, the formation of their societies, and the establishment of their organization were evidently reckoned as privileges and not as the rights of ordinary citizens. The idea of privilege constantly expressed itself. When

[1] *Benjamin Gregory D.D. Autobiographical Recollections*, p. 379.
[2] *The Village Blacksmith*, by James Everett, p. 339.
[3] *ibid.*, p. 129.

the Methodists decided to take part in the 'Accession Day' celebrations connected with the fiftieth year of the reign of King George the Third, the true reason was not merely to join in the general thanksgiving, but also to express their gratitude 'for the manifold civil and religious privileges' conferred upon them.[1] With the passing of Lord Sidmouth's Bill in 1812, legalizing their position in the State, they rejoiced greatly over the unexpected benediction, and freely circulated the news to all their people. 'We have received benefits,' said the Conference declaration, 'let us be grateful. Those benefits have been confirmed with good will, and confidence in our integrity; let us receive them with satisfaction and affection.'[2] 'In their congregations, their assemblies, and in private families, the voice of thanksgiving was heard, and the most lively gratitude to their civil governors was felt, for the late Act of Parliament, securing to them and their descendants liberty of conscience. This Act, the result of an enlightened policy, will be considered as an additional motive to attach them to the Government, and to their country, and will call forth their most ardent endeavours to inculcate a spirit of peace, and obedience to the laws.'[3] The benign results were received with thankfulness, for in 1814, the Prince Regent was publicly thanked for the part he had played in the matter. The Conference members assured him of their 'thankful recollections of the privileges' thus conferred. 'For this extension and establishment of religious liberty', they hastened to exclaim, 'we are solicitous to express our warmest gratitude to your Royal Highness under whose counsels the measure was introduced into Parliament, and unanimously passed into law.'[4] Similar sentiments were indicated in 1817 and 1819 by the Committee of Privileges, and again in the 'thirties by the Conference.

The idea of privilege left no doubt about Methodist duty toward the rulers of the land. This duty resolved itself into submission and obedience to lawful authority, afterwards described by the critics (*Wooler's British Gazette*, January 21, 1821) as 'those murderous doctrines of passive obedience and non-resistance'. According to these doctrines the subject had no rights, and the State had no duties. Existing institutions had to be accepted without question, and religion seemingly had nothing to do with

[1] *Methodist Magazine*, 1809, p. 400.
[2] *ibid.*, 1812, p. 720.
[3] *Leeds Mercury*, Aug. 15, 1812.
[4] *Methodist Magazine*, 1814, p. 870.

administration and precious little to do with legislation. Hence it was easy for apologists to exclaim, 'We teach love to God, obedience to the laws of our land, loyalty to our King, honour to whom honour is due, and respect for all authority'.[1] And it was no empty boast to say in 1816, 'Our venerable Sovereign never had a more faithful subject than our great founder, Mr. Wesley; and we, as a body, have given the Government such proofs of our loyalty during seventy years, that they have long been convinced of the rectitude of our political principles, and regarded us as firm friends to the British Constitution, and the present august family of the Throne'.[2]

The Methodist loyalty also had a prudential basis. For a religious minority movement to seek the reform of the Church and the nation appeared to be a very dangerous task. It was similar in the early days of Christianity. Under the paternal Government of the Roman Empire the first Christians while desiring to establish a new kingdom were freely permitted the exercise of their religious customs. But on no account could these customs be used as a cloak for political sedition. In order therefore to avoid suspicion of ulterior purposes the founder of the new religion was careful to announce at the onset of his campaign that his kingdom was not of this world. It was heavenly and not earthly. It was spiritual and not political. When asked in later days to define more clearly his attitude to the civil power, he uttered those memorable words, 'Render to Caesar the things that are Caesar's and to God the things that are God's'.[3] His enemies laid the charge against him 'that he claimed to be king of the Jews'. This was sufficient for the Roman authority. He was crucified on that count.

The adherents of the new religion had to guard against a similar fate. So their leading exponent defines more fully what ought to be the attitude of Christians to the State. Writing from prison, he advises Titus, who was exercising the office of a bishop, to put the Christians 'in mind to be subject to principalities and powers, to obey magistrates, to be ready to every good work'.[4] This was excellent advice from a man who was awaiting his trial at the hands of the civil authority, and who was writing to a eader of a minority movement.

[1] *Methodism Defended*, Wesleyan Tracts, p. 23.
[2] *ibid.*, p. 23.
[3] Mark xii. 17.
[4] Titus iii. 1. Also Romans xiii. 1–7.

If it be remembered that Methodism, throughout the whole of the first half of the nineteenth century, was undoubtedly a minority religious movement, then its ideas concerning duty toward the State become more intelligible. One cannot be charged with misrepresentation in saying that it carried on its operations for many years under the suspicious gaze of officials in high places. It was tolerated but not welcomed by them. Therefore its purpose had to be adequately defined, and its relation to the ruling authority clearly stated. A prudential policy was already formulated in Scripture. To adopt such a policy was both easy and natural.

With the Bible and common prudence behind them the Wesleyans left no doubt about their loyalty. Through their devotion to this ideal they created a working-class bourgeoisie from which the established order had nothing to fear. As Halévy points out (*History of the English People*, Vol. I, 401–2, French Edition), 'the despotism of the new habits rendered almost useless the despotism of the laws'. Working men learned to govern themselves instead of being governed from above. Under the influence of the Wesleyan revival, one can follow from 1792 to 1815 'the decadence of the revolutionary spirit among the Dissenters'. All this might explain why among all the countries of Europe England was the least revolutionary, and the most exempt from violent change. The complete explanation is not to be found in the political institutions nor in the economic organization of the time.

During the critical years of the Luddite revolt and the later disturbances the Methodist proletariat must have been constantly tempted to join the disaffected. But the loyalist attitude prevailed. Generally speaking the working-class portions of the community that came under the influence of Methodism were conspicuous, not by their alliance with, but their aloofness from, the agitations. If it be recollected that all the ebullitions reviewed in the previous chapter, except the Labourers' revolt of 1830, occurred in districts where Methodism was exceptionally strong, then the Methodist aloofness appears more amazing still. It becomes less surprising that a few individual Methodists and ex-Methodists should be implicated. Dr. Coke, for example, quotes in 1801 the case of the three Methodists who had been arrested on suspicion of disaffection, and he was pleased to acknowledge that they had been expelled from the Wesleyan Connexion solely for their democratic sentiments. Among the seventeen men reserved for execution in connexion with the Yorkshire disturbances of 1812, one at least was indirectly associated with Methodism. During the trial, 'it was observed to James Hey, that it was very extraordinary, that he who had had the advantage of a religious education, his father being of the Methodist Society, should have come to such a disgraceful situation; to which he replied, "the son's crimes will never be imputed to his father".'[1] According to one authority two of the executed men in the Derbyshire insurrection of 1817 had been successful local preachers among the Methodists in the vicinity of Belper.[2] Two other Methodists were among convicted insurgents, one of them being sentenced to transportation. In the preparation for the Cato Street Conspiracy of 1820, two of the companions of Thistlewood were associated with Methodism. One of them became alarmed at the prospect of open violence. He reported his fears to his class leader who escorted him to the house of Mr. Butterworth, M.P., in order to give information. The other had left the Methodist Connexion and finally became so implicated in the conspiracy that he suffered incarceration in Toothill's prison. A poem of fifty verses written by him was sent to the Home Office. What the Home Secretary thought of them is not placed on record, but the following selection reveals what the writer felt about him and his class.

> Tyrants. Ye fill the poor with dread
> And take away his right
> And raise the price of meat and bread
> And thus his labour blight.
>
> You never labour, never toil,
> But you can eat and drink;
> You never cultivate the soil,
> Nor of the poor man think.
>
> Tyrants. No longer be deceived
> The time will surely come
> When mankind whom you've aggrieved
> Will see your awful doom.[3]

[1] *Leeds Mercury*, Jan. 16 and 23, 1813.
[2] *Autobiographical Recollections of Benjamin Gregory*, pp. 126–9. The Primitive Methodists got their nickname 'Ranters' at Belper. The Ludlams and Turners were Methodists. See *Leeds Mercury*, Nov. 1, 1817.
[3] H.O. 44. 5, 1820.

A new situation arises in 1826. Some Methodist 'captains of industry', the Whitehead Brothers of Rossendale, who were graciously eulogized by Cooke Taylor in 1842 for their paternal care of their workmen, were threatened with murder and had their factories attacked. This, however, was not the work of fellow Methodists.

No evidence of Methodists participating in the riots of 1830 and 1831 has so far been found. The situation was different in 1842. When the Rev. Dr. Vale's house was attacked and his furniture set on fire at Longton, Staffordshire, in the August of that year, Joseph Whiston was arrested along with others for complicity in the outrage. At the trial Whiston was described by a witness as 'a member of the Primitive Methodist Connexion'. Chief Justice Tyndal, referring to the unfortunate man, avowed he had been 'most actively engaged in setting fire to the furniture in front of the house'. No mercy was shown, and although several witnesses testified to the excellence of his character, he was sentenced to twenty-one years' transportation.[1] Joseph Armitage of Leeds was another Methodist selected for judicial rebuke. He was charged at the York Assizes in 1842 for his share in the riots of August. Lord Denham confessed that it gave him great pain 'to see in such a situation a person so well esteemed and highly respected, and who had been entrusted . . . with one of the most important situations that man can fill towards man . . . that is, an instructor of youth in a Wesleyan school'. 'What was more likely', adds his lordship, 'than that the mob should be led astray when they saw such men as he acting in such a manner.' And although Armitage denied taking any part in the disturbances, he was sentenced to six months' hard labour.[2]

Methodist implication appears to be more evidenced in the Manchester outrages. In a correspondence between the Revs. Hugh Stowell and James Gwyther carried on through the columns of the *Manchester Guardian* of 1843 (June 7), the former charges the Dissenters with being conspicuous in the riots of 1842, and offers to supply a list of fifteen names as evidence. The latter seeks to refute the charge and asks for the promised list. Six of the names were described as Methodist, most of them being local preachers. To support his defence he supplies a counter list which described the religion of 425 prisoners, 213 of whom belonged to

[1] *Staffordshire Examiner*, Oct. 8, 1842. [2] *Bradford Observer*, Sept. 8, 1842.

the Church of England while only 92 were classified as Dissenters. Among the latter, 63 were listed as Methodist.

Conspicuous among the ex-Methodists who were arrested on charges of inciting to riot were the Rev. J. R. Stephens of Ashton-under-Lyne, the Revs. W. V. Jackson and W. Scholefield of Manchester, and the Rev. W. Essler of Stockport. The two former suffered imprisonment in 1839–40, while the two latter though arrested in 1842 escaped this penalty. John Skevington, an ex-Primitive Methodist minister, was imprisoned at Loughborough during 1842, and Joseph Capper, a local preacher, together with John Richards and Thomas Cooper, both ex-Methodist local preachers, were sent to prison for their share in the Pottery disturbances.

Although this list of Methodists and ex-Methodists charged with offences against law and order might appear convincing to the critic that Methodism was a disruptive force, yet a review of the evidence against the arrested, together with a knowledge of the way Methodism disciplined its members, should demonstrate the contrary. A large number of untutored individuals were constantly brought under the influence of the Methodist teaching. That so many wild and unlearned people should be kept quiet and submissive in the days of intense suffering and agitation is one of the marvels of English social life. A casual review of the records found in Quarterly Meeting, Local Preachers' Meeting and Leaders' Meeting Minutes Books would give an insight into the method of success. Rules and regulations had to be obeyed. Violation and disobedience were severely censured or punished. In many instances expulsion was imposed. By this means respect for authority and obedience to law were both taught and enforced.

PART II

METHODISM AND THE POLITICAL SOCIETIES OF 1816–1850

CHAPTER I

THE RADICAL SOCIETIES OF 1816–1823

WORKING-CLASS agitation for Parliamentary Reform goes back to 1792, when the London Corresponding Society was organized by Thomas Hardy. As its name suggests, one of its objects was to get into touch with similar institutions. Political societies had already been established at Manchester, Stockport, Norwich, and Sheffield. The Sheffield Society was said 'to be two thousand strong'. 'To link together all such local efforts in the pursuit of common aims was the object, from its inception, of the London Corresponding Society.'[1] Its members were pledged to work for 'a Thorough Reform in Parliament' by demanding 'equal representation, Annual Parliaments, and Universal Suffrage'.[2] One of its first resolutions expressed the opinion that 'every individual had the right to share in the Government of that society of which he is a member, unless incapacitated'.[3] Its numbers continued to grow until the December of 1795, when the Seditious Meetings Bill was passed.[4] On April 19, 1798, the whole of the London Committee were seized by order of the Government, and a few months later the Society was effectually suppressed.[5]

Although political quiescence was enforced among the lower classes from 1798–1816, discontent did not remain silent. As already noted it lifted its voice against the high prices that obtained in 1800–1, and broke out into violence during 1811 to 1814. Turning from industrial violence in 1816 it entered the political arena once more.

The outer history of the Radical agitation is concerned with public meetings, Parliamentary petitions, and mob demonstrations. In the later months of 1816 public demonstrations

[1] *The Age of Grey and Peel*, H. W. Carless Davies, pp. 77–80.
[2] Place MSS. 27812, p. 50.
[3] *ibid.*, p. 3.
[4] An Act for the more effectually preventing Seditious Meetings and Assemblies. U.K. Statutes. 39 George III. Cap. VIII.
[5] Place MSS. 27808, p. 111.

began to be held in different parts of the country. Important gatherings took place at London, Leeds, Liverpool, Sheffield, and other places, and in every case the prevalent distress was considered. London took the lead in this activity. At a meeting held in the Palace Yard, Westminster, early in September, it was unanimously resolved 'that to obtain relief from their present distress, and to prevent forever a return, it is necessary the people, in their respective counties, cities, towns and villages, should cordially co-operate in the measures adopted by the cities of London and Westminster for the salvation of their country, in firmly and perseveringly claiming by petition their right to a real representation annually elected'.[1] A similar meeting was held at Spa Fields on November 15 'to take into consideration the propriety of petitioning the Prince Regent upon the present distressed state of the country'. During the same day mob violence broke out in several parts of the city.[2] Another meeting was held a fortnight later, when Henry Hunt described his visit to the Prince Regent. Before the arrival of Hunt, the assembled people were addressed by a young person who said among other things, 'They have neglected the starving people, robbed them of everything, and given them a penny. Is this to be endured? Four millions are in distress'. 'If I jump down will you follow me?' 'Yes! Yes!' cried the angry mob. A number of people followed him into the city and committed various acts of outrage.[3] *The Morning Post* (December 3, 1816) described the affair as 'little short of Treason stalking forth to open day, setting all law at defiance, and daringly and infamously unfurling the flags of Resistance and Rebellion to the land'.

Greater importance was given to the movement for reform by the decision of 'the Lord Mayor, Aldermen and Commons of the City of London, in Common Council Assembled' to take an address to the Prince Regent in order 'to represent our national sufferings and grievances, and respectfully to suggest the measures which we conceive to be indispensably necessary for the safety, the quiet and the prosperity of the Realm'. On December 9, 'his Royal Highness held a Court at Carlton-house, for the purpose of receiving the address'. 'The Corporation of the City of London

[1] *The Times*, Sept. 12, 1816. Also *Leeds Mercury*, Sept. 14, 1816.
[2] *Leeds Mercury*, Nov. 23, 1816. Also *The Times*, Nov. 16, 1816. And Place MSS. 27809, p. 21.
[3] *The Times*, Dec. 3, 1816.

arrived in Grand State procession about two o'clock at Carlton-house followed by a concourse of people huzzaing, and were received in Pall-mall by a flourish of the trumpets of the Life Guards. On their entrance into the Court-yard, and descending from their carriages, the band of the Guard of honour played an excellent march.' In their petition they boldly asserted that 'our grievances are the natural effect of rash and ruinous Wars unjustly commenced, and pertinaciously persisted in, when no rational object was to be obtained'. Other evils were indicated and said to have arisen 'from the corrupt and inadequate state of the Representation of the People in Parliament, whereby all constitutional control over the servants of the Crown has been lost, and Parliament have become subservient to the will of Ministers'. 'Nothing but a reformation of these abuses,' they declared, 'and restoring to the People their just and constitutional right in the Election of Members of Parliament, can afford a security against their recurrence—calm the apprehensions of the People—allay their irritated feelings and prevent' a continuance of discontent. No wonder the Prince Regent expressed 'strong feelings of surprise and regret', but he afforded no relief when he confessed 'I deplore the prevailing distress and difficulties of the country'. They are chiefly 'to be attributed to unavoidable causes'.[1]

Through examples of this kind, the working-class portion of the community gained increasing courage in formulating their demands. Many petitions against the use of machinery, and in favour of Parliamentary Reform, reached the House of Commons in the early months of 1817. The boldest project emanated from Manchester. At a meeting held on March 3, it was decided to present a petition to the Prince of the Realm. It was also determined 'that in order to "undeceive" the Prince Regent, and to bring him acquainted with the real state of the country, a large deputation of the people should be dispatched to London, to present their own address'. An appeal was made for volunteers to join in the contemplated march. Every man was invited to 'assemble peaceably and orderly, and provide himself with the necessary means of support requisite to bear him through this loyal and necessary undertaking'. Between 10,000 and 30,000 people gathered near St. Peter's Church on March 10, in order to give a hearty send-off to the marchers. While the leaders were

[1] *The Times*, Dec. 10, 1816.

addressing the assembled crowd, the platform was surrounded, and Drummond, Johnson, and Baguley were arrested. Already 'about a thousand men, provided with knapsacks, containing blankets, and such provisions as they could take, had withdrawn a short time before to Piccadilly, from where they set out soon after on their political pilgrimage to London'. A troop of cavalry followed 'the migratory reformers who had set out on their way to London. Before they arrived at Longsight, a number of stragglers were overtaken and secured; and at Stockport Bridge, the cavalry surrounded a great number, all furnished for bivouacking, and in the travelling equipage of this party, two unusually large knives were discovered. In the course of the day the number of persons apprehended and lodged in the New Bayley amounted to two hundred'.[1] I. Silvester informs the Home Office on the next day 'that all the Gaols of the County and especially the New Bayley Prison are and were previously to the present occasion remarkably crowded', while the Rev. W. R. Hay reports his regret 'that of those who marched as toward London, only a rear detachment was taken'.[2] 'Not more than 500, out of the many thousands assembled in the morning, penetrated so far as Macclesfield.'[3] A few eventually arrived at a place near Ashbourne in Derbyshire. The latter, weary and footsore, were stopped by the Rev. W. Powis, 'a most active magistrate from Leek', and 'although the mob was unarmed and conducted themselves quietly', the shepherd of human souls terminated their long march by the help of the military.[4] During the next three months a climax was reached. Some of the misled reformers made attempts at rebellion, but they were quickly arrested and three of their number beheaded.

After the explosions of 1817 quietude reigned for a time. Apparently it was the calm before the storm. Discontent had not been allayed by reaction and repression. It had been driven underground only. In the winter of 1818 and 1819 the Radicals came into the arena again. They held both private and public meetings, always with the same purpose, to relieve their distress by a reform of Parliament. While a minority that attended these gatherings might be described as 'very seditious, designing and

[1] *Leeds Mercury*, March 15, 1817. Also H.O. 40. 5, 1817.
[2] H.O. 42. 161, 1817.
[3] *Leeds Mercury*, March 15, 1817.
[4] H.O. 42. 161, 1817.

dangerous characters', yet 'the great mass of the population' were 'by no means disaffected'.[1] The Government thought otherwise and sought to prevent their meetings. In a proclamation dated July 30, 1819, 'the wicked purposes' of 'seditious and treasonable speeches' are publicly condemned. Such speeches, declared the official publication, tend 'to bring into hatred and contempt the Government and Constitution', and seek 'to excite disobedience to the laws and insurrection against His Majesty's authority'. His subjects are therefore warned against 'all proceedings tending to produce the evil effects described'.[2] Irrespective of this advice the Reformers of Lancashire held a great demonstration at Manchester on August 16, 1819. Henry Hunt, the great exponent of political reform, processioned through the streets on his way to address the meeting. Contingents of supporters came from other places in the vicinity. The magistrates had already gathered in council before the meeting began. As soon as the speakers appeared on the platform the military were ordered to arrest them. Various accounts have been given as to what followed. The majority of reports, however, agree that the unarmed multitude, without any provocation whatever, were attacked by the troops acting on the instructions of the magistrates. Hunt and his companions were arrested, while at least five or six people were killed and two or three hundred wounded.

This ferocious onslaught against a peaceful assembly inflamed and embittered working-class feeling. Protest meetings against the action of the magistrates were held in various parts of the country. Whigs joined with Radicals in denouncing the magisterial attack. In some districts county meetings were held and a determination to protect the right of public speech was repeatedly expressed. On Thursday, September 9, 1819, the Court of Common Council declared that Englishmen had a right 'to assemble together for the purpose of deliberating upon public grievances as well as on the legal and constitutional means of obtaining redress'. In view of this right the people of Manchester were justified in meeting together and 'were therefore acting under the sanction of the laws, and entitled to the protection of the Magistrates'.[3] At a county meeting in York on October 14,

[1] Lord Fitzwilliam's letter in *Newcastle Chronicle*, Aug. 7, 1819.
[2] *The Times*, Aug. 2, 1819.
[3] *Leeds Mercury*, Sept. 18, 1819.

practically the same decision was reached. Lord Fitzwilliam was deprived of his Lord Lieutenancy for attending the meeting and signing the requisition that made it possible.[1]

Reference has already been made to the disturbances of 1820. These, however, did not tend to increase the influence of the diminishing number of Radical reformers. With Hunt and his companions in prison the movement for reform had languished for a time. But Hunt was not idle while in confinement. By formulating a plan for the re-organization of reformers he inaugurated the Great Northern Union. In 1821 a branch of the Union had been formed in Manchester, and the resurrected *Manchester Observer*, now called '*Wooler's British Gazette*', became the unofficial organ of the new association. After the repulse of reform in the House of Commons in 1823, the agitation in the country died down for a while. It revived again in later days.

The inner history of Radicalism is connected with the activities of reform clubs and unions, and with the stories of conspiracy and sedition. On Tuesday, February 18, 1817, the 'Secret Committee of the House of Lords' presented their report 'Respecting Certain Dangerous Meetings and Combinations'. The evidence which they examined left 'no doubt in their minds that a traitorous conspiracy has been formed in the metropolis for the purpose of overthrowing, by means of a general insurrection, the established government, laws, and constitution of this kingdom, and of effecting a general plunder and division of property'. Plans for this project were made last autumn, and Spa Fields was fixed upon as 'the place affording the greatest facilities for entering the town, and attacking the most important points in the city'.[2] On November 15, 1816, it was intended 'to set fire to various barracks', to make 'an attack upon the Tower and Bank, and other points of importance'.[3] Had the plan 'even partially succeeded, there seems much reason to believe that it would have been the signal for a more general rising in other parts of the kingdom'. 'Under pretence of Parliamentary reform' the minds of the lower classes of the community are infected 'with a spirit of discontent and disaffection, of insubordination, and contempt of all law, religion, and morality', while holding 'out to them the plunder and division of all property, as the main object of their

[1] *Leeds Mercury*, Oct. 30, 1819.
[2] *Hansard's Parliamentary Debates*, 1817, Vol. xxxv, p. 412.
[3] *ibid.*, p. 413.

efforts, and the restoration of their natural rights'.[1] With this object in view 'Hampden Clubs', 'Union Clubs', and 'Spencean' societies have been established principally 'in the neighbourhood of Leicester, Loughborough, Nottingham, Mansfield, Derby, Chesterfield, Sheffield, Blackburn, Manchester, Birmingham, and Norwich'.[2]

The subject of a general rising is considered again on Wednesday February 19, when the report of the House of Commons Secret Committee was presented. 'Attempts have been made,' says the report, 'in various parts of the country, as well as in the metropolis, to take advantage of the distress in which the labouring and manufacturing classes of the community are at present involved, to induce them to look for immediate relief, not only in a reform of Parliament on the plan of universal suffrage and annual election, but in a total overthrow of all existing establishments, and in a division of the landed, and extinction of the funded property of the country.'[3] The members of the committee were quite satisfied that in the Metropolis certain people intended 'a sudden rising in the dead of night, to surprise and overpower the soldiers in their different barracks . . . to possess themselves of the artillery, to seize or destroy the bridges, and to take possession of the Tower and the Bank'.[4] Evidence of this wicked plot is seen on a placard which had been found. 'Britain to Arms' read the headline. 'The whole country awaits the signal from London to fly to arms, haste, break open gun-smiths and the places likely to find arms, run all constables who touch a man of us; no rise of bread; no Regent; no Castlereagh; off with their heads; no placemen, tythes, or enclosures; no taxes; no bishops, only useless lumber, stand true, or be slaves for ever.'[5]

Reports of this nature made it more easy to secure the passage of the Habeas Corpus Suspension Bill. When a further suspension was required, the presentation of the second reports paved the way. On Thursday, June 12, the House of Lords were informed by the Secret Committee that the papers which had been examined 'afford but too many proofs of the continued existence of a traitorous conspiracy for the overthrow of our established government and constitution, and for the subversion of the existing

[1] *Hansard's Parliamentary Debates*, 1817, Vol. xxxv, p. 415.
[2] *ibid.*, p. 416.
[3] *ibid.*, p. 438.
[4] *ibid.*, p. 440.
[5] *ibid.*, p. 440.

order of society'. In the proceedings that took place in Manchester, Nottingham, Sheffield, and Birmingham, 'the pretence of parliamentary reform appears to have been almost wholly discarded; they evidently point to nothing short of revolution'. 'On one occasion it is stated to have been proposed, that Manchester should be made a Moscow.' 'It was on the night of March 30 that a general insurrection was intended to have commenced at Manchester. The Magistrates were to be seized; the prisoners were to be liberated; the soldiers were either to be surprised in their barracks, or a certain number of factories were to be set on fire, for the purpose of drawing the soldiers out of their barracks.'[1] Although this plan was foiled by the vigilance of the magistrates, 'another general rising appears to have been fixed for as early a day as possible after the discussion of an expected motion for reform in Parliament. Nottingham appears to have been intended as the headquarters upon which a part of the insurgents were to march in the first instance'.[2] This plan was eventually postponed until June 9.

The idea of a general rising received further evidence from the Second Report of the Secret Committee to the House of Commons. From papers dealing with the proceedings of the disaffected in the counties of Lancashire, Leicestershire, Nottinghamshire, and some parts of Yorkshire, together with the towns of Birmingham and Stockport, 'a general idea seemed prevalent, that some fixed day, at no very great distance, was to be appointed for a general rising'.[3] When the Manchester marchers set out on their journey to London, they felt sure 'that their numbers, which, in the course of their progress, would amount to not less than 100,000, would make it impossible ultimately to resist them'.[4] The plan fixed for March 30, 'was, to assemble as many as could be collected, in the night, at Manchester; to attack the barracks, the police office, the prison, the houses of magistrates and constables, and the banks in separate parties; and to set fire to the factories in the town'.[5] 'Expectations were held out, that a general insurrection would take place, at the same time, in

[1] *Hansard's Parliamentary Debates*, 1817, Vol. xxxvi, pp. 949, 953.
[2] *ibid.*, pp. 954–5.
[3] *ibid.*, p. 1089.
[4] *ibid.*, p. 1090.
[5] *ibid.*, p. 1092. This part of the report is based upon the evidence supplied by the agents of the magistrates in the Manchester area. See Hammonds *The Skilled Labourer* for a description of the activities of these agents, pp. 350–3.

different parts of the counties of Lancaster, York, Warwick, Leicester, Nottingham, Chester, and Stafford.' In the month of May delegates from Manchester, Birmingham, Nottingham, Derby, Leeds, Sheffield, Wakefield, Huddersfield, and other places met together and agreed 'to foment the irritation among the disaffected, and to combine some general plan of simultaneous, or connected insurrection; the object of which was, after consolidating a sufficient force, to march upon London, and there to overturn the existing government, and to establish a republic'. 'The utmost confidence prevailed among the delegates, as to the ultimate attainment of their object.'[1] Eventually the plan was held in abeyance till June 9, when attempts were made in Yorkshire and Derbyshire to put it into execution.

Whether the Government honestly believed that insurrection was the general purpose of Radical activities, or whether in order to crush reform, which they hated, they deliberately deceived both Houses of Parliament by supplying them with carefully selected dubious papers, opinions may differ. If the former view be accepted, then the Government were obviously duped by their own emissaries. What the editor of the *Leeds Mercury* said about the Manchester plot of March 30 can be applied to all the plots reported to the Home Office. Writing on April 12, he says, 'another week has passed, and we have heard nothing, except on paper, of the rebellion with which we are told that the manufacturing towns in this part of the kingdom were threatened. Indeed it has been altogether a paper insurrection'. Where disturbances actually took place, the agents of the local and central authorities were largely to blame. When the Second Report of the Secret Committee was under consideration in the House of Commons, Lord Milton observed 'that much of the disturbances in Derbyshire and Yorkshire had been produced by the arts of Government emissaries'.[2] A study of the Home Office Papers leads one to the same conclusion.[3] Edward Baines and others brought to public notice evidence of the machinations of

[1] *Hansard's Parliamentary Debates*, 1817, Vol. xxxvi, pp. 1092–3.
[2] *ibid.*, p. 1083.
[3] The Hammonds adopt this view. See *The Skilled Labourer* for chapter on 'The Adventures of Oliver the Spy'. They trace the movements of the Government 'provocateurs' in the vicinity of Manchester, as well as in Yorkshire and the Midlands, pp. 341–6.

Oliver the spy. He was described 'as a person of genteel appearance and good address, nearly six feet high, of erect figure, light hair, red and rather large whiskers, and a full face, a little pitted with the small pox'. This man, in the pay and with the authority of His Majesty's Ministers, inveigled himself into the confidence of illiterate and distressed reformers. Having gained their confidence, he told them fantastic stories of insurrectionary preparations in various parts of the country. 'All the metropolis', he is reported to have said, 'were favourable to a change in the Government.' 'Everything was organized.' 'It was absolutely settled, that on the night preceding the trial of the state prisoners (the night of June 8) a general rising would take place.' 'The same plan should be simultaneously acted upon in all parts of the country.' 'His friends in London', he once affirmed, 'were almost heart-broken that the people in the country were so quiet.'[1] How the Yorkshire dupes responded has already been described, but through the activities of the *Leeds Mercury* they were saved from the severest penalty. Not one prisoner was executed. The matter was different in Derbyshire. Brandreth, Ludlam, and Turner were hanged while others were transported.

The defeat of feeble attempts at rebellion did not relieve the prevailing distress. In their desperation working men turned to industrial action then back again to political reform. Sometimes both methods were tried in conjunction, but the law was against them. How to get round the law was always a difficult task. A new endeavour to do this was made in July, 1818, when the Political Protestants were organized at Hull.[2] Commenting on the formation of this society, the editor of *The Black Dwarf* (Aug. 19, 1818), hopes it will have the same success 'which has attended the "Religious Protestants" in the defeat of every system of oppression, and the exposure of every public delusion'. 'That the example will be followed', he had absolutely no doubt. In the 'Rules and Regulations', which he prints in their entirety, the mind of the working-class politicians is clearly revealed. While protesting against the 'mockery' of representation they are resolved 'to rescue the House of Commons from the . . . Borough Merchants, and to restore it to the people'.

'We sincerely believe', declared the promoters, 'that political ignorance has been the cause of all our national misery and

[1] *Leeds Mercury*, June 14, 1817. [2] H.O. 42. 179, 1818.

degradation, and that nothing but a firm and extensive Union of the people to promote and diffuse a correct knowledge of our immediate rights, can possibly protect our Country either from absolute despotism on the one hand or a dreadful Revolution and anarchy on the other. We shall, therefore, meet once a week, in small classes, not exceeding twenty in each class, and subscribe One Penny each, for the purpose of purchasing such means of information as may be required; in which way we exhort all friends of Radical Reform throughout the kingdom to associate.

'The leaders of each class shall hold a meeting once a month to report the progress of the Institution; and in order to do away all ground of accusation, against our proceedings, we declare that we will not have any secret transactions whatever, and that our meetings, our books and accounts, of every description, shall at all times be laid open for the inspection of the Magistrates or others, who may request the same.'[1] Shortly after the publication of these rules, both Cleary and Wooler commend their acceptance to the readers of *The Black Dwarf*. The former with his eye upon the law, and not forgetting the need of co-operation among political reformers, regards 'the plan of the Political Protestants, established at Hull', as 'a good model for proceeding upon in these times'. 'We hope,' he confidently asserts, 'we shall shortly be able to announce the formation of clubs of Political Protestants everywhere. We must not correspond with them, we suppose; but they may write to us, if they please; and any publicity we can give to their proceedings may be commanded in the columns of *The Black Dwarf*.'[2] The latter, remembering the events of 1817, announces with a sort of triumphant optimism that 'this association is proceeding with some rapidity in the town where the idea was first conceived'. 'Against them,' he says, 'spies will be useless; and the agents of a Sidmouth and a Castereagh will be as harmless as the scowling fiend that was startled at the ear of Eve by the touch of Ithuriel.' He confidently declares that 'we will destroy all pretence for the use of the bayonet'. In order to accomplish these objects, 'small associations' and 'small subscriptions' are necessary. 'Such is the practice of the "Political Protestants". If every man convinced of the necessity, and

[1] *The Black Dwarf*, Aug. 19, 1818. Also H.O. 42. 179, 1818.
[2] *The Black Dwarf*, Sept. 2, 1818.

wishing for the accomplishment of a radical reform, would but sign his name, and the lists would be laid before the borough-mongers, their nerves would shake to dissolution, and their fancied sceptre of iron would crumble into dust.' 'Those who condemn clubs,' he adds, 'either do not understand what they can accomplish, or they wish nothing to be done. Larger meetings are not so well calculated for discussions or deliberation; and if they were, is there a better mode of securing large meetings than a previous combination of smaller ones.'[1] In addition to these sentiments, the editor of *The Black Dwarf* published an abridged list of the 'Rules of the Political Protestants'. These rules are ordered to 'be written in the class book of every class of Political Protestants throughout the kingdom', and are 'most earnestly recommended to the strict observance of each individual who unites himself to this most important institution'. One of the rules declares that 'we engage to form the —[2] Class of Political Protestants, which class shall not contain more than twenty members; and to use all the influence in our power, to cause as many more classes to be formed as possible'.

Receiving the constant commendation of the pages of *The Black Dwarf*, the Hull Union continued to exercise an increasing influence. In less than twelve months, similar societies were formed at Crediton, York, Leeds, Wakefield, London, and Coventry. Crediton established a society of Political Protestants in the October of 1818. A member of the new society informs *The Black Dwarf* (Nov. 11, 1818) 'that the laudable example which has recently been set by the patriots of Hull, in forming a Political Protestant Association, for the purpose of endeavouring to procure a radical reform in the Commons' House of Parliament, has been followed by the inhabitants of this town'. In a footnote he says, 'We meet regularly once a week, for the purpose of perusing such periodical and other works as are calculated to afford political information'. The York Society of Political Protestants was established in the early part of December. A correspondent, reporting this fact (*The Black Dwarf*, December 9, 1818), announces that 'they have adopted the "declaration" before inserted in *The Dwarf*, and are proceeding with spirit and success towards importance and effect'. A few months later, the York

[1] *The Black Dwarf*, Sept. 9, 1818.
[2] The number of the class was inserted here, *The Black Dwarf*, Sept. 9, 1818.

Society receives the blessing of T. J. Wooler. He commends them because of their 'desire for political information'. Believing that the weight of oppression must soon be removed, he adds, 'The means you have adopted for that purpose are some of the most efficient. Nothing can be accomplished but by Union. . . . Men must meet each other, unite their knowledge and their powers, compare their sentiments, weigh together the force of opposite statements—and draw the pure gold of truth from the dross of the inferior ore with which it is generally combined. . . . Your meetings', he declares, 'are legal; and the justice of your cause will vindicate your proceedings. Continue to transact your business in the public eye. Concealment is not requisite. Invite your enemies to scrutinize your conduct. You can fearlessly look them in the face, and tell them you defy their malignity'. After promising to publish their second declaration, he says, 'I am happy to inform you, that the order of Political Protestants is rapidly increasing. In all parts of the country, similar societies are forming; and the plain dealing of the parties, the undisguised avowal of just principles, and the open pursuit of general good, must ensure them respect if they fail, and the general gratitude of their country if they succeed. Societies under other denominations are also adopting the same sentiments'.[1]

An 'Association of the Friends to Radical Reform' had been established at Leeds in the middle of February, 1819. Though not bearing the name of Political Protestants when it published an address in the *Leeds Mercury* of February 20, its organization, objects and declaration were the same as the Hull Society. The instruction given to the class-leaders is also the same.[2] In an address to 'the Friends of Radical Reform', after describing the abuses of the present system of government, it definitely declares that 'the diffusion of Political Knowledge' is 'essentially necessary'. In pursuit of this object, the members agree to 'meet once a week in small classes, not exceeding twenty-five each class, and subscribe one penny each'.[3] A similar union had been inaugurated at Wakefield by the beginning of June, 1819. An ex-chief constable, reporting its existence, declares that 'the disaffected act more systematically throughout this part of the county. They

[1] *The Black Dwarf*, April 21, 1819.
[2] Compare *The Black Dwarf*, Aug. 19, 1818 with the *Leeds Mercury*, Feb. 20, 1819.
[3] *Leeds Mercury*, Feb. 20, 1819.

are formed into classes of twenty-five each'. Each has a leader and consults with other leaders.[1]

The Hull Political Protestants were by no means inactive during the early months of 1819. Although the Rev. Joseph Harrison had been instrumental in forming a similar union in Stockport, under a different name and with slightly different rules, a correspondent writes him concerning the Hull Society, and asks for his co-operation. 'We have formed ourselves', he declares, 'into an institution of Political Protestants, which we most earnestly recommend to be adopted in every town and village in the nation. We divide ourselves into classes of twenty each, and each class meets once a week, where they think proper; the members subscribe a penny each weekly, and read Cobbett, and Sherwin's Registers, Wooler's *Black Dwarf*, and other works, calculated to diffuse political knowledge; the leaders of each class hold a meeting on the first Monday in every month, to report the progress of the institution to the chairman.' 'We declare that we will continue to use every means in our power, to establish a real protecting Parliament, instead of the borough-mongers destroying Parliament. We do not dictate any creed, we do not insist upon annual or triennial Parliaments, universal suffrage, or voting by house-keepers; we only require that every person who acknowledges the necessity of a reform in any shape will prove their sincerity by joining with this union, and when this institution is sufficiently extensive we shall then determine what system of reform we shall declare for, by referring it to the majority of each class. The members of the class can then write all their names upon one sheet of paper, and each individual can specify opposite his name, what system of reform he prefers.' The writer adds, 'I have written to Sir Charles Wolseley, Bart., in Staffordshire . . . to solicit his patronage and co-operation with us; and I have received his answer wherein he says "the institution is excellent, and you may rely upon my willingness to co-operate with the Political Protestants of Hull, to the utmost of my power".' Addressing Mr. Harrison, the correspondent says, 'You, Sir, are most sincerely entreated by the Political Protestants, on behalf of themselves and their much injured country, that you and all the friends to reform, in your neighbourhood will join with us to form a temperate, rational and firm union throughout the nation,

[1] H.O. 42. 188, 1819.

as the only means of effecting our political salvation. With such a union we shall become omnipotent against either despotism or anarchy; but divided, or single-handed, we remain imbecile and incapable of doing anything'.[1]

At the beginning of June, Political Protestants were reported to be established in Coventry and London.[2] Before the end of the month, the societies at Leeds and Wakefield were congratulated 'on the progress of their institution'.[3] Although direct evidence is not yet available, it is nevertheless highly probable that societies of Political Protestants were formed at other places by this time. At the Hunslet reform meeting, held on June 7, delegates from the following places attended—Manchester, Rochdale, Huddersfield, Stockport, Oldham, Stalybridge, Barnsley, New Mills, Royton, Bury, Heywood, Todmorden, Blackburn, Leeds, Wakefield, Macclesfield, Ashton-under-Lyne, Gee Cross, Lees, Morley, Holmfirth, Failsworth, Heyside, Whitfield, Leigh, and Middleton.[4] A letter from the Hull Society was read at the gathering advising the formation of societies in order to fight the 'borough-mongers' and 'the black hypocrisy of our false priests'. James Mann, the Leeds representative, informed the delegates 'that Unions on the principles of Radical Reform are formed in almost every part of England; and without Radical Reform our country will be ruined'.[5]

It was only after the Hunslet meeting that the Hull papers began to discuss the Political Protestant Society. The editor of the *Rockingham and Hull Weekly Advertiser* (June to Dec., 1819) proudly announced his great pleasure in learning that 'our institution of Political Protestants is making such progress in Leeds, Wakefield, &c'. A very different sentiment is expressed by the *Hull Packet* (June to Dec., 1819). The editor is alarmed at the purport of the letter sent by the Hull Political Protestants and cynically exclaims, 'from such reform, good Lord, deliver us'. According to the *Hull Advertiser and Exchange Gazette* (June to Dec., 1819), 'a Revolution, and one of the most extensive nature, is the object of these pretended reformers'.

Greater prominence came to the York Political Protestants through the Hunslet demonstration. Their principles are regarded

[1] *The Black Dwarf*, April 14, 1819.
[2] *ibid.*, June 2, 1819.
[3] *ibid*, June 23, 1819.
[4] *ibid.*, June 16, 1819.
[5] *ibid.*, June 16, 1819.

as 'popular' by the editor of the *York Herald* (June to Dec., 1819), and he gladly announces that they are 'rapidly spreading and assuming everywhere a definite form'. One of the proprietors of this paper is charged by the *Yorkshire Gazette* (June to Dec., 1819) with attending a meeting of the York reformers 'whose creed' is described as 'Annual Parliaments and Universal Suffrage'. Following on this charge a fierce discussion ensues between the two papers. *The Herald* is so annoyed at the charges that it descends to the use of objectionable invective by repeatedly describing its opponent as 'the Soot-Bag Gazette'. The *York Chronicle* (June to Dec., 1819) takes no part in the quarrel, and says very little about the new society. Most of the provincial papers comment on the Hunslet gathering. A correspondent to the *Worcester Journal* (July 1, 1819) appears to be greatly alarmed at the activity of the Radicals. Writing from Leeds, he says, they 'are so completely beset and hemmed in . . . with Union and Reform Societies and the members of them are known to be so numerous, that the best informed persons, men who are by no means Alarmists, are apprehensive that some dire commotion will ere long take place. Mischief is certainly brewing'. These reformers, he avows, amount to 'more than 120,000', and have associations in most of the towns of Lancashire, Yorkshire, and Cheshire.

It is very probable that the Political Protestants were already established in most of the twenty-seven localities represented at Hunslet. A similar union for the promotion of human happiness had been formed at Stockport on October 30, 1818. Its motto was extracted from the Bible—'Do unto others as you would they should do to you'. In its declaration it calls attention to 'the ill-spent years of our history', 'the constant and rapid decrease of private morals', 'the oppression, slavery, and cruelty that everywhere abounds', and 'the greatest suffering and affliction both of body and mind' 'arrived at a pitch of severity never before equalled'. Faced with 'a continuance, if not an increase' of this privation of life, mainly due to the mismanagement of a 'sordid Aristocracy and corrupt system of Government', the rules of the society declare among other things that men are born free, sovereignty lies with the people, and an association is necessary to preserve human rights. In order to make such a union permanent and powerful, the town is arbitrarily divided into twelve sections or districts, and each section is divided into classes. Rule 7 declares that 'all members of the Union shall be divided or classed with twelve members to each class; they shall elect a leader from amongst themselves every three months; every class shall meet once every week at the house of the leader or some other of the members of the class, or at the Union Rooms, as may be most convenient to them, for the purpose of reading any political, or other books, papers, &c., &c., or conversation upon the best practical mode, according to the exigency of the time, of obtaining a free and good Government, which is the primary and principal step to the attainment of human happiness. Each member shall pay weekly to his class leader, at the time of the meeting, one penny, for the purpose of carrying into effect the object of the Union, viz., that of obtaining Political Liberty and Universal Freedom. The class leaders shall write down the important proceedings of every class meeting, in order that it may be reported to the body of the Union'. The eighth rule ordains that 'the class-leaders shall meet the general committee and officers at the Union Rooms every Monday evening at 8 o'clock, for the purpose of paying to the general fund their respective class collections; and of reporting the progress of their respective classes in moral and political information; for stating what they consider to be necessary for the further promoting of the general object; to receive instructions from, and advice with, the general committee respecting the welfare and further promoting the object of the Institution'. Rule 14 empowers the general committee, or any part thereof 'to visit each and every class at the time of its meeting, for the purpose of rendering all the assistance he or they can, for the promotion of the objects of the Union'. The 15th rule relegates 'the transaction of local business' to a 'Section Committee' comprised of two representatives from each Section together with the class leaders. In the 17th rule it is required that the names of the candidates for the general committee shall be delivered 'to each class leader of the Union, who shall fully canvass the merits or demerits of each candidate in their respective classes'. Altogether there are twenty-six rules governing the society, and the 25th rule affirms it to be impossible, while the corruptions of government continue, to 'do unto others as you would they should do to you'. Every member, therefore, is expected to seek 'a radical reform of Parliament, by means of suffrage in all male persons of mature age and sane minds, who have not for any crime forfeited the right of Parliament having a duration not exceeding one year, and of elections by ballot'.[1]

In the April of 1819 a political society for the promotion of human happiness is formed at Macclesfield. The Stockport plan is adopted in its entirety.[2] A member of the Stockport Union, writing a few weeks later in *Sherwin's Political Register*, gives an account of the political class meeting. 'We generally read at a class meeting,' he says, 'for about half an hour.' 'After reading, a general conversation takes place for about half an hour more, when each member states his opinion and ideas of the Government.'[3] Shortly after the appearance of this article, a union is reported from London. At the inaugural meeting the members agreed to form themselves into sections of twelve to each leader. Every group had to choose its own leader, and each member was asked to subscribe a penny a week to the general fund.[4]

The Radical females of Stockport followed the example set by the men-folk. They too formed themselves into political classes. Rule 1 of their society ordains 'that the members shall be classed, with twelve members in each class, who shall select a leader or collector amongst themselves every fourteen weeks; also, every female on becoming a member, shall pay weekly to her collector, one penny, for the purpose of assisting our male friends in obtaining their object'.[5] According to the *Leeds Mercury* (July 21, 1819), the females at Stockport had followed 'the example set by Alice Kitchen and her associates at Blackburn'. *The Newcastle Courant* account (July 24, 1819) of the Stockport Female Union also assumes it was influenced by the Blackburn Female Union. In an earlier report (*Manchester Observer*, July 17, 1819), the secretary of the former union announces that 'at the first meeting on Thursday the 1st instant . . . thirty-six females entered the lists, and were formed into classes pursuant to the rules of the union. At our second meeting last Monday evening but one, five classes were formed; at our third meeting last Monday evening seven classes were formed'.

[1] *Wooler's British Gazette*, April 25, 1819. Also *Manchester Observer*, May 8, 1819. *The Black Dwarf*, April 28, 1819. H.O. 42. 184, 1819.
[2] H.O. 42. 186, 1819.
[3] *ibid.*, 42. 188, 1819.
[4] *ibid.*, 42. 190, 1819.
[5] *Wooler's British Gazette*, July 25, 1819.

Reports to the Home Office indicate the spread of Union Societies in the county of Lancashire. 'The town of Manchester is divided into sections. Each person pays a penny a week into the general fund', and every section has a leader.[1] According to Fletcher, several classes had been established at Bolton. Every class consists of twelve persons, and 'each person contributes one penny per week'.[2] The Union Society at Wigan meets regularly at the house of Henry Haselden. Instead of the usual twelve people comprising a section, the number here is twenty-five. Each section meets once a week 'for the mutual edification and instruction of its members'. An address, bearing the title 'Britains be Free', is published by the medium of a handbill. Henry Haselden, who apparently was the leader of the society, suffers the usual penalty for Radical leadership. He is eventually arrested.[3] According to a correspondent in *The Black Dwarf* (June 2, 1819), the political reformers in Oldham had been driven from the public houses because the publicans were threatened with a suspension of their licence if they continued to house the Radicals. Under these conditions, the latter hired a room of their own and formed themselves into a union 'similar to the Stockport Union'. 'The room also serves for a place of resort for reading political tracts', and occasionally 'a gratuitous sermon' was preached. A school for instructing the young had likewise been opened. Over 200 scholars were registered in a few weeks. Political debates regularly took place on the premises. The correspondent wanted to know from the editor of *The Black Dwarf* 'whether they are acting in conformity to law'. Public meetings were not held because they incurred too much expense. 'Petitioning is of no avail', he exclaims, 'while the House of Commons is constituted as at present and while Sidmouth stands sentinel before the ears of the Prince Regent, like the three-headed dog who guards the entrance to the realms of Pluto. We are endeavouring most assiduously to inform ourselves and others, by all the means in our power, that when we are called upon by circumstances we may be able to act as lovers of our country, and mankind.'

Among the results of the Manchester Peterloo, the increase of Union Societies and political class meetings were not the least. Associations for the promotion of human happiness are reported

[1] H.O. 42. 188, 1819. [2] *ibid.*, 42. 190, 1819. [3] *ibid.*, 42. 189, 1819.

from Nottingham, Blackburn, Bury, Wolverhampton, Manchester, Warwick, St. Neots, Barnsley, and New Mills. The society at Nottingham is divided into sections of twenty-five, and each section has a representative on a committee 'for the management of the whole society'.[1] Reporting two months later (H.O. 42. 197, 1819), J. H. Barker announces that 'they have formed themselves into a body . . . divided into classes of twenty-five, with a leader or deputy to each class'. 'I do not yet know', he confesses, 'how many classes are formed, but I know of one person being in number eight.' At one of the meetings delegates were appointed 'to go to the neighbouring populous villages to recommend the formation of classes'. According to another account, class tickets were issued to the class members, and each one had to show his ticket when attending the class meeting. 'District Committees' were sometimes held in the room belonging to the Blackburn Society, and the question of a 'national meeting' was occasionally discussed. A letter from the Bury class leader R. D. Fletcher, a woollen weaver, admits that 'he is a class leader to a section of Reformers at Bury', and that 'George Taylor of Bury, hatter, is the President of the Union Soct.'. At Wolverhampton 'those principles of reform exhibited to the County by that veteran of reform, Major Cartwright', were accepted as the defined object of the association. In order to achieve the object with 'greater facility', the town and neighbourhood is divided into sections of thirty members, each section being 'directed by a leader'.[2] The Manchester Union is divided into sections of twenty-five. An agent from the Police Office, writing on December 4, says 'I was at a section meeting last night, they are the same as class meetings among the Methodists'.[3] No secrecy is attempted in connexion with the Warwick Association. A printed handbill declares the object to be the attainment of 'Civil & Religious Liberty'. For the accomplishment of this purpose it was decided 'that each member shall contribute not less than one penny per week'. It was also arranged 'that the members be divided into classes'.[4] An ingenious method is adopted at St. Neots, Huntingdon, to increase the number of Radical supporters. According to the Rev. R. Gee, private meetings are held regularly, and any man who can produce twenty-six receipts representing

[1] H.O. 42. 195, 1819.
[2] *ibid.*, 42. 198, 1819.
[3] *ibid.*, 42. 200, 1819.
[4] *ibid.*, 42. 198, 1819.

twenty-six penny contributions 'is appointed Class Leader of twenty-six men'. He is then authorized to meet his contributors 'every Saturday night either in his own house or in some house fixed on by him'.[1] At Barnsley the reformers are said to be identified 'with a religious sect called Kilhamites'.[2] The secretary of the union after his arrest describes the activities of the political classes when being examined by a magistrate.[3] Through the medium of a spy the existence of the New Mills Society is revealed to the authorities. When faced with the possibility of disbanding because of the Government hostility, they decide to meet 'in classes in one another's houses'.[4] The London sectional meetings, which apparently had begun in June, 1819, continue till the end of the year.[5]

While the Union Societies continued their activities in the various places already named, the Political Protestants were spreading into the Midlands and the North East. According to *The Black Dwarf* (Sept. 1, Oct. 6, 20, 1819) the latter had established themselves in Coventry, Walworth, Leicester, and other places. The Leicester reformers, being 'convinced that the diffusion of political information is the best means' of obtaining their objects, formed themselves into societies for that purpose. Birmingham Radicals had also organized a union by this time. Their members were grouped in sections, and they met in a house of their own. T. J. Wooler announces his intention of attending a Radical dinner in their room, and he takes the opportunity of recommending through the pages of *The Black Dwarf* (Sept. 15, 1819) the abstention from 'all excisable articles as much as possible'. He also advises his readers 'to assemble in places of their own, and to form unions upon the principles of radical reform, divided into classes, and sections, with their meetings open, and their proceedings at all times open for inspection'.

A society of Political Protestants was established at Newcastle on August 3, 1819. The Hull declaration and resolutions were adopted in their entirety. In the usual way classes, class leaders, class leaders' meetings, and the penny weekly subscription were inaugurated. When the declaration was posted throughout the town and the neighbouring villages, it 'excited considerable

[1] H.O. 42. 200, 1819.
[2] *ibid.*, 42. 200, 1819.
[3] *ibid.*, 40. 16, 1821.
[4] *ibid.*, 42. 203, 1820.
[5] *ibid.*, 42. 195, 198, 199, 1819.

attention'. The Mayor of the town, who was described as 'brother-in-law to the Lord Chancellor, and one of the receivers of the revenues of Greenwich Hospital estates', was 'roused into activity against the reformers. Some of the police he employed to deface the political declaration posted up in the street, others of them' he 'cashiered for meeting amongst reformers and reading' *The Black Dwarf*.[1]

The Rev. Dr. Gray of Sunderland had flattered himself 'that Sunderland might escape the contagion'. Nevertheless, a union had been established in that town. Its promoters declared that its existence was 'necessary to dispel political ignorance'. Hence they formed themselves into classes of twenty members, and decided to meet every week 'at their class room' and 'to subscribe one penny each'.[2] The same gentleman sends to the Home Office a handbill containing the 'Declaration of the Political Protestants of North and South Shields'. In the customary way they engage to meet in classes of twenty members, and to pay a weekly subscription of one penny each. A monthly meeting of class leaders is also arranged.[3]

The strength of the Political Protestants in the North-East at this time was demonstrated by the size and enthusiasm of a meeting held on Newcastle Town Moor during the Monday of October 11, 1819. The following societies attended and processioned to the meeting place—Benwell, Fawden, Newcastle, Winlaton, Gateshead, North and South Shields, Sunderland, and East Newcastle. The committee of management walked in front, 'after which came the classes into which the societies are divided, each being headed by a class leader'. 'The classes walked four abreast, holding each other's hands.' According to another account, 'the heads of classes carried white or black wands. Every class had its distinctive ensign, bearing the initials of the place, and the number of the class. Many of the class leaders wore black, and a few had white hats'.[4] The Rev. C. Thorpe of Winlaton reckoned that 7,000 reformers took part in the procession, while from 50,000 to 70,000 attended the demonstration.[5]

[1] *The Black Dwarf*, Aug. 11, 1819.
[2] H.O. 42. 195, 1819.
[3] *ibid.*, 42. 196, 1819.
[4] *Newcastle Courant*, Oct. 16, 1819.
[5] H.O. 42. 197, 1819. Also *Manchester Observer*, Oct. 23, 1819. *Newcastle Chronicle*, Oct. 16, 1819. *Newcastle Courant*, Oct. 16, 1819.

This huge political gathering, organized by the Political Protestants, was fully reported by all the local papers. The *Newcastle Chronicle* asserts that 'the events of the day will long be impressed on the memory of the inhabitants of this town'. As an example of the spirit that actuated the reformers, the editor refers to those that came from Shields. When halted at the Ballast Hills, they refused 'to partake even of a barrel of ale provided for them, after a walk of eight miles in a warm day', 'determined not to be diverted from their purpose, nor to do anything that might endanger the harmony of the day'. Together with the *Newcastle Courant* (Aug., 1819 to Feb., 1820) and the *Tyne Mercury* (June, 1819 to Feb., 1820), the *Chronicle* (Aug., to Dec., 1819) regularly reports the activities of the Political Protestants in the Newcastle area and along Tyneside.

Perhaps it was in reference to the October meeting that Mr. Wawn, a prominent methodist at Newcastle, writes in a melancholy tone to Jabez Bunting. 'It is to me,' he says, 'at this time, a subject of painful and depressing concern that two of our local preachers (from North Shields) have attended the tremendous Radical Reform meeting just held here, and one of them spoke at some length, and quite in the spirit of the assembly.' He confesses with some amount of sadness that 'a small number of our leaders are among the most determined friends, to their spirit and design, and . . . measures'; and that 'some of the really pious, misguided sisterhood have helped to make their colours'. After expostulating with some of them, he reports with gladness that 'several members have quitted their classes'. The Radicals, he adds, 'have adopted almost the whole Methodist economy, the terms "class leaders", "district meetings", &c. &c., being perfectly current among them'. He expresses alarm in the concluding portion of the letter when he says, 'if men are to be drilled at missionary and Bible meetings to face a multitude with recollection, and acquired facility of address, and begin to employ the mighty moral weapon thus gained to the endangering of the very existence of the Government of the country, we may certainly begin to tremble for the consequences'.[1] Information of this kind no doubt influenced the Methodist authorities, and helped to call forth in the November of 1819 the notorious circular from the Committee for Guarding the

[1] *The Life of Jabez Bunting.* By his son Thomas Percival Bunting, Vol. II, p.167.

Privileges of Methodists.[1] T. J. Wooler (*The Black Dwarf*, July 26, 1820) charged William Wilberforce with being the instigator of this document. 'Although it bears the signatures of Charles Atmore, and Thomas Blanshard,' writes Wooler, 'it is in reality a pure essay for treasury favour, by Mr. Wilberforce.' 'It has all the peculiar characteristics of your style about it.'

According to reports to the Home Office, the Tyneside Radicals were very active at this time. The Rev. C. Thorpe of Winlaton Parish informs the Home Secretary of the activities of the reformers in his area. 'There are several classes,' he says, 'each class consisting of twenty men, and a presiding leader, which are assembled in rotation nightly in a room hired for the purpose.' 'This system,' he believes, 'to be already in operation among the pitmen on the river Wear.'[2] A report from Mr. Buddle affirms that 'the majority of the workmen of almost every colliery on both rivers, are formed into classes of twenty, with a leader to each class'. The Newcastle Mayor confesses that 'the dissatisfaction, and I most truly lament to add, the disaffection of the pitmen rapidly increases; at one colliery (Mount Moor) near to Gateshead Fell, all the pitmen, except five, have joined the Radicals'. 'Heaton Colliery now has twelve classes, each class consisting of twenty men.' In a further report he tells the Home Office 'that nearly all the labouring people' of Swalwell, Winlaton, Blaydon, and other places 'have joined the Radical class meetings'.[3] Toward the end of November, he announces that it affords him 'great satisfaction in stating that the pitmen at Percy Main Colliery have broke up their classes, divided their fund, and the furniture in the private room in which they held their meeting'. Yet in spite of this assurance, the Earl of Darlington reports that 'meetings of class leaders from the different collieries were held on the 13th, 20th, and 22nd inst. in Newcastle'.[4] On December 31, the Mayor of Newcastle is not so optimistic as he was at the end of November. He wants to retain a naval force, in addition to the military, because 'the Radical classes have not broke up', and because 'nothing but the Military and Naval force preserves the tranquillity of this part of the kingdom'.[5]

Although Union Societies and Political Protestants continued

[1] *Methodist Magazine*, 1819, pp. 942–4.
[2] H.O. 42. 196, 1819.
[3] *ibid.*, 42. 197, 1819.
[4] *ibid.*, 42. 199, 1819.
[5] *ibid.*, 42. 201, 1819.

to be very active until the end of 1819, the information concerning their existence in 1820 is rather meagre. Possibly they were feeling keenly the adverse effects of Government hostility. Several Acts had been passed in order to limit their activities, and many of their leaders were already under arrest and awaiting their trial. Apparently they were quietly dissolving their classes. On January 26 (*The Black Dwarf*), T. J. Wooler finds it necessary to emphasize the value of 'reformers meeting with each other and harmonizing their views in such a manner as to be ready to take whatever measures may be deemed advisable, promptly, loyally, safely, and effectually. For this purpose Union Societies, and Societies of Political Protestants are peculiarly qualified. It is by union alone great things can be accomplished; and it is the want of co-operative union, that renders reformers inefficient. What enabled the Methodists and Dissenters to dictate toleration to the State and the Church, united against them? Nothing but that union, which originated in their class meetings, and daily and weekly associations'. 'The effects of this union are finely displayed, when Sidmouth made his demonstration against the mode of licensing dissenting teachers. The signal of resistance was no sooner given in the metropolis, but it spread with electric rapidity through the provinces.' 'Sidmouth was frightened at the unexpected opposition he had raised. Like a boy surrounded with a swarm of wasps, he ran howling from the storm he had provoked.' 'Let the reformer', added Wooler, 'take the lesson which this curious circumstance holds out to them. Let them be prepared for business when it calls on them; and not have to devise operations when their liberties are invaded.'

The advice of Wooler apparently did not achieve the purpose for which it was given. While reform societies continued their existence in some localities, they were not so numerous and vigorous as hitherto. When the question of the Queen's relationship with the King assumed a national importance, they co-operated with the Whigs in opposition to the Government. Practically no information is available at present concerning the last days of the Union Societies and the Political Protestants. In the month of January, Jonathan Holmes of New Mills reports the tendency of the union in his locality to break up because of the new Act. At present 'they are meeting in classes in one another's houses'.[1]

[1] H.O., 42. 203, 1820.

Though the Radical Associations had changed their name by the beginning of 1821, the political classes still continue. On the second day of January at George Leigh Street, Manchester, a 'Permanent Fund for the Relief of the Sufferers in the cause of Parliamentary Reform' is formally inaugurated. The question was discussed: 'Is the purchase of liberty worth a penny a week?' 'Is it worth a halfpenny?' The third resolution passed at the meeting ordained 'that in order to procure the pecuniary means for carrying the above resolution into effect, the town of Manchester shall be divided into twenty-four districts, each of which shall have its own treasurer; that the subscribers in each district shall form themselves into classes of twenty each, who shall choose their own collectors'. The next resolution determines 'that the collectors of classes in every district shall appoint the receiver of the said district, into whose hands they shall pay weekly the amount of their collections, and the receivers of each of the twenty-four districts, shall pay into the hands of the general treasurer every Tuesday evening, the sums they have received'. Resolution five decides 'that every collector of classes, shall have a class paper with his own name and the number of his class, and the names of the members, and the amount of their weekly subscriptions, which class paper shall be given in to the receiver of the district every week, with sums collected, and shall be produced by him every Tuesday evening, to the secretary of the fund, for inspection, who shall give a printed receipt signed by himself, for the amount of each class paper, which receipt shall be given to the district receiver, and by him forwarded to the collectors when their class papers are returned to them'. The following resolution is a disciplinary one. It is decided 'that every collector of classes, and every district receiver who shall neglect, for more than two weeks together, to bring or send in the amount of their subscriptions and their papers shall be dismissed; and their names, together with the amount of their defalcations, publicly advertised'. When the accounts are printed, 'copies shall be given to the collectors in each district, for distribution amongst the classes'. Resolution sixteen determines 'that the proceedings of this meeting be recommended to every city, town and village in the kingdom in order that similar proceedings may be adopted for a union of sentiment, and the creation of power in pecuniary matters that may command respect'. Finally a committee of twenty-two is appointed to work the whole scheme.[1] The income for the first quarter amounted to £37 12s. 1d., all of which except £5 came from the classes.[2] Nottingham established a similar fund, and although no information is to hand to show whether its members were divided into classes, evidence is available to prove that they were grouped into districts.[3] This union continued to operate until 1823.[4]

Political classes are once more recommended when Henry Hunt, writing from prison, outlined a scheme for the organization of the Great Northern Political Union. 'My plan', he says, 'would be to concentrate and consolidate the union by sections of one hundred and six men in each. At the head of each section should be a centurion; under him five trusty men; each of these trusty men will enrol twenty men in his neighbourhood. I propose that each centurion shall subscribe sixpence a week towards the the general fund; each trusty man threepence a week; and each brother on the remaining hundred (for they shall all be called and known to each other by the endearing name of brother) one penny a week. Each trusty man to collect the pence from the twenty that have enrolled themselves under him, and hand it over, together with his own threepence, weekly, to the centurion, which sum when collected, will amount, with the centurion's sixpence, to ten shillings and one penny each week. As soon as this is accomplished and paid to the sub-treasurer of the central committee, this section shall be complete, and shall be enrolled as No. 1, with the centurion's name and residence attached to it, and so on to the extent of any number of sections.'[5] Central committees, he asserts, are established 'at Manchester for the county of Lancaster', 'at Leeds for the county of York', and at Taunton 'for the county of Somerset. . . . And it is proposed to establish a Central Committee in each county in England and Scotland'. Hunt was rather doubtful about Ireland.[6] In reply to Hunt's letter, John Butler suggests 'it would be better to divide the members of the Great Northern Union into classes of ten men each, to meet at each other's houses one evening every week;

[1] *The Black Dwarf*, Feb. 28, 1821.
[2] *ibid.*, April 18, 1821.
[3] *ibid.*, March 21, 1821.
[4] *ibid.*, May 23, Nov. 21, 1821. Feb. 20, June 12, Aug. 21, Nov. 27, 1822.
[5] *ibid.*, Oct. 10, 1821. Also *Wooler's British Gazette*, Oct. 7, 1821.
[6] *ibid.*, Oct. 10, 1821.

each class to choose one man from among them for the purpose of conducting the meeting and over so many classes to place as you stated, trusty men over twenties'. 'The use I would make of the classes would be, to effect a reform in the conduct of professing Reformers.' Hunt, 'acknowledges his conviction of the improvement suggested by Mr. B. which he recommends for immediate adoption'. The editor of *Wooler's British Gazette* and *Manchester Observer* (Dec. 8, 1821) recognizes the utility of Butler's plan for new branch unions, but for the Manchester branch he advises a continuance of the old scheme.

The revived political union received the benediction of the veteran reformer Major Cartwright, while the columns of *The Black Dwarf* and the *British Gazette* were frequently used to espouse the cause. In spite of the hostile attitude of the 'Secretary for the Hypocrite's Department', and 'the cobbling at reform' recommended by the Whigs, the union made rapid progress. Within three months branches had been established at Manchester, Nottingham, Taunton, Leeds, Bolton, Blackburn, Barnsley, Royton, Stockport, and Carlisle.[1] Before the end of January, 1822, new branches had been formed at Preston, Sheffield, Oldham, Ashton-under-Lyne, Halifax, Bradford, Wakefield, and Rochdale.[2] An enthusiast from Leicester, writing to his fellow townsmen, recommends the formation of a union on Hunt's plan. 'An easy method', he says, 'of carrying into effect the plan proposed by Mr. Hunt is to form a general committee of trusty men, each being responsible for the subscription of twenty reformers: every member of the committee paying fourpence weekly for himself, and twenty pence for the class he represents, would pay to the treasurer two shillings every week. When five classes were thus formed, a centurion should be elected; and the first division would be complete. A second would succeed in like manner, and in the full maturity of the plan the centurions might form the acting committee; the collectors of classes, the general committee of management; while the concerns of the society would be submitted to the general body of subscribing reformers, at regular intervals. Thus a regularly organized political and rational militia might be formed throughout the kingdom, with one purpose and one means of pursuing it, until the desired reform were accomplished.'[3]

[1] *The Black Dwarf*, Nov. 14 and 28, 1821. [2] *ibid.*, Jan. 30, 1822.
[3] *ibid.*, Jan. 16, 1822.

During the whole of the year of 1822 the union apparently was extending. In the early part of July both Birmingham and Coventry are reported to 'have formed' a union 'upon the just principles of first relieving the wants of those who are suffering, and of forwarding the surplus, if any, to the funds of the Northern Union'.[1] The surviving group of Political Protestants in Newcastle, Northumberland, and Durham, having established a central committee of the Great Northern Union at Newcastle in November 1821, are still exercising their right of political agitation in the September of 1822. A letter from the *Manchester Observer* was submitted on September 3, 'to the consideration of the general committee, composed of class-leaders, from North and South Shields, Winlaton, Swalwell, Stella, Gateshead, . . . who expressed unanimously their opinion of the necessity of union, and their determination to open a correspondence' with the paper.[2] The union was still in a vigorous condition when Hunt was liberated from Ilchester gaol at the end of October, 1828, and proceeded to Glastonbury to take over the lordship of Glaston Manor.

Radical enthusiasm was still alive in the May of 1823. During that month they were able to send £100 to Spain for the purpose of 'furnishing the Spaniards with arms to repel the banditti of the Holy Alliance'. This generous action received the commendation of the editor of *The Black Dwarf* (May 28, 1823). After publishing the amount of the gift, he exclaimed, 'The Reformers of Manchester have nobly performed their duty'. With the release of the Rev. J. Harrison from gaol in October, 1823, most of the Radical leaders had regained their freedom and naturally their independence of Radical charity. The need of subscriptions therefore was not so pressing. Whether this was a cause or a coincidence, historians alone can decide. Nevertheless, Radical activities became less vigorous after this time. T. J. Wooler apparently lamented this discouraging fact. At the beginning of 1824, he announced the approaching decease of *The Black Dwarf*. He confesses that when he commenced his newspaper, he imagined there was a 'Public in Britain' 'devoutedly attached to the cause of Parliamentary reform. This', he declares, 'was an error'. 'It is true, that hundreds of thousands have petitioned and clamoured for reform; but the event has

[1] *The Black Dwarf*, July 10, 1822. [2] *ibid.*, Sept. 18, 1822.

proved what their enemies asserted, and what *The Black Dwarf* treated as a calumny, that they only clamoured for bread. And if they were only stimulated by hunger and the influence of despair and distress upon the animal passions, they were not reformers, but bubbles thrown up in the fermentation of society.'[1]

The utility of these classes is best seen in their educational effect. Untutored working men in those days knew very little about the secrets of successful collective action and still less about the intricacies of class-made laws. They needed to be instructed in these matters. Hence they came together in small groups, not only to pay their weekly subscriptions, but also to get useful information concerning political questions. This was probably the main, though not the only, value of the class meeting. It was in reality a school of political education. In the rules and practices of the Political Protestants this fact is clearly manifest. According to T. Walker, the Hull Society was in the habit at the class meeting of reading '*Cobbett and Sherwin's Registers*, *Wooler's Black Dwarf*, and other works, calculated to diffuse political knowledge'.[2] The Newcastle Union may be taken as an example of other unions in the North. In the weekly class the class leader was expected to 'read or cause to be read, interesting extracts from papers and political publications'. He had to 'encourage the members to make remarks', and to 'repress any violent or improper expression'. It was also ordained that 'the class leaders shall determine what papers and books shall be purchased'. 'The works recommended are *Cartwright's Bill of Rights*, which ought to be had in all classes—also *The Black Dwarf*—*Bentham's Reform Catechism*—and other works—*Ensor's Works*—Cobbett's Paper against Gold, and his *Weekly Register*—also the publications of Wooler, Sherwin, &c.'. 'Useful cheap tracts when sent to a class-leaders' meeting, are to be distributed to his class as soon as possible; and each member to exert himself in circulating papers friendly to the public cause.'[3] Similar practices were adopted in the Union Societies. In the Stockport Union the classes met weekly 'for the purpose of reading any political, or other books, papers, &c.'.[4] The Radical class was undoubtedly

[1] *The Black Dwarf*, 1824, Preface.
[2] *ibid.*, April 14, 1819.
[3] *Newcastle Courant*, Dec. 11, 1819.
[4] *Wooler's British Gazette*, April 25, 1819. Also *Manchester Observer*, May 8, 1819.

a useful instrument for dispelling political ignorance, and at the same time a channel of useful information.

As a financial agency the class served a beneficial purpose. The collection of the weekly penny subscription was invariably associated with the class meeting. Where no regular meeting existed the income was always uncertain. When a class was established, the matter was different. As a rule the leader was expected to collect the members' subscriptions. Meeting his class every week made it more easy to gather the necessary contributions. Although the amount that each member gave might be considered small, yet the regularity of the gift and the number that subscribed made the total a substantial one at the end of every quarter or year. An examination of a union balance sheet would make interesting reading. The Manchester branch of the Great Northern Union, for example, remitted £40 to the general treasurer in six months.[1] Another £10 was sent five weeks after.[2] The income of the Nottingham Union Fund from November 1820, to November 1821, amounted to £93 15s. 4d.[3] Several other unions were receiving subscriptions at the same time toward political Radicalism. Most of this money came by the medium of weekly subscriptions. Considered therefore from the standpoint of finance, organization, or tuition, the class meeting occupied a very important place in working-class politics.

[1] *The Black Dwarf*, Jan. 30, 1822. [2] *ibid.*, Feb. 6, 1822. [3] *ibid.*, Nov. 21, 1821.

CHAPTER II

THE POLITICAL UNIONS OF 1831–1835

THE working-class political unions of 1831 to 1835 can be regarded as a revival of the suppressed societies of 1820 to 1823. In 1829 discontent against the prevailing political system began to show itself again. It was inspired by the deep depression among certain sections of the community. No relief could be afforded until the mismanagement of public affairs was corrected. Once more the cry for reform was clearly heard. The people must have their own representatives in the House of Commons. For this purpose reform meetings were held in different parts of the country. Weekly gatherings were organized at Leeds for a time. London had its Reform Association which met monthly to discuss Parliamentary Reform. Through its agency the labouring portions of the community were invited 'to form associations', and 'to lose no time in proclaiming' their 'attachment to Universal Suffrage', 'Vote by Ballot, and Annual Parliaments'.[1]

With the advent of 1830, a definite attempt was made to unify the Whig and the Radical forces in the work of reform. The alliance of 1816 and 1820 was revived again by the formation of the Birmingham Political Union on January 25. Provision was made by this association for the co-operation of the middle and working classes. Although the complete Radical programme was not accepted, members of the union pledged themselves to work for a measure of political reform. While doing this, they were expected to prove themselves 'good, faithful and loyal subjects of the King', to 'obey the laws of the land; and where they cease to protect the rights, liberties, and interests of the community, to get them changed by just, legal and peaceful means only'.[2] On this basis political unions were established in different parts of the country. Through the influence of the London Reform Association the Metropolitan Union was formed, and a more Radical programme than the Birmingham one was adopted. Many of the provincial unions followed London, among

[1] *Leeds Patriot*, Sept. and Oct., 1829. [2] H.O. 44. 19, 1830.

which were Almondbury, Hunslet, Honley, and Manchester. In the October of 1831, the National Political Union, based on the Birmingham plan, was established in London. Similar unions had already been formed in Newcastle and Bristol, provision being made in every case for an equal number of middle and working-class representatives to be on the Council.

This unity of Whig and Radical forces made more certain the passage of the Reform Bill in 1831–1832. But it was not achieved without fierce opposition from the 'diehards' in both Houses of Parliament. The forces for reform, however, were very powerful in the land, and their determination was shown in many ways. Violent demonstrations against their opponents were not infrequent, the most disastrous occurring in Bristol during the October of 1831.

The Reform Bill, which was finally passed in 1832, did not satisfy the ultra Radicals among the working classes. Only the middle classes had been appeased for the moment. The former felt they had been betrayed. So they continued their fight for reform. The betrayal of the lower classes had been foreseen by some of their leaders, and a working-class political society was formed in London as early as April 2, 1831. According to William Lovett, 'The National Union of Working Classes' sprang out of another society called 'The British Association for promoting Co-operative Knowledge'.[1] The latter was a branch of Robert Owen's plan for establishing a new order. It was formed on May 11, 1829, principally by some people who belonged to the London Co-operative Trading Association. Those who took a prominent part in the movement were James Watson, William Lovett, John Cleave, George Foskett, Robert Whigg, Philip and George Shene, William Millard, Thomas Powell, Henry Hetherington, and Benjamin Warden, all working men.[2] These men endeavoured to form co-operative societies on those parts of Owen's scheme which they believed would be acceptable to the people. This was done while Owen was in America. 'Many persons who were strictly religious were alarmed at some of the proceedings of the British Association, especially at many of its members attending and supporting Mr. Owen's Sunday morning lectures.'[3] A few months before the dissolution of the British

[1] Place MSS. 27791, p. 243. Also 27822, p. 17.
[2] Place MSS. 27791, p. 243. Also *Weekly Free Press*, Jan. 16, 1830.
[3] Place MSS. 27791, p. 246.

Association, some carpenters named Hetherington, Warden, and Foskett met at Argyle Street on April 2, 1831, and called themselves the 'Metropolitan Trades Union'. The name was afterwards changed into 'The National Union of Working Classes'. They met for three weeks at Argyle Street, then on April 20, they moved to 36, Castle Street, Oxford Market. On May 25, a declaration and rules were brought forward by Hetherington and his two companions. The British Association having terminated its existence, some of its members joined the new society. William Benbow afterwards became a member, and the meeting place was transferred to his Coffee House at Temple Bar.

Within a few months of the passing of the Reform Bill, the London Union practically became extinct. 'Even the Birmingham Union, now sank down like the rest of the unions, lost its power and its influence and was of very little importance in any respect.'[1] Most of the Provincial Unions of the Birmingham type had been dissolved by the spring of 1833. The National Union of Working Classes still continued its activity, but Francis Place believed that it 'never consisted of a large body of members, though it had considerable influence at particular moments'.[2] Yet after twelve months existence its leaders were holding their meetings at a dozen different places in the Metropolis. At these centres they held both private and public gatherings. Their private meetings were called classes, and were confined to members. It was otherwise with their public meetings. Occasionally their language against the authorities was violent, and apparently for this reason spies were sent among them to report their plans. One of these spies, a policeman named Popay, had to appear before a Select Committee in 1833 to give an account of his conduct. It appears from the evidence that he was instructed to 'attend their public meetings', but he went beyond his orders and participated in their proceedings.[3]

Popay's adventures were only one phase of the police action in relation to the political societies. On May 12, 1833, a public meeting had been arranged to take place at Cold Bath Fields. The object of the gathering was 'to make preparation to carry into effect the necessity for a National Convention'.[4]

[1] Place MSS. 27796, p. 206.
[2] *ibid.*, 27791, p. 242.
[3] Select Committee Report on the Petition of Frederick Young and others. *Parliamentary Papers*, 1833, Vol. xiii, p. 579. Popay was a member of several classes.
[4] *The Poor Man's Guardian*, May 4, 1833.

The meeting having been banned by a Proclamation of the Government, an attempt was made to hold it. As a consequence, a conflict ensued with the police and one policeman was killed while several civilians were injured. At the inquest on the deceased policeman the jury returned a verdict of justifiable homicide. This verdict was later quashed by the Court of the King's Bench. A Select Committee was appointed to inquire into the affair, and one writer describes its purpose to be 'to whitewash ministers'.

In the summer of 1833 the Union began to lose some of its members. On July 15, those who remained were asked at the weekly meeting 'to exert themselves individually and collectively to strengthen and increase the members of the classes of this Union and urge their fellow workmen to aid them in this important object'. At the quarterly meeting in October, J. Russell, the secretary, volunteered a reduction of his salary from £1 to 15*s*. a week, 'because of reduced income'. A committee, which reported on the decline of the union, attributed the decrease 'to the dissipated habits of the people, and the apathy consequent thereupon'. On January 13, 1834, the general committee ascribes the decline partly to the increase of Trade Unions. Throughout the whole of this year the Union continued to exist, though with diminishing numbers and decreasing income. Some consolation is afforded by the knowledge that 'The Trade Unions have taken one at least of the objects of this Union, viz: to obtain for the working man the full value for his labour'. The last public notice of the movement appeared on November 14, 1835, when the committee was urged to meet on Monday, November 15, 'on business of much importance'.[1]

Working-class political unions also existed in the provinces. As early as August, 1831, the North-Western District of the National Union of Working Classes sent an address to a public meeting held under the auspices of the Manchester and Salford Union of Working Classes. At a meeting held in the Rotunda about the same time, it was decided to hold a Grand National Conference 'to devise the best methods of obtaining the rights of the labouring part of society'.[2] A correspondent, writing about the suggested Conference, wants a branch of the National Union of Working Classes formed in every town and village. Information

[1] Place MSS. 27797, pp. 20-306. [2] *Poor Man's Guardian*, August 27, 1831.

from Brighton tells of a union being formed there, and a request for the rules of the parent body to be sent to them is being forwarded to London. A month later the Radical reformers of Blackburn sent an address to London. It arrived in the course of a fortnight. Before the end of the year, a branch of the union had been established in Bristol, the rules of the National Union of Working Classes being read and adopted. On the authority of *The Poor Man's Guardian* (Jan. 21, 1832), the 'Female Radical Reformers' of Manchester decided in January, 1832, to form 'a branch Political Union, as an Auxiliary to the National Union of Working Classes—upon the just principles of Universal Suffrage—Annual Parliaments—and Vote by Ballot'. Two months later the London Union had further relations with Manchester. Some of the delegates from the latter place came to London to explain the conditions under which they laboured in Manchester, and the 'Manchester Brethren' are recommended to meet on Sundays.[1] A sum of money is raised in London for the purpose of assisting the Lancashire men who had been cast into prison. Working-class unions are reported from Oldham, Bolton, Macclesfield, Radford, Norwich, Yeovil, Frome, and Somerton.[2]

Some of the working-class reformers of Birmingham are apparently not at all satisfied with the results achieved by the Birmingham Political Union. A public meeting therefore is arranged to take place at Newhall Hill on Monday, October 29, 1832. Delegates from London are invited to this assembly. Hetherington, Cleave, and Mee are sent to represent the parent body. On account of the rain, the meeting is held in Beardsworth Repository, and a Political Union of Working Classes is formed.[3] Dr. Wade took a prominent part in the proceedings and was consequently censured by the Birmingham Political Union, of which he was a member. The London delegation, while in the Midlands, paid a visit to Northampton and helped to establish a branch of their union in that town. On Monday, November 10, the Manchester Union of Working Classes adopts the London rules.[4]

As already indicated the private meetings of the National Union of Working Classes were called classes. They were similar

[1] Place MSS. 27791, p. 361.
[2] *ibid.*, 27796, p. 320–4. Also *Poor Man's Guardian*, 1832–3.
[3] *The Poor Man's Guardian*, Nov. 3, 1832.
[4] *ibid.*, Nov. 10, 1832.

to the class meetings of the Political Protestants and Union Societies of 1818 to 1823, and were introduced to the members on October 24, 1831. A committee had gone carefully into the matter and recommended them at a meeting in the Rotunda. John Cleave read the resolutions which were as follows:

To the National Union. We, your Committee, hereby inform you that, in order that this Society may be a real Union, and not a mere chaos, we propose—

1. That you should appoint class leaders for the different districts of the metropolis and its vicinity.
2. That there should be on an average twenty-five members to each class, so that there may be forty class leaders to 1,000 members.
3. That every member should call, or leave his name at the residence of his class leader, once a week, or the class leader on the members, if more convenient.
4. That the list of class leaders be read over in the first general meeting of the Union every month, and, that each class leader be then either continued, or changed, according to the meeting.
5. That each class leader shall keep a list of the names, and residences of the different individuals, who leave their names with him, and that he shall receive their monthly subscription and send it to the secretary.
6. That the services of the class leaders be perfectly gratuitous.
7. That the class leaders constitute a committee, which shall meet once every week at such times and place as shall be deemed most convenient.
8. That all the branches of this Union, who adopt the resolutions submitted to them by this committee, be requested to send class leaders to this meeting, at the rate of one person to twenty-five members, on Friday evening, November 4 at eight o'clock.

Daniel O'Connell who was at the meeting supported the committee and added 'the organization recommended, was the same as that which was so successfully followed and pursued by the Wesleyans, and he thought the same sauce that so well answered the goose, might with a certainty be applied to the gander'. William Benbow, as chairman, also approved of the resolutions and remarked, 'if they wished to judge of the comparative value of any measure by its effects, they had only to refer to the Methodist body as a practical illustration of the Wesleyan rules and regulations'. He also expressed the hope 'that in a few days London alone would produce from 500 to a thousand such leaders—each at the head of twenty-five men'. '*He had no hesitation in saying that if the Union of the Working Classes followed up the plan laid down and established by Wesley—, they would in one short year be able to build themselves a Rotunda to meet at and debate, and enable them to laugh at their enemies, as well as to establish the liberties of their country.'* [1] The recommendations of the committee were apparently accepted by the union, for class meetings became a part of the constitution. In the published 'Objects and Laws' of the movement it was decided that the general committee should 'be empowered to nominate to the Union, for its approval or rejection, a list of such persons as may be recommended to them as fit for class leaders or collectors to the amount of one for every twenty-five members of the Union'. Once a fortnight the members of the committee had to 'meet the class leaders or collectors' in order 'to receive the subscriptions or collections of the members, and see them handed over to the Treasurer'. 'The class leaders or collectors' were expected to 'call upon the members on their list (or the members on them, as may be most convenient) once a week, to receive the contributions; which list they shall make up, and hand over the monies received at their fortnightly meetings to the General Committee.' [2] By the month of November, 1831, twenty-four class leaders had been appointed and their names placed on record. [3] At another meeting in the Rotunda, Benbow 'recommended them to join classes and propagate the class system. There were 500 and upwards already formed and he believed these would soon be 1,000'. [4]

William Lovett, when writing an account of the National Union of Working Classes, asserted that 'the most useful of their meetings were the classes. Thus conducted, persons were selected by the committee on account of their intelligence, moral fitness, and activity to be class leaders. Whenever the committee decided that a certain member should be a class leader, the secretary wrote to him, requesting him to accept the appointment, gave him the necessary instructions, and the names of twenty other members whose residences were nearest to him. A printed form was also given to him signed by the secretary, on this he was to enter the names, &c., of the members of his class, he was to receive their weekly subscriptions and enter them in their proper place, the sum he received every time the class met was to be added up

[1] Place MSS. 27791, pp. 308–9. Also *The Poor Man's Guardian*, October 29, 1831.
[2] Place MSS. 27835, p. 251.
[3] *The Poor Man's Guardian*, Nov. 26, 1831. Also Place MSS. 27791, p. 318.
[4] *The Poor Man's Guardian*, Dec. 10, 1831.

and named to the class; at the second meeting the sum received was added to the first and the whole declared. There was a meeting of the class leaders every fortnight attended by the secretary, and to him each class leader paid the two weeks' money he had received. The class leader was supplied with authenticated cards of admission; each of these cards authorized the person who took one, on payment of sixpence, to attend the class for three months'.

'The class meetings were generally held at the house of some member. The class leader was the chairman and some subject, either for conversation or discussion, was selected. Sometimes selections were made from books. The works of Paine—Godwin—Owen—Ensor—and other Radical writers were preferred. The unstamped periodicals of the day were also subjects of conversation and discussion, and in this manner hundreds of persons were made acquainted with books and principles of which they were previously ignorant. They were made more social, also, and better disposed towards one another. In addition to these useful attainments the conversations and discussions generated and encouraged the talent for public speaking, so useful in a country of corruptions and abuses of all kinds, whence its exercise become a duty.'[1]

It is perfectly clear from the evidence available that the class system became an essential part of the organization of the National Union of Working Classes and that it was copied from the Methodists. When the Select Committee met in the early part of 1833 to consider the conduct of Policeman Popay in relation to the private meetings of the National Union of Working Classes, James Brown, a class leader, admitted that their union was divided into classes. The classes were twenty-five in number. They consider as working men that they produce all the wealth of the nation and therefore they ought to be represented in the House of Commons. 'This is the nature of our conversation,' he frankly declares. 'We read newspapers and proceedings in Parliament and comment upon them.' 'A man may join that class where his friends reside.' Any person who desires to join the union 'gives his name, his address and his occupation, and he is registered in the class paper . . . then he receives a card, and that always recognizes him as a member'. 'The person who

[1] Place MSS. 27791, pp. 250–2.

holds the paper sheet' sees that every man's name and subscription are put down. 'He is called the class leader, just in the same way as the Wesleyan Methodists do; that is how the mode originated.' 'We meet as friends and brothers to lighten each other's minds.' Brown asserted that on one occasion he went with Popay to visit a class at Richmond. John Simpson, another class leader, asserted that Popay used to assist in the writing connected with the class. Shem Shelly, a class mate of Popay, declared that unemployment created the political agitation. 'If there had been plenty of work I dare say there never would have been anything of it. If every man could keep the wolf from his door there would be no meetings of any sort. It is poverty that has brought the people together.' William Woodford, a carpenter, held a responsible position in his class. The duty of reading *The Poor Man's Guardian* was usually relegated to him. Another class leader, John Simpson by name, acknowledged that the union was divided into classes. The class 'meetings', he says, 'are certainly private; they are like a family; they meet and consult to devise the best manner of drawing up petitions for grievances'. At these meetings, which are usually held in a public house, 'we read political works', 'or draw up resolutions, or comment upon any Act that is brought into the House'. In fact, 'it is merely a family social meeting for reading, discussing, and nothing more'.[1]

William Cobbett, who was mainly responsible for getting the Select Committee appointed, published in his Register a report of the proceedings. Some of the facts he elicits from the evidence are: '1st. That the title of the association is "The National Political Union of Working Classes". 2nd. That the Central Committee or body of managers, meet at a place in Theobald's Road. 3rd. That the body, or the whole of the members of the association, divide themselves into classes after the manner of the Wesleyan Methodists. 4th. That each class has, after the manner of these Methodists, what is called a "leader" who collects the contributions, pays the expenses and manages the business of the class. 5th. That the class meetings are confined to members of the union exclusively; but, two or more classes very frequently meet at some place, and then the meetings are

[1] Report from the Select Committee on the Petition of Frederick Young and others. *Parliamentary Papers*, 1833, Vol. xiii, pp. 423–517.

called public meetings, and to these meetings any person whatever might be admitted.'[1]

The Poor Man's Guardian, acknowledged to be the semi-official paper of the Union, constituted the most reliable source of information. Toward the end of 1831 two or three notices appear in this paper announcing class-leaders' meetings. The first intimation is found in the issue of December 17. Class leaders are asked to attend the Leaders' Meeting on December 22 at the Philadelphian Chapel, Windmill Street, Finsbury Square. A second class-leaders' meeting was announced in the last issue of the year, and from that time onward, notices of class meetings and leaders' meetings frequently appear.

Numerous class meetings were held during the year 1832. Francis Place, who was not very sympathetic toward the Union, acknowledged the fact that in the month of July, eighty-six classes existed, which yielded an income of £30–9–4½ for the quarter at the rate of one penny a week per member. Nine months after that date, the number of classes had declined to thirty-nine, with a quarterly income of £13–3–7½.[2] This account of the number of classes underestimates the position. At one period there were more than 100 classes operating in the Metropolis.

The issue of *The Poor Man's Guardian* for 1832 is replete with information about the working of the class system. Practically every week some public notice is given to class leaders or to class meetings. A typical announcement to the class leaders is the following: 'The next class-leaders' meeting will be held on Thursday, January 19, at the Commercial Coffee House, Temple Bar, when all class leaders are requested to attend.'[3] At least twenty-five similar notices to class leaders are found in its pages throughout the year. Most of these announcements were signed by James Osborne, general secretary, till the middle of October, 1832. He was succeeded by J. Russell who adopted the same practice of public notices to class-leaders.

Very little information is given about individual classes till toward the end of the year. One or two general announcements are made in the earlier editions. For example, reference is made in the issue of April 7 to a resolution passed at the ninety-second class that a subscription be made for Mr. Boreham. In the same

[1] Place MSS. 27797, p. 150.
[2] *ibid.*, 27791, p. 242.
[3] *The Poor Man's Guardian*, Jan. 14, 1832.

issue 'members are particularly requested to attend in their class meetings, as the visiting committee will go round to renew the cards, class papers, &c'. When the general meeting of members was held at Saville House, Leicester Square, 'several of the classes, from various parts of the town, marched to the meeting in procession. The one from Finsbury was joined by others till their numbers amounted to upwards of a hundred. They walked two-a-breast, with military step and excited considerable attention'.[1] On July 30, the Eastern Classes and the Western Classes joined together at Copenhagen House to celebrate the second anniversary of the French Revolution. 'Several of the classes marched in procession from different parts of the Metropolis to the place of meeting, accompanied with bands of music, and carrying innumerable banners with flags.'[2]

The first notice to the individual classes appears in the issue of August 18, 1832. The following announcement is made: 'the members of the Fifth Class are urgently requested to attend at 27, King Street, Snow Hill, on Sunday morning next at Ten o'clock.' Another intimation follows: 'The 1st, 2nd, 7th, and 35th Classes will meet in the Institution on Sunday morning at 11 o'clock. All the members of those Classes are earnestly requested by their Leaders to attend.' From this time onward notices to members of individual classes constantly appear. Before the end of the year, public announcements similar to the above were made to the following classes: 38th, 69th, 34th, 63rd, 96th, 42nd, 29th, 32nd, 39th, 41st, 78th, 106th, 73rd, 10th, 92nd, 5th, 45th, and 22nd. The order of the above classes is that in which they appear in *The Guardian*. In some cases the class leaders append their name to the notice calling the class together.

The 1833 issue of *The Guardian* follows the practice of the 1832 edition. Numerous announcements to class leaders and classes are to be found. 'Class leaders' are urged sometimes 'to send in the class papers and receipts', to attend some particular meeting 'on business of great importance to the Union', to forward 'their nominations for the new committee', 'to make up their accounts', or to 'give a report of their classes'. The public notices to the individual classes appear practically every week. It is impossible to reprint all that appeared from time to time, but in the course of the year, the following classes received

[1] *The Poor Man's Guardian*, March 3, 1832. [2] *ibid.*, August 4, 1832.

definite intimations:—1, 3, 4, 6, 7, 9, 10, 11, 12, 16, 20, 21, 23, 25, 26, 29, 30, 32, 35, 36, 37, 40, 41, 42, 43, 46, 47, 51, 52, 62, 64, 66, 67, 71, 72, 73, 77, 78, 82, 90, 91, 92, 93, 95, 96, 97, 99, 100, 105, 106, and 107. It may be mentioned in passing that quite a number received no public notice whatever in 1833. In this category, the following classes were advertised in 1832: 5, 22, 34, 38, 39, 45, 63, and 69. If we assume that at least 107 classes existed in 1833, a very large number of them did not trouble to advertise their meetings in *The Guardian*. Perhaps they relied entirely on the announcement at the weekly meeting. One of the class leaders, when giving evidence before the Select Committee, declared that his class never advertised in *The Poor Man's Guardian* 'nor any class about Camberwell and Walworth'.[1]

1833 was the high water mark for the activity of the classes. Toward the end of the year the numbers show a steady decline. Signs of the decline must have been seen before the autumn. In the month of July, the members of the committee considered the situation and advised the classes to greater exertions to increase their numbers. A general conference of class leaders and committee was held in the following month to examine the position. A later committee reported spies amongst their number, and Samuel Dean, a class leader, is singled out and condemned for betraying the high confidence placed in him. J. Russell at this committee voluntarily accepted a reduction of salary in order to help the financial position.

The year 1834 seems to have been a lean one for the Union. Reports of meetings and notices to class leaders are fewer than in 1833. At the quarterly meeting of members held on January 13, the report indicated that the past quarter had been destitute of political news. The next quarterly meeting rejoiced at the increase of Trade Unions. This increase of Trade Unions became a contributory cause for the decline of the Political Unions.

A number of classes continued to meet in certain areas, but they met less frequently than formerly. Only ten classes publicly announced their meetings in the course of the year in *The Poor Man's Guardian*. Those that received intimation are the following: 10, 13, 20, 23, 25, 35, 64, 67, 88, and 92. Most of these announcements appeared at the beginning of the year in the first three

[1] Report from Select Committee on the Petition of Frederick Young and others. *Parliamentary Papers*, 1833, Vol. xiii, p. 516.

months. Between March 31 and July 26, no public notice appeared in *The Poor Man's Guardian.* On the latter date the 64th Class is informed of a special meeting at the Knave of Clubs, Club Row, Church Street, Shoreditch on business of importance. On August 9, the 92nd Class receives an intimation of a meeting to be held at the Patriotic Coffee House, Union Street, Bishopsgate Street 'for the purpose of receiving the report of Brother Stanman'. The only other notice is given on November 22 to the 20th, 10th, 64th and 67th classes. They are asked to meet on the following Monday 'on business of the greatest importance'. This notice is signed by Thomas Sharman and F. Brian, two class leaders.

The year 1835 witnesses the termination of the classes and the Union. Classes continue to meet until the middle of July, but their number is rather small. During the first six months, public notices are issued through the pages of *The Poor Man's Guardian* to the following classes: 1, 6, 7, 10, 23, 67, 83, and 92. On January 24, the members of the 67th Class, 'in conjunction with the Friends of the Human Race' are reported having subscribed 3s. and 4s. 3d. respectively on the day George Harney was released from 'his most sacred Majesty's College, Cold Bath Field'.[1] An address from the National Union of Working Classes to the unrepresented of Great Britain and Ireland advises the latter to 'begin at once to establish Unions in every town in the United Kingdom, on the principle of the National Union of Working Classes in London'.[2] In the issue of February 28, the 92nd, 10th, 83rd, and 67th classes are asked to meet in the course of the week. At three of the class meetings the laws and objects of the Union are to be explained.

The last public intimation of class meetings is to be found in the issue of July 18. 'The friends of freedom' are invited to the 6th Class which meets every Monday night at the Star Coffee House, Star Street, Paddington. The members of the first class are advertised to consider at their meeting on the following Monday at the Patriotic Coffee House, Union Street, Bishopsgate Street, the subject 'Is National Education Beneficial to the Working Classes?' The final meeting of the Union is held on

[1] *The Poor Man's Guardian*, Jan. 24, 1835. Apparently, this money was for the support of those who had suffered imprisonment.
[2] *ibid.*, Jan. 31, 1835.

November 16, and no further notice appears in the pages of *The Poor Man's Guardian.*

Information concerning the political class meetings in the provinces is very scanty. Evidence shows that quite a number of centres adopted the rules of the London Union. Class meetings therefore would be most likely established. In a report from Blackburn to Colonel Shaw, Dixon Robinson affirms that 3,000 to 4,000 members subscribe to the Union at the rate of a penny or half-penny per member each week. 'The money', he says, 'is collected by persons who are called class leaders (a class meeting consisting of twelve persons) who pay the money over to the treasurer of the district.' 'Each of the class leaders has a sheet of paper, partly printed, and ruled in a particular form. The names of the twelve persons comprising the class are inserted on the paper, and there is a column for every week to the end of the year, commencing in August last, in which the sum received is put down. Every class is numbered.'[1] A political meeting is reported from Great Bridge in Staffordshire and Quarterly Meetings are held. Probably the provincial unions, like the London Union, were adversely affected by the growth of Trade Unions.

[1] H.O. 40. 30, 1832.

CHAPTER III

THE CHARTIST ASSOCIATIONS OF 1836–1850

THE political societies of 1836 to 1850 had a complex origin, and in spite of the many attempts at unity they remained complex in their practice and organization. As Birmingham had played a conspicuous part in the reform agitation of 1831 and 1832, so her representatives became prominent in the Chartist agitation of 1838 and 1839. They drew up the terms of the first 'National Petition' and sent an important delegation to the first 'National Convention'. When the Assembly decided to support methods of violence, their delegates withdrew, and this constituted the first step toward the formation of a separate reform movement. Three years later they were responsible for the organization of the Complete Suffrage Association.

The industrial areas of the North supplied another factor in the complexity of working-class politics. Aggravated by the enforced application of the Poor Law Amendment Act of 1834, large numbers of distressed labourers supported the repeal agitation led by the Rev. J. R. Stephens and Richard Oastler. With their passions enflamed by stories of cruelty imposed upon their unfortunate poor through the orders of the Poor Law Commissioners, these enraged workmen presented prepared material for the acceptance of Chartist propaganda. Political reform coupled with passionate denunciation never lacked supporters among these folk.

London added its quota to the complexity of the situation. The National Union of Working Classes, which had dwindled in numbers during 1834 and 1835, allied its forces in December, 1835, with the newly formed Radical Association. The secretary of the former accepted the same position in the organization of the latter. A few months later the first Working Men's Association, with William Lovett, an ex-class-leader of the National Union of Working Classes, as secretary, was established in the Metropolis. Aided by a few Radical Members of Parliament this society summarized its needs in a bill, intended for Parliament, and afterwards called 'the People's Charter'. In due course large political meetings were held in different parts of the country for the support of the 'Charter'. The first climax came in 1839 when the National Convention met at the British Hotel, Cockspur Street, Charing Cross. Several months were spent in needless discussion on the methods of enforcing their demands. In the meanwhile the National Petition was presented to Parliament and laid on the table. This unexpected blow annoyed the delegates of the Convention, and the possession of arms, which meant resort to physical violence, was advocated by the Assembly. The Birmingham delegates, being opposed to such measures, withdrew from the Convention. Those who remained appealed to their supporters, and the possession of arms became a major issue among reformers.

Notwithstanding the dissension at the Convention and its ultimate decease, the National Chartist Association was formed at Manchester in 1840, and this became the main organization for working-class political agitators. For our purpose here three phases of its activity need a brief review.

The talk about the use of physical force greatly affected the movement. This line of action was taken by those who had lost patience because of Government inaction, or were driven to despair by distress and reactionary measures. The Rev. J. R. Stephens apparently belonged to this group. As early as 1836 he is reported to have declared that 'there was no hope of anything being done for them unless they resorted to physical force and that the only question was when they should begin. The question was when should they commence burning and destroying mills and other property'.[1] At this time, according to Francis Place (Place MSS. 27820, p. 219), 'the Rev. J. R. Stephens was moving about from place to place, preaching to the people the necessity of their resorting to physical force'. 'His followers', he contends, 'were never exhausted with bawling his praises and never tired of contemplating the mischief he constantly proposed to them'.[2] A witness avowed that he said in a sermon preached at Stalybridge in 1839, 'I will help the poor; I will plead for the poor . . . when talking and pleading and praying are at an end, and found to be of non-effect, then I will fight for the poor; the poor shall have their own again'.[3] At a meeting held at the

[1] Place MSS. 27820, p. 141. [2] *ibid.*, 27821, p. 226. [3] H.O. 40. 43, 1839.

Crown and Anchor, London, in the May of 1839, he informed his audience that he never told the people to arm against the laws, 'but against the accurst factory system, against that cruel system of child working, and mother working. I have told the people they had a right to arm against the Poor Law system—the three Commissioners with their prisons and bastilles'. 'I told the people it was high time to arm, and I repeat it now.'[1] Another report says that 'Richard Oastler is day after day and time after time advising the people to organize and arm', and 'the traitor Stephens is preaching up that it is the Law of God, and the Bible'.[2] When Stephens was placed under arrest in the early part of January, 1839, Capt. H. J. Clark reported as a result, 'a great feeling of safety'.[3] Many angry threats were uttered when it became known that he had been committed. At a meeting in Birmingham where Attwood was chairman, Brown, a notorious Chartist, told his audience that 'the Government had let loose their bloodhounds. The Rev. Mr. Stephens', he declared, 'had been seized and committed for trial, but let them touch a hair of his head, and woe be to them, his oppressors'.[4] When certain tradesmen were called to witness against him, they not only began to lose their trade, but their lives were also threatened. Such was the feeling expressed against them that one witness asked to be relieved of the onerous task. He exclaimed in his appeal that, in consequence of his evidence against Stephens, 'both my life, and property, and the property of my esteemed partner, have been, and are still in danger of being destroyed by the Chartists, and their credulous adherents'. Sixty pounds were given to the three witnesses as a compensation for their loss of trade. The magistrates of Ashton recommended '£30 to Ripley, £20 to Boardman, and £10 to Marples'.[5]

There were many expressions of violence in the early years of the movement. Drilling took place round Ashton and Oldham in the spring in 1839. Bearing arms was declared illegal at Oldham. On June 29, a Cheshire constable was badly assaulted at Dukinfield. Ten days later, two specials were thrown into the canal. About the same time the Working Men's Association of Stockport asked a noble Lord for 'eleven thousand stand of arms,

[1] H.O. 40. 44, 1839.
[2] *ibid.*, 40. 52, 1839.
[3] *ibid.*, 40. 37, 1839.
[4] Place MSS. 27821, p. 7.
[5] H.O. 40. 37, 1839.

&c., for the use of the Working Men's Association'.[1] The Rev. W. V. Jackson, a Methodist minister, is reported to be busy during this period. He talks about 'bullets and lead and guns and pistols and pikes'. Col. Wemys reports him employing 'unusual inflammatory language, exciting the people to go to the meetings armed, and to make use of their arms, if any attempt was made by the police or military to interrupt them'.[2] The Convention on Wednesday, July 10, asserted that, in case of attack by the police or others on a legally assembled meeting, the members of the meeting were 'justified upon every principle of law and self-preservation in meeting force by force. Even to the slaying of the persons guilty of such atrocious and ferocious assaults upon their rights and persons'.[3] According to reports, there was a great deal of talk about arms during this period. Col. Macerone's pamphlet on 'Defensive Instructions for the People', with 'Instructions on the Subject of Arms and Ammunition and Horse Fighting', was widely circulated.[4] The Justices of the Peace of Mansfield inform the Home Office that the Chartists in several districts possess 'guns, pistols, and other weapons'.[5] In a manifesto from the General Convention, Chartists are asked to exercise their 'ancient constitutional right, and provide themselves with the Arms of Freemen'. At Trowbridge three to four thousand agitators are expected to march from the district with '*pikes*, *swords*, *pistols* and other *kinds of weapons*'. When describing the activities of the Working Men's Association of Wiltshire, the magistrates assert that 'the delegates and leaders of such Association have induced the members thereof to arm themselves, and pikes, daggers, pistols, guns and other offensive weapons have been manufactured and distributed amongst many of the labouring classes who have enrolled themselves members of such Association'.[6] Drilling and talk of arms and ammunition are reported from Birmingham. T. Burgess, the Police Commissioner, has no doubt about the 'Drillings by the Chartists'.[7]

After the attempts at violence in Sheffield and Bradford in the January of 1840 no further disorders were reported till 1842. In that year disturbances took place in many districts. The second

[1] H.O. 40. 41, 1839.
[2] *ibid.*, 40. 43, 1839.
[3] *ibid.*, 40. 44, 1839.
[4] *ibid.*, 40. 48, 1839.
[5] *ibid.*, 40. 47, 1839.
[6] *ibid.*, 40. 48, 1839.
[7] *ibid.*, 40. 50, 1839.

week in August apparently was the critical period. Major T. Strenger from Macclesfield reports 'several thousands of men and boys armed with bludgeons' on their way from Stockport. They 'succeeded in stopping every factory in the town, turning out the hands and putting out the engine fires'. The Congleton Mayor informs the Home Office that the town was invaded by ten thousand individuals armed with bludgeons.[1] An attempt to burn the effigy of Sir Robert Peel is made at Northampton, and when the police take it away the crowd attack the Town Hall.[2] News of 'great destruction at Hanley, Stoke, Lane End and Longton' comes from Staffordshire.[3] At Huddersfield thousands of men are said to be 'putting an end to work whereever they go'. In Bradford the people are 'resolved not to work again until the Charter was established'. J. Waterhouse reports from Halifax 'that disturbances' in that town were to 'continue until the Charter is granted'. The rioters are going about 'with strong sticks and bludgeons'. Troops have to be sent to Tadcaster, Wetherby, Leeds, Aberford, and York. At Holmfirth 'a lawless mob consisting of upwards of 2,000 people armed with bludgeons, sticks, &c. went to the mills and collieries round the neighbourhood, and compelled the workpeople to discontinue their work'. A number of rioters were wounded at Halifax. The military charged the mob at Skipton. Sixty prisoners are taken at Bradford. Among the 300 prisoners tried at York in September, '212 of them' were rioters.[4] Such is the state of things in Lancashire that troops are wanted at Oldham, Rochdale, Heywood, Bolton, Blackburn, Bury and other towns.[5]

After the explosions of 1842, when many of the Chartist leaders had been cast into prison, peace was established for a few years. Violence, however, began to show itself again in 1848. On March 17, Armitage reports 'that the repealers of Liverpool and Manchester in conjunction with the Chartists were concocting mischief and entertained the idea of setting fire to these towns probably to-day'. This report appears to have been sent by way of Dublin Castle Constabulary Office. On account of

[1] H.O. 45. OS. 242, 1842. This is the first time that the contents of H.O. 45 have been made public.
[2] *ibid.*, 45. OS. 256, 1842.
[3] *ibid.*, 45. OS. 260, 1842.
[4] *ibid.*, 45. OS. 264, 1842.
[5] *ibid.*, 45. OS. 268, 1842.

the danger, the Ordinance Office, 'on the authority of the Lieutenant-General commanding the District', 'issued to the Mayor of Manchester for the use of the Police 500 cutlasses complete'.[1] A month later, Horsfall, the Mayor of Liverpool, sends by electric telegraph to the Home Office the following message: 'Just communicated. Good authority. Chartists at Manchester are organized, armed with pikes & muskets. Mode of attack arranged. Special Constables to be first overpowered'. E. Armitage, the Manchester Mayor, also used the new form of transmitting news and says, 'Report of Mayor of Liverpool not confirmed by any information received here and such extent organization doubted'.[2] This appeared to contradict a previous message that he sent through the usual channel affirming his expectancy of a general disturbance after the presentation of the people's charter.[3]

Whether these messages were responsible for the alarm that existed in Government circles at this time, it cannot be definitely proved. But it is certain that a great deal of consternation was manifest concerning the proposed Chartist demonstration at Kennington Common. Though three members of the Chartist Convention wrote to Sir George Gray, the Home Secretary, 'that the National Convention never had advised and utterly repudiates the idea of an armed assembly being called or an armed Procession taking place', every preparation was made for a grand defensive. Thomas Atchison suggests the dismounting of all guns, so that they cannot be used, ostensibly by the invaders. The Lord Mayor wants 'a sufficient number of hand grenades and such ammunition as may be considered necessary for the protection' of the Mansion House. Henry Ellis at the British Museum desires muskets, ammunition, arms, cutlasses and pikes for defensive purposes. The Bank is carefully guarded, and in addition to the ordinary troops and police, 22,853 special constables are sworn for the Metropolitan area. The Lord Mayor sent to the Home Office the following return of specials appointed for the city; Aldersgate 554, Aldgate 653, Bassishaw 112, Billingsgate 441, Bishopsgate 604, Bread Street 368, Bridge Street 255, Broad Street 1,200, Candlewick 297, Castle Baynard 518, Cheap 396, Coleman Street 635, Cordwainer 335, Cornhill 530, Cripplegate 1,732, Dowgate 400, Farringdon within 683, Farringdon without 1,760,

[1] H.O. 45. OS 2410A, 1848. [2] *ibid.*, 45. OS. 2410, 1848.
[3] *ibid.*, 45. OS. 2410A, 1848.

Langbourn 570, Lime Street 317, Portsoken 417, Queenhithe 6,500, Tower 2,144, Vintry 21, Walbrook 352, Bank of England 670.[1] According to the *Halifax Guardian* (April 15, 1848), a well-informed Tory paper, 150,000 specials were appointed for the London area alone. Yet in spite of such excessive preparations, the Chartists marched to Kennington Common without incident. An observer watching the procession, sent the following message to the Home Office, 'not the slightest appearance of arms or even bludgeons'. Neither the Bank nor the Mansion House was attacked by the enemy. About 15,000 to 20,000 people attended the demonstration. Before the start of the meeting, the Chief Commissioner of the Police had an interview with O'Connor, the Chartist leader. Reporting the interview, Mr. R. Mayne said, 'I never saw a man more frightened than he was, and he would I am sure have promised me anything'. Nothing of a desperate character happened at the Common. Those in charge of the petition were allowed to cross the bridges on their way to the House of Commons. The rest of the demonstrators dispersed quietly at the end of the meeting. Some of those who had shown zeal in the defensive preparations had their names forwarded to the Queen, and Her Majesty thanked them graciously. A few of the members of the Metropolitan Police got a better reward. £99 were distributed among 15 of them.[2]

Although the Government had achieved a glorious victory over an imaginary enemy in London, the foe in the provinces was not yet defeated. Alarming news continued to be sent from Lancashire. On May 31, E. Armitage reports that a number of men came along Oldham Road 'armed with pikes and other weapons'. A few weeks later, the Rev. Thomas Mills sends a message to the Home Secretary announcing the fact that many people 'are enrolling as Chartist Guards'. He encloses a bill which informs the public about the formation of a 'National Guard', 'for the Protection of the Middle and Working Classes of Oldham'. Conditions are so difficult at Bacup and Burnley that special constables are appointed. A public meeting advertised for Bolton is banned by the magistrates because 'organized and Confederated Clubs and Associations have been formed' 'for the attainment of illegal and Treasonable Objects', and

[1] H.O. 45. OS. 2410AD-AL, 1848. [2] *ibid.*, 45. OS. 2410, 1848.

because 'these clubs avowedly intend to disturb the Public Peace'. The Chief Constable of Ashton in his report for June 16, says, 'We have what is called a National Guard formed in this town numbering from 300 to 400 persons, all of whom are very young men—they meet about three times a week in the Chartist's Room in Bentinch Street, they are arming themselves with pikes, pistols and some few with rifle pieces, and I have no doubt that this is going on throughout the country, where they have formed a National Guard—pikes are privately made and sold in this town and it is in contemplation to begin training and drilling privately'. Drilling is carried on at Liverpool. One man is arrested in the act of carrying a hundred pikes in a sack. A committee of magistrates report the existence of many secret clubs where 'the question of arming and fighting is discussed'. Armed insurrection is regarded by the authorities as not only possible but probable.[1] About the same time, a police report concerning London informs the Home Secretary of a planned outbreak by the Chartists and Confederated Clubs. The police are to be attacked, and churches together with public buildings are to be burned. Another objective of the armed associates is for '*the Government to be taken by surprise at midnight and to be done within ten days from this time*'.[2] The danger in the country continues throughout July and into August. In the early part of the summer the chairman of the Burnley magistrates believes he has 'unquestionable evidence that the Chartists intend to attack barracks and manufactories'. He wants Sir T. Arbuthnot to send military assistance. Large numbers of specials are appointed for Manchester, Bradford, and Halifax. Another reporter believes that in case of disturbance in Ireland there would be an outbreak in Liverpool, Manchester, Bradford, Leeds, Halifax and other places.[3] Matters take a serious turn at Ashton. A mob armed with pikes and guns come into conflict with the police. One constable is shot and two men wounded. Specials and military are called out, and the mob is put to flight. Twenty men are arrested. Seventeen are sent to the Assizes at Liverpool on a charge of 'Seditious Conspiracy', and two for murder. Many other prisoners are tried at Liverpool. O'Brien is among those charged with the intent 'to riot and levy war'. The expenses

[1] H.O. 45. OS. 2410A, 1848. [2] *ibid.*, 45. OS. 2410, 1848.
[3] *ibid.*, 45. OS. 2410AB-AC, 1848.

for defensive precautions at Liverpool were rather heavy. That for the military amounted to £1,099 10s. 11d., while the specials cost £2,103 19s. od.[1] According to the *Bolton Chronicle* (July 29, 1848), 21,000 special constables were appointed for Liverpool alone. What the defensive preparations cost at other places cannot be ascertained, but it must have been considerable.

Another phase of Chartist activity that greatly affected the movement was its peculiar form of political propaganda. In the early years of the agitation, open-air demonstrations, drawing immense crowds, were often held in populous centres. But when the Government banned such meetings in 1839, the Chartists had to change their tactics. Endeavouring to avoid the law, they copied the example of the Primitive Methodists and held Sunday meetings in the fields or on the moors, usually outside the jurisdiction of the magistrates. Like the Methodists they designated their gatherings as 'camp meetings'.

The first reference to Chartist Camp Meetings so far revealed by research was made at the Rochdale Conference of June 25, 1839, when a number of Chartist delegates considered the formation of a national organization. According to the *Manchester Guardian* (June 29, 1839), 'camp meetings for political purposes were recommended' by the assembled Chartists. Whether this recommendation was actually adopted at that time cannot as yet be certified. On Sunday, September 22, however, a Chartist Camp Meeting was held at a place midway between Sheffield and Barnsley. The *Northern Liberator*, when reporting the event, says, 'On Sunday Afternoon the men, and men they may emphatically be called, of Sheffield, joined by immense assemblages from Barnsley and the surrounding districts, held a religious camp meeting on Hood Hill; and never before was such a religious meeting held in Yorkshire. The Rev. Mr. Thornton, of Bradford, preached a sermon that must have gone witheringly to the souls of the magistrates and minions of power that were present. Sure enough he did tear up by the roots the abomination of the State Church, plurality of livings, and blasphemous mammon worshippers'.[2] The *Northern Star* (Sept. 28, 1839) describes it as a 'Great Chartist Camp Meeting', at which 5 to 10,000 people

[1] H.O. 45. OS. 2410A, 1848.

[2] *Northern Liberator*, Sept. 28, 1839. Thornton had been a delegate at the Rochdale Conference. *Manchester and Salford Advertiser*, June 29, 1839.

assembled. The *Sheffield Mercury* (Sept. 28, 1839) thinks of it in other terms. According to the editor's account, great alarm had been created by this meeting in the mind of the Tory Press. 'The Chartists', he says, 'appear to have set at nought the warnings and threats of the magistrates. On Sunday they held —according to public announcement, "a Chartist Camp Meeting", at Hood Hill, a place on the road between Sheffield and Barnsley. Several thousands of these misguided persons, including, of course, all the idlers of the neighbouring villages, were present, and were addressed by a person from Bradford, who holds similar sentiments with themselves. Thus not only was the Sabbath desecrated by this noisy gathering, but the sacred formulas of Divine Worship were parodied by giving to the proceedings the appellation and method of a religious service. What the "sermon" was we know not, except that in it the Speaker abused the Clergy. But of the shocking mockery of devotional exercise which was practised, in the presence of several magistrates, it seems, our readers will judge from the following "Hymn", which with others of a like bearing, were "sold", and sung on the ground.'

Sad oppression now compels,
Working men to join themselves;
Ye sufferers don't no more delay,
Work with might while it is day.

Chorus.

I a Chartist now will be
And contend for liberty.

The Charter springs from Zion's hill,
Though opposed, go on it will;
Will you serve its sacred cause,
And receive its equal laws?

Chorus.

Union is our Captain's name,
By just laws he'll rule the main
Before his face he'll make to flee,
All bad laws of tyranny.

Chorus.

Brothers and sisters now unite,
And contend for your just rights;

Then soon the poor will happy be,
Glorious times we all shall see.
And the Chartists' song will be,
My country and sweet liberty.

'The Sunday's rehearsal', adds the editor, 'all of which went off peaceably—that is, the Chartists assembled in thousands—shewed their strength and their union—fraternized themselves by singing songs of self-devotion and resolution to a purpose inconsistent with the very existence of the present state of society—and the magistrates looked quietly on—this peaceable Sabbath day's rehearsal, we say, prepared for Monday evening's meeting in the Square, when, conformable to announcement, Feargus O'Connor, the great Chartist leader (who had only been apprehended and bailed three days before for a conspiracy, unlawful assemblies and seditious speeches at Manchester), addressed the assembled thousands.'

In spite of the adverse criticism of the *Mercury* editorial, further camp meetings were held in the vicinity. Two were held on the first Sunday in October, and two on the second Sunday.[1] In the issue of the *Northern Star* of October 12, 1839, the following account is given. 'According to custom, the Chartists held a camp meeting at Loxley, a wild romantic village four miles from Sheffield, but in consequence of the situation not generally being known, the attendance was not so numerous as it otherwise would have been, although the congregation consisted of some thousands. These politico-religious meetings are becoming very popular in Sheffield, and we understand there will be one held to-morrow at Attercliffe.' A fortnight elapses before another report appears. This time the readers of the *Northern Star* are informed that 'meetings of this description continue to be held every Sunday. Last Sunday, there was one held at Attercliffe, a considerable village one mile from Sheffield. These meetings have been productive of much good, for they have not only kept the agitation alive in Sheffield but also enlightened the ignorant rustics of the villages where such meetings have been held. We recommend this practice to other large towns'. A later report from Sheffield announces another type of meeting. 'On Sunday week, the Chartists of this town held what is

[1] *Sheffield Iris*, Oct. 8, 1839. *Sheffield Independent*, Oct. 12, 1839 and *Northern Liberator*, Oct. 19, 1839.

called a lovefeast, after the style of a body of religionists called Methodists.'[1]

At least another town adopted the new method of public meeting before the end of 1839. The *Northern Liberator* (Nov. 9, 1839) announces that at Loughborough on 'Sunday last, the patriots held a camp meeting, when Messrs. Barratt and Black, from Nottingham, attended and preached Chartist sermons, to the gratification of the friends of equal laws, but to the annoyance of the oppressors and their tools'.

From 1839 to 1850 the Chartist Camp Meeting remained the most regular and important form of political propaganda among the lower classes. Contemporary newspapers show how popular they were. Nearly 400 reports are to be found in the *Northern Star* during this period. As the semi-official organ of the movement it often gave glowing accounts of these demonstrations, avowing that 50,000 to 70,000 people sometimes attended. The year 1842 appears to have been a time of great political activity, ninety Chartist Camp Meetings being reported between April and September. Excitement was less intense in 1843, seventy-three Camp Meetings having been held. From 1844 to 1847 the number was less still, though a few were held each year. Early in 1848 political agitation once more revived, no doubt inspired somewhat by news of revolution on the Continent. Immediately after the information came to England of the Paris Rising, Chartist Camp Meetings began to be held in Lancashire and Yorkshire. Most of the speakers at these demonstrations sympathized with the revolutionaries, and demanded redress of their own wrongs. Within the space of five months sixty-eight Chartist Camp Meetings were reported by the *Northern Star*.

The accounts in the local press were usually coloured by political party feeling. Some of the Tory papers gave long and alarming reports of these Sunday gatherings. Others simply ignored them. Among the former the *Halifax Guardian* stands conspicuous, thirty-one Camp Meetings for Yorkshire and Lancashire alone being reported. A great deal of space is allotted to an account of the three Chartist Camp Meetings at Cronkeyshaw, near Rochdale, on Sunday, August 14, the eve of the general strike of 1842. According to the *Guardian* (Aug. 20,

[1] *Northern Star*, Nov. 9, 1839.

1842) reporter, James Mills of Whitworth asserted at the morning gathering that 'every chapter of the Bible breathed nothing but freedom and liberty'. A woman read from Luke XIV. 13, which says, 'But when thou makest a feast, call the poor, the maimed, the lame, the blind; and thou shalt be blessed; for they cannot recompense thee'. All this was preceded by a hymn sung to the tune 'Old Hundred'.

> They call the earth and land their own,
> And all they give us back's a stone.

When the Bradford Camp Meeting was advertised to take place at Pudding's Hill for Sunday, May 27, 1848, such was the alarm created among the local authorities that 2,000 special constables were appointed. Several units of the Cavalry and Artillery were called to assist, and although 10,000 reformers gathered at the meeting no disturbance took place. Disorder, however, broke out next day. At a later meeting held at Wibsey Slack on July 2, the Chartist preacher, a Mr. Lightowler, spoke on the text, 'if this work be of man it will come to naught, but if it be of God ye cannot overthrow it'.[1]

Like the *Halifax Guardian* the *Bolton Chronicle* is very critical of all the Chartist activities, and especially of the Sunday demonstrations. A sample of its attitude (June 18, 1842) is found in its estimate of the Pendle Hill Camp Meeting, held on Sunday, June 12, 1842. It contends that 'no man, no peaceably disposed subject of these realms will read this report without feeling both pity and disgust at the vile treason which is so insidiously wormed into the ears of the working classes'.

Among the Whig papers that were hostile to the Chartist Camp Meetings, the *Manchester Guardian* stands supreme. From 1839 to 1848 it reports twenty-seven such meetings, most of which were held in Lancashire. Ten of these took place in 1842, while eleven are reported for 1848. In several cases a very long account is given, the length usually being determined by the greatness of the alarm which these meetings created. The *Leeds Mercury* emulated the *Manchester Guardian* in its hostility to Chartist propaganda, though not so much pace is allotted to Chartist news of this sort. From 1839 to 1848 only eight Chartist

[1] *Halifax Guardian*, July 8, 1848.

Camp Meetings are reported, three of which are given in 1848.

Notwithstanding all this hostility, the Chartist movement received sympathetic consideration from some of the local newspapers. Amongst this class the *Manchester and Salford Advertiser* is important. Altogether it reported nineteen Camp Meetings, eight of which were held in 1842, four in 1843, two between 1845 and 1847, and five in 1848. The *Bradford Observer* also appears to be somewhat sympathetic to Chartism. It reported fourteen Chartist Camp Meetings, three of which were held in 1842, one in 1843, and the remainder in 1848. The majority of these gatherings were held in the vicinity of Halifax, Huddersfield, and Bradford.

Only a few Chartist Camp Meetings are reported by the *East Midland Press*. The *Nottingham Review*, having for its motto, 'England, with all thy faults, I love thee still', reported four Camp Meetings, although it gives much space to Chartist activities. The *Leicestershire Mercury*, while not so sympathetic as the *Nottingham Review*, reports six Camp Meetings for the Leicester area. A very long account is given of 'The Three Counties Camp Meeting', held at Loughborough on Sunday, April 9, 1848. The *Leicester Chronicle* and the *Leicester Journal* scarcely notice the Sunday demonstrations, only three being reported between them.

Perhaps the most important form of Chartist activity, and the least noticed, is the political class meeting. Like their ancestors, the Radicals of 1818 to 1823 and the Political Unions of 1831 to 1835, the members of the National Chartist Association organized themselves according to the Methodist fashion on class meeting lines.

The first intimation that Chartists had adopted the system of political class meetings comes from a letter to the Home Office on May 17, 1839. Jos. Wild, constable of Manchester, reports that the Chartists at Oldham are meeting in houses, and that their society consists 'principally of working men', the 'Chartists and the members of the Political Union' being the same people. Enclosed with this letter is a list of the rules of 'The Great Northern Union of the Borough of Oldham Political Association'. The declared purpose of this union is said to be the establishment of 'Universal Suffrage, Annual Parliaments, Vote by Ballot, no Property Qualifications'. After dividing the town into a number of districts, it was arranged 'That each of the above-mentioned districts be sub-divided into as many classes as may be deemed convenient, for enrolling members' names and the more easily conducting the affairs of the Union'. The next rule desires 'That each of the above-mentioned divisions elect as many leaders or collectors as they have separate classes; such class leaders or collectors to form a committee for collecting subscriptions and contributions and passing the same into the hands of the treasurer'.[1]

Before the end of the year, classes had been formed at Bolton, Manchester, Bradford, Barnsley, Birmingham, Bristol, Huddersfield, South Shields, Sheffield, and certain places in Leicester, Derbyshire, Nottingham, and Staffordshire. On Tuesday, June 25, a delegate meeting of reformers was held at Rochdale in Robert Hall's house better known as 'Hark-up-to-Glory public house'. Twenty-eight places from Lancashire, Yorkshire, Derbyshire, and Staffordshire were represented. At this meeting it was unanimously decided that 'the system of classes' 'should be adopted by the Chartists in every district. Several of the delegates stated that this system had already been acted on by the political unions of their own town. The delegates from Bradford, in particular, reported the success with which this system was attended'. Every member present pledged himself to form classes in his own district where they were not already established. Mr. Roberts, the chairman of the conference, 'drew a striking picture of their success in Hulme and Chorlton-upon-Medlock since they had adopted this plan'. 'Mr. George Lloyd, of Bolton, said the system had been also tried in their district, and attended with some success.' Mr. Hollingsworth, of the Potteries, stated 'that if something of this kind were not adopted, he very much feared that the cause of the people would go down'.[2]

Classes had been established in Bradford as early as June, 1839. Apart from the statement of the Bradford delegate at the Rochdale Conference of June 25, Samuel Smith, in his evidence at the trial of the Bradford Chartists (when they were charged with riot and conspiracy) at the York Assizes, 1840, confessed that

[1] H.O. 40. 37, 1839.
[2] *The Manchester and Salford Advertiser*, June 29, 1839.

he was a class leader up to August 12, 1839, when 'the National Holiday' was begun.[1] He admitted that 'Classes were first established among the Chartists in June or July last'. 'My class', he said, 'was a moral force Chartist class.'[2] Owing to the ban imposed by the magistrates in the August of 1839 on open-air gatherings in Sheffield, the Chartists as a kind of counter-move organized themselves into political classes. A placard posted on the walls announced this innovation. It stated that 'In consequence of our worthy? magistrates having determined in their wisdom upon suppressing our legal and peaceable meetings, we have resolved upon holding small class meetings, similar to the Methodist class meetings, for the purpose of concentrating our strength, for the holy purpose of effecting our just, legal, and constitutional object—The People's Charter'.[3] The editor of the *Sheffield Independent*, writing on August 24, after announcing that the Chartists 'have devoted several evenings this week to the organization of classes', advises his readers 'to avoid connecting themselves with these classes'. He tells them such 'proceedings will not be regarded with indifference, and no man can be safe in going further than he can be well assured is within the law'. In spite of this ominous warning the *Sheffield Iris* was able to announce a fortnight later (Sept. 3) that the classes 'have been established in almost every part of the town'. 'We understand there are upwards of a hundred classes of the above description already formed in Sheffield.'

It is certain that these classes continued to exist until January, 1840. Ere that month had terminated, the Chartists of Sheffield got into prominence by a foolish attempt at insurrection. On the Saturday evening of January 11, they decided to attack the town, hoping to capture the Town Hall and the Tontine Hotel. 'To carry this plan into effect, the various classes were ordered to be at their place of meeting by ten o'clock and to take with them what arms they could secretly carry.' 'It seems that the classes were to join each other in different places on the outskirts, prior to their descent upon the town, for the purpose above mentioned. Several of the classes seem, by the evidence given before the magistrates, to have met together, but not, however,

[1] *The Sheffield and Rotherham Independent*, Feb. 29, 1840.
[2] *Northern Star*, March 21, 1840.
[3] *The Sheffield Mercury and Hallamshire Advertiser*, Aug. 24, 1839.

in anything like the force which was calculated upon.' 'Several classes assembled in Daisy-walk or the neighbourhood, but whether any of the others assembled in any other part of the town cannot be ascertained.'[1] This hazardous attempt at insurrection was frustrated by the preparations previously made by the magistrates. Most of the class leaders were arrested and Samuel Thompson, one of the prisoners, described at the trial the work of the classes. 'The Chartists', he said, 'are divided into classes, meeting at different houses, under leaders. These meetings are usually held at the houses of the leaders. There are six or seven class leaders in Sheffield.' He mentions the names of several of the leaders, he himself being in charge of a class. In the course of the trial, a great deal of evidence is given concerning the operations of the various class meetings.[2] Further information about the classes was presented at the trial of the second batch of Sheffield prisoners. Foxall, another insurgent to give evidence against his class mates, confessed that he 'belonged to Daniel Hand's class, at John Clayton's in Porter Street'. 'Clayton was a member as well.' 'At the class meeting there were frequent discussions about the best mode of attacking the military.'[3] In the following March, when the prisoners were finally tried and sentenced at the Yorkshire Assizes, the Attorney-General in his statement for the prosecution said among other things, 'there was established in the town of Sheffield societies called Chartists'. They had 'a plan of the most dangerous and mischievous character. They were resolved, not by constitutional and legitimate means, but by force and violence, to carry out that plan into effect. For this purpose they were divided into classes —each class had a leader—and they met at certain places in Sheffield and the neighbourhood and orders being communicated to them by the leaders who conducted these persons who were in these classes'. In their attack upon the Town Hall and Tontine Hotel, 'the class leaders were to bring them to the appointed place'.[4] At the same Assizes, some Chartists from Bradford were tried for seditiously conspiring to create a riot, and once again the work of the classes was described.

[1] *The Sheffield Mercury*, January 18, 1840.
[2] H.O. 40. 57, 1840. Also the *Sheffield and Rotherham Independent*, Jan. 18, 1840. And *Sheffield Mercury*, Jan. 18, 1840.
[3] *Northern Star*, Jan. 25, 1840.
[4] *ibid.*, March 21, 1840.

Classes existed at other places in Yorkshire besides Sheffield and Bradford. Some were found at Attercliffe and Rotherham. When Samuel Thompson gave his evidence at Sheffield, he affirmed that 'the Rotherham people and the Attercliffe class were to meet at the Railway Tavern', apparently to take part in the general attack on the town of Sheffield.[1] During the month of October, 1839, the Huddersfield Northern Union was very active in the organizing of class meetings and the appointment of class leaders. A correspondent reported that at the weekly class meeting 'class leaders were appointed to commence new classes in their several districts in the town'. 'We hope', he exclaims, 'to be able in a short time to announce them in full operation in all the out districts.'[2] Toward the end of January, 1840, the two constables of Keighley, E. Laycock and T. Wall, sent information to the local magistrates concerning a number of Chartist leaders who were 'acting in concert with Chartist Associations, in different Towns in the Riding, by forming those, who are in membership into classes and meeting such classes secretly, at different places in the Town, and neighbourhood'. The ulterior purpose of these activities is to make 'a sudden and simultaneous outbreak in different towns in the Riding, similar to what has occurred at Sheffield and Dewsbury and other places'.[3]

Leicester and Nottingham were among the counties infected by the new mode of political activity. 'The friends of equal laws' at Loughborough, not content with holding 'camp meetings', instituted in the autumn of 1839 the system of classes and 'class-leaders' meetings'. A meeting for class leaders was announced for the evening of December 2, 1839. A report sent to the *Northern Liberator* on the next day says that 'the class-leaders' meeting has been held; they have given a good account of their classes', and 'have agreed to push organization'.[4] Class meetings were established in Nottingham during the latter part of September, 1839. A correspondent from Birmingham, having visited the town, asserts that 'it is inhabited by Radicals, and so far as the honest working people are concerned, by Radicals alone. They meet every evening in large numbers to read the newspapers'. 'They, too, are forming into classes, and look little inclined to

[1] *The Sheffield and Rotherham Independent*, Jan. 18, 1840.
[2] *Northern Liberator*, Oct. 12, 1839.
[3] H.O. 40. 57, 1840.
[4] *Northern Liberator*, Dec. 7, 1839.

submit to Lord John's supper of bayonets and skilley.'[1] The Mayor of Nottingham, a few months later, refers to the same people when he affirms that 'the Chartists are now conducting all their proceedings here with great secrecy, having adopted a plan similar to the Wesleyans, dividing themselves into classes, each class having a Leader and meeting under his direction and are directed by him what to do. The Leaders have their meetings . . . and none but those who are in the Society are allowed to attend'.[2] A similar organization was introduced among the Chartists at Basford in the latter part of November. At a meeting held in the 'Sign of the Red Cow', the members of the union decided to form themselves 'into classes of tens, appointing one man to each class, to be called a committee-man, and that meetings be held at the above-mentioned house on any day or evening, once a week, at the hours of seven, for the despatch of business'.[3] The Radicals of Sheepshed were not to be outdone by their neighbours. On December 14, Major-General Sir Charles Napier sends a letter to the Home Office from the Rev. J. H. Hamilton, the Vicar of Sheepshed. The letter is described as 'this excellent note' displaying 'sound judgement'. In this 'excellent note', the Vicar says, 'the Chartists here as elsewhere hold regular meetings of about ten persons which they call classes . . . and at these meetings they read communications from the Chartists elsewhere and "transact business", generally paying each a certain sum towards the expenses'.[4]

Indications of the existence of classes in the neighbourhood of Newcastle are found as early as the second week of August, 1839. The Duke of Northumberland, writing to the Home Office on August 13, speaks of the concern among his viewers and agents because of the political activities of the colliers who work in his mines. 'At Cooper', according to J. Jobling, 'they are organized into Societies of twenty, and a leader to each, the chief leader is also a preacher.'[5] Six weeks later, at a public meeting held in the New Lecture Room, Nelson Street, Newcastle, E. Charlton, the chairman, 'called upon all present who could form a class of twelve, to attend in the anteroom and enrol their names'. 'A large number attended for the purpose of enrolment

[1] *Northern Liberator*, Sept. 28, 1839.
[2] H.O. 40. 55, 1840.
[3] *Northern Star*, Nov. 30, 1839.
[4] H.O. 40. 53, 1839.
[5] *ibid.*, 40. 46, 1839.

as class leaders accordingly.' When the Council of the Northern Political Union met on the following Wednesday, 'a large number of class leaders were present, many of whom announced the completion of their respective classes'. The hope was expressed 'that every man deserving the name of patriot will form around him, if possible, a class of twelve. There are already fifty classes formed in Newcastle. Let the most active spirits in town and country embrace the opportunity which now offers, and before six weeks goes round the Union will be far more numerous and far more firmly united than ever it was before'.[1] 'A considerable number of class leaders were present' at the next Council meeting and duly 'paid in the subscriptions of their respective classes'.[2] Before the end of October, the Council apparently were having some difficulty in their financial arrangements. At one of their weekly gatherings it was resolved 'that all class-leaders who should be defaulters for four successive weeks, without offering a satisfactory explanation, should be published in the *Liberator* as defaulters, and be no longer considered class leaders till they received new authority from the Council. It was urged in support of the motion, that any man whose other business prevented him acting efficiently as a class leader, could at once release himself from the duty by coming and making a statement to that effect to the Council'.[3]

Classes were also established at South Shields in the early part of October. At a meeting of the Political Union in Dr. Thoburn's Chapel on Monday, October 7, the following rules were adopted: '1. That the members of the Union be enrolled in classes of tens: each class to be under the management of a leader. 2. That every five classes, or fifty men form a section; each section to be under the control of a marshalman.' '8. That each leader collect the weekly contributions of his class; and to summon the said class together when and where the marshalman of this section may appoint. 9. That the contributions of each member be one penny per week; the leaders to pay the contributions of their respective classes to the Council on their weekly night of meeting.' Quarterly meetings were also appointed to be held on the first Tuesday in January, April, July, and October, 1840.[4] A month later, 'the staunch democrats' of the 'patriotic district' of Usworth

[1] *Northern Liberator*, Oct. 5, 1839.
[2] *ibid.*, Oct. 12, 1839.
[3] *ibid.*, Oct. 19, 1839.
[4] *ibid.*, Oct. 12, 1839.

accepted the South Shields plan. On Saturday, November 2, a meeting was held 'for the purpose of class enrolment, in accordance with the newly adopted plan of organization'.[1] Whether the South Shields plan was adopted by other localities or not, the results of the latest research have so far not revealed. Classes were, however, probably formed in other villages of the neighbourhood.

At Birmingham, toward the end of 1839, classes had become a regular institution among the reformers. During the month of October reports of class meetings held at Allison Street and other places were constantly sent to the Police Office by spies and police agents. According to one report sent on October 24, a committee man requested 'that every class leader would furnish a return of the number of arms and the quantity of ammunition'. On October 29 another report says, 'the meeting was called for the purpose of filling up the classes and forming fresh ones'. Admission to these meetings was usually by ticket. 'Two men were placed at the door to examine the tickets of each member previous to their being admitted.' One of the spies attending these meetings says 'they wanted money and class leaders and some were for having the leaders to be known by numbers, others by letters'. Sometimes they had singing and prayers at their gatherings. One night when they thought 'there was a spy in the room', they prayed 'that God would turn his heart toward their most righteous cause'. Shortly after this episode, they decided that 'on account of spies attending the meetings, they are in future going to transact their business in the classes . . . meetings of ten at the houses of class leaders'. One of the spies named Tongue reported on November 10 that 'Brown met his class of sixteen, each member paid his 1d. toward the society and 6d. towards getting arms'. A fortnight afterwards, he reports two speakers from Yorkshire advising them 'to arm themselves and form into classes'. One of the visitors 'told them how they met in Dewsbury in nines and every nine had a leader'. At a meeting in Lawrence Street Chapel, W. H. Green advised those present 'to organize themselves at their own homes and form classes and there they can talk about private things without anyone interfering'. As a result of this advice, 'W. Wilson then began . . . forming classes at . . . the same as W. Green'.[2]

[1] *Northern Liberator*, Nov. 2, 1839. [2] H.O. 40. 50, 1839.

Further evidence of the existence of classes among the Chartists at Birmingham is found in the report of F. Burgess to the Home Office on December 19, 1839. 'I have been using', he affirms, 'my best endeavours to ascertain the nature of the organization here, and of that of the connexion with other districts, and as far as I can judge, it is simple in its nature, calculated well to elude immediate detection, not very extensive in its operations here, but certainly in connexion with other quarters, particularly with the North, where it is said to be extensive. . . . There are committees formed from the General Association and a select committee chosen from that body consisting entirely of class leaders or managers of classes of small numbers who are associated together in small bodies in the neighbourhood where they live, so as to be able to meet at the shortest notice when required by their leaders . . . there are many of these classes. . . . These class meetings are held at the houses of various members at the will of the leader who names the time of meeting and house selected for it on so short a notice that the members if they wish have not time to give us notice of these meetings.'[1]

A copy of the Chartist rules and regulations of the Birmingham Association had preceded the receipt of the above letter at the Home Office. Rule 8 says, 'That for the better promulgating truth, this Association shall be divided into classes, each class to have a leader, who shall give into the committee a weekly report of the members and contributions of their respective classes'. The next rule requires that 'the secretary shall take down their names and residences of every committee and class leader, and every class leader shall take the name and residence of every member of his class'. Rule 10 ordains that 'any member of this committee or any class leader changing his residence shall inform the secretary of the same. Any class member changing his residence shall acquaint the leader of his class'. General meetings of members in times of emergency are to be called by the secretary who then informs 'each class leader to wait upon their respective classes'. A public meeting is to be held every Sunday evening 'for reading and lecturing from the Scripture at half past 6 o'clock'.[2]

Classes had been established by the Chartists at other places by this time. Through the influence of the Birmingham

[1] H.O. 40. 50, 1839. [2] *ibid.*, 40. 50, 1839.

Association, classes had been formed at Dudley, Bilston and Lyewaste in the Black Country. A correspondent, reporting from Bristol on behalf of the Working Men's Association, affirms on October 29 that 'we are organizing here into classes, with great rapidity; in fact, we are at the present moment in a better condition than we have been since the commencement of the National movement'.[1] At Middleton, in Lancashire, Butterworth of Manchester and Bairstow of Yorkshire, when speaking at the Radical chapel, advised the Chartists 'to unite and join their classes'.[2]

Not much information is available concerning the class system in the early months of 1840, except that which is connected with the Yorkshire Chartists. During the first few days of April the Northern Political Union in the Newcastle area reorganizes itself, and a new set of rules is accepted. Rule 4 declares 'that to ensure regular payment of subscriptions, every twenty members shall be a class, and pay their subscriptions to a collector, who shall pay the same to the treasurer monthly'.[3] In the course of the summer, the political class is more widely accepted. On July 11, 1840, at Chapel Row, South Durham, the Chartists are reported 'getting into their classes'. The hope is expressed that every man 'who is a Chartist at heart will get enrolled. If he is not in a class, his light is under a bushel'. A correspondent sends the information from Barnard Castle, that some classes have been formed there, and he 'anticipates a formidable organization'. South Church is optimistic. Several classes have been organized. The writer of the report issues an appeal saying, 'let the classes be attended to, for unless classes are formed, funds raised, missionaries employed, tracts published, it is no use. Get into your classes, men of South Church. You were the first to take the field, see that you are the last to leave it'. Evenwood also 'has classes formed at last'. An enthusiast exclaims, 'Come forward, ye trampled sons of evil'. 'Come Wesleyans, Ranters, Baptists, all sorts.' 'Press forward, press forward, the prize is in view. A crown of bright glory is waiting for you.'[4]

Toward the end of July, 1840, a notable step was taken by the Northern Chartists. At a delegate meeting in the Griffith Inn, Great Ancoats, Manchester, 'The National Charter

[1] *Northern Liberator*, Nov. 2, 1839.
[2] *ibid.*, Dec. 7, 1839.
[3] *ibid.*, April 11, 1840.
[4] *Northern Star*, July 11, 1840.

Association of Great Britain' was formally inaugurated and a list of regulations adopted. Regulation 7 definitely includes the system of classes. It provides that 'wherever possible, the members shall be formed into classes of ten persons, which classes shall meet weekly or at other stated periods as most convenient; and one out of, and by, each class shall be nominated as leader (and appointed by the executive as hereinafter ordered) who shall collect from each member the sum of one penny per week to the funds of this association'. In an address published by the delegates the hope is expressed that there will 'not be a working man, a working woman, or child, who is not a member of this great and glorious Association—properly arranged in classes and other divisions'.[1] When the organization was discussed in detail, several comments were made upon the proposal to form classes. Mr. Leach thought 'the system of classes might do well for the country where the population was thinly scattered', but would not work so well in the towns. Mr. Morgan commended the system. It worked all right in Bristol where some classes were established, 'and they met once a week for instruction'. 'Mr. Philip said the class system had been attended with a most beneficial result in Wiltshire.' 'Since the class system had been adopted, the money came in to a considerable extent. It was also found effective in calling meetings; each leader called on his class and in two hours they could be assembled.' Mr. Smart asserted 'they had so much difficulty in getting in money, that, without the class system . . . they would not get it in for any purpose whatever'. Mr. Barker reminded the delegates that 'various religious bodies, whose members were very poor, managed to raise a penny a week for them, and he thought they might do the same'. Mr. Spurr referred to the Methodists and said, 'Among the Wesleyans where some were poor, those that were better off made up the difference so that there was no loss. They must try to do likewise'.[2]

Immediately after the organization of the National Charter Association was confirmed, the plan began to be adopted by associations in different parts of the country. The Manchester plan was accepted by the Sunderland Chartists and regarded by them as a sure foundation. Every honest man is recommended to 'enrol himself in the classes', and to make them 'an important

[1] *Northern Star*, Aug. 1, 1840. [2] *ibid.*, July 25, 1840.

medium for the diffusion of intelligence'.[1] The members at South Church are told to 'keep up the classes, they are the sinews of a giant and will, if carried on, give a speedy triumph to the Charter'.[2] Although the leaders of the Newcastle Union are in prison, the Manchester plan is accepted.[3] A few weeks later the fact is announced that 'a great number of class leaders came forward and reported they had got new classes'.[4] A Durham delegate meeting commends the scheme in a published address which says, 'Men of Durham, it is for you to follow up the work so ably begun by the Manchester delegates, as propounded in their plan of organization. Let every village throughout the country immediately engage itself in the formation of classes. Few individuals in this country can be so poor as not to afford one penny a week to purchase their freedom with. The cause never had a more prosperous appearance than at present'.[5] Stockport Working Men's Association is dissolved and the National Charter Association takes its place. The usual classification is agreed upon. Two hundred members immediately enrolled. 'The application for class books was most flattering.' London, Loughborough, Rochdale, and Frome also adopt the the Manchester scheme.[6] Extra classes are formed at Salford. Chartists are advised to 'get formed into classes as speedily as possible'. Middlesbrough Chartists are organized into classes.[7] Places as far distant as Brighton, Liverpool, Plymouth, and Gateshead accept the Manchester plan. Middleton, Huddersfield, South Hetton, Gloucester, Sutton-in-Ashfield, Bristol, Nantwich, Worcester, and Tower Hamlets also report the formation of classes, while Bradford, Oldham, and Newcastle report continued progress.[8] 'Female Chartist classes' are being established at Oldham. Dewsbury announces that they 'have formed a teetotal class and a great many of the teetotallers have joined us'.[9]

The general acceptance of the class-meeting system by the Chartists aroused the fears of some of the officials in high position. Writing from York Street, Westminster, J. Johnson affirms that 'a council of seven' sit at Manchester and direct the proceedings of the whole. The country is divided into 'Ridings', 'Divisions',

[1] *Northern Star*, Aug. 22, 1840.
[2] *ibid.*, Aug. 29, 1840.
[3] *Northern Liberator*, Aug. 15, 1840.
[4] *Northern Star*, Sept. 5, 1840.
[5] *Northern Liberator*, Sept. 19, 1840.
[6] *Northern Star*, Aug. 29, 1840.
[7] *ibid.*, Sept. 5, 1840.
[8] *ibid.*, Sept. 12–Dec. 12, 1840.
[9] *ibid.*, Dec. 19, 1840.

'Districts', and 'each district into classes, each class will consist of ten, who have a leader and he has the name and residence of each member of his class, he calls at their house and collects the money. A card is given to each member so that every one is known, and can be called together at shortest notice, and when the organization is complete the Council of seven will appoint a dictator (it is expected)' who will have 'the power of directing the whole of England, Ireland and Scotland. They meet privately and nothing can be known by the police of any consequence'.[1]

Had the Manchester plan continued to be operated by the Chartists, it is difficult to estimate what might have been the result. Great progress was registered and much enthusiasm displayed while the scheme remained in existence, but apparently it came within the 'mesh of the law'. William Lovett and others declared the new organization to be illegal. Consequently, at the National Delegate Meeting held in Manchester on February 20–23, 1841, a new plan of organization was accepted in place of the old one. Among other things, the class meetings were left out, but the penny weekly subscription was maintained.[2] The editor of the *Northern Star*, in the issue of March 6, discusses the new situation and laments the abolition of the classes, wards, divisions, and local officers. He believed the Chartist principles to be religious principles and desired Chartists to declare them to be such, and thus place themselves in the same category as the Methodists, Baptists and others. Prohibition by the Government of the Chartist propaganda would carry similar action against the Methodists. His plan, however, was not accepted. The natural result was foreseen by the Rev. W. Hill. Chartism began to wane for a time.

After the stormy period of 1842, when Chartism received a heavy blow from the authorities, and when many of the leaders had been cast into prison, the reformers went into their shell once more. Nothing was heard of class meetings until August, 1843,[3] when the editor of the *Northern Star* once again refers to his plan of Chartists declaring themselves to be a religious society. 'I hold the principles of Chartism,' he exclaims, 'to be Religious

[1] H.O. 40. 57, 1840.

[2] *Northern Star*, Feb. 27, 1841.

[3] An exception was found at Stroudwater where the Chartists were reported in July, 1843, to be forming themselves into classes. No. 1 class met every Monday night. *Northern Star*, July 8, 1843.

principles and every Chartist Society to be consequently a Religious Society; and I would gladly see them so declare themselves; and leave to the vile herd of despots the option of openly and manifestly trampling on their own laws, or of crushing with Chartism, Methodism in all its various shapes and all the other isms of dissent in all its varieties of aspects.' He then expounds his new scheme which provides for an Annual Convention, a General Executive, District Councils, Branch Boards, and Classes. In regard to classes, he says: 'Whenever the members of any Branch determine that it might conduce to the welfare and advantage of the Branch to be divided into classes, the Branch Board have hereby the power to constitute them of as many members as may be determined on, according to locality. Each class, when constituted, shall choose for itself a leader subject to the confirmation of the Branch Board. The duties of the leader will be to arrange for conversational meetings with his class at a place of meeting most convenient; to hold a friendly discussion relative to the principles and objects of the Association, to read the tracts and authorized documents and reports of the general body; to collect the subscriptions of the members and weekly hand them over to the Branch Secretary; and generally to infuse a spirit of kindness and forbearance amongst the members.' Commenting on the scheme, he further adds, 'we shall have classes of tens or twenties with their class leaders forming in the whole a perfect system of communication from head to body, and from body to head; an indispensable in all efficient Organization'.[1]

At a meeting of delegates in Birmingham a few days after this publication, the editor's plan is accepted.[2] Although adopted by the Birmingham Conference very little information can be obtained concerning its application in the different localities. This may be due to the lack of news from the *Northern Star*, or perhaps to the waning influence of the Chartist movement. Some light is given on the situation at a delegate meeting held in the West Riding of Yorkshire during October, 1844. The general apathy abroad is lamented and a call to action is sounded. The officers of the National Charter Association are asked 'to appoint visiting committees, or class leaders, according to the rules and advice of the Executive'.[3]

With the revival of Chartism in the early part of 1848, a new

[1] *Northern Star*, Aug. 26, 1843. [2] *ibid.*, Sept. 16, 1843. [3] *ibid.*, Oct. 12, 1844.

plan of organization is accepted by the Conference of the National Charter Association. The country is to be divided into districts, localities, wards, and classes. A ward will 'consist of 100 and classes of ten members'. Among the local officers there are to be class leaders. Their duties will be 'to make themselves acquainted with residences of members composing their respective classes, and to communicate to them, the instructions received from the wardmen'. Camp meetings and public meetings are to be held forthwith in order that 'the plan or organization may be confirmed'. One of the delegates in the discussion declared 'it was a return to the good old plan of 1839 of having class leaders which he was very sorry that they had ever departed from'. A proclamation, issued by the Provisional Executive Committee, contained the following call, 'Rally, rally, in your classes. . . . Chartists, these are times to try men's souls'. The Metropolitan area immediately accepts the new plan. Districts and localities are formed, each locality being divided into wards of one hundred members, and 'each ward into classes or sections of ten each'.[1]

Within a month of the termination of the Birmingham Conference, Ernest Jones, a member of the Executive, had to answer, along with others, a charge of uttering seditious words at a meeting on Clerkenwell Green on May 26. He is reported to have said in the course of his speech, 'Where are your classes? Have you made your ward mates? Have you made your class leaders? Have you perfected your organization? If not, call public meetings and elect your class leaders. Do not let the classes be formed before you have your class leaders. You will find it much easier to form a class after the class leader is appointed. For if you form classes, and then afterwards appoint leaders, you may spend two or three hours or more upon the formation of every class, and never come to a fixed determination with regard to it, as one man may live here and another there. Elect the leader, and he knows the men likely to form the class living in his neighbourhood. There will be no improper assumption of that power, because you all elect the class leaders at the public meetings. Rest assured if each locality elects 100 class leaders, you will soon have 1,000 men under the banner. This is the only way to get up the organization'. 'Commence at the foundation—namely, the classes and the wards and all the rest will follow of itself'.[2]

[1] *Northern Star*, May 20 to June 3, 1848. [2] *ibid.*, June 10, 1848.

At a meeting held in Hyde at the beginning of July, Dr. McDouall, another member of the Executive, advocated the acceptance of the new scheme. He is reported to have said that their intention was 'to strike terror into Little John and the Government of this Country by our great numbers'. 'They must form themselves into sections of tens, and over the sections there will be a captain.' About the same time information is sent to the Home Office that secret indoor meetings are held by the Irish Repealers and Chartists at Bolton, and a special meeting is to be held by their chiefs at which only 'wardsmen and class leaders' can be admitted.[1] A report from Leicester says, 'They have carried out their plan of organization to some extent by dividing themselves into classes with leaders to each class'. At a Chartist meeting in Darlington on June 21, William Bryne explains to his audience that 'all towns are to be divided into Districts, each District is to have a wardsman who is to form the members into classes of ten each'. Every class must have 'a class leader who is to summon the members of his class on all occasions when they are required to assemble'. 'Only by these means, they could ever obtain their rights.'[2] Class meetings are being formed at Farringdon Hall, Holborn Hill, London.[3] Class leaders are still exercising their functions in the R Division of the Metropolitan Police area,[4] 'being very active in the Lambeth and Finsbury districts'.[5] Bury Edge in Yorkshire accepts the new plan of organization. In one week 'eighteen classes have been formed, twelve of which were filled up, and the remainder in a fair way of filling up'.[6] A correspondent to the *Northern Star* (June 24, 1848), quotes the Wesleyans as an example to follow in the matter of organization. 'Where there are no Chartist class leaders,' he says, 'let one settle down and become an ardent propagandist, and when the tens have got together, let them call on the butcher, baker, &c.' for help. Bury Edge continues to make progress, 'A most favourable report having been received from the different class leaders'.[7]

Once again the good old plan is abandoned. This happened in October, 1848. On the eleventh of the month, an address from the Executive of the Chartist Association, signed by Samuel

[1] H.O. 45. OS. 2410A, 1848.
[2] *ibid.*, 45. OS. 2410B–Z, 1848.
[3] *ibid.*, 45. OS. 2410AD–AL, 1848.
[4] *ibid.*, 45. OS. 2410, 1848.
[5] *Northern Star*, July 1 and Aug. 19, 1848.
[6] *ibid.*, June 10, 1848.
[7] *ibid.*, July 1, 1848.

Kydd, contained the information that the Attorney-General, at the late trials in the Old Bailey, had said 'the plan of organization lately adopted by the Chartist body was illegal'. In consequence of this the Chartists are advised 'to abandon such parts of the new plan as may have been adopted and fall back upon the old system of organization so well understood by you all'.[1] That recommendation marked the decease of the political class. Another plan was therefore adopted by the London section of the Executive. No classes are included in this plan, but the weekly penny subscription is retained.[2]

[1] *Northern Star*, Oct. 14, 1848. [2] *ibid.*, Dec. 2, 1848.

CHAPTER IV

THE MOTIVE OF THE POLITICAL SOCIETIES

THE motive behind the political societies was mainly economic, with the political as secondary. Although the Government might at times regard their purpose as seditious and revolutionary, an analysis of their activities shows that view to be entirely mistaken. The Radicals of 1816, accepting the programme of Major Cartwright and his supporters, demanded Universal Suffrage, Vote by Ballot, and Annual Parliaments. While the political purpose might be variously described at different times, the working-class reformers never departed from its fundamentals. Even when their societies were suppressed by Government reaction, the political principles remained as an ideal to be revived again when circumstances became favourable. This happened in 1831, and again in 1836.

Throughout the whole of the period covered by the Chartist agitation, the political objective was never forgotten. The six points of the Charter were in reality a natural extension of the programme accepted by the Radicals of 1816 to 1823 and adopted by the Political Unions of 1831 to 1835. When the Complete Suffrage Movement was inaugurated by Joseph Sturge in 1842–3, it deviated from the Charter, not because it objected to the use of physical force, but through its refusal to accept Universal Suffrage.

While all this may be true, the economic motive of the political societies always appeared to be the dominant factor. By most of the working-class agitators the political was regarded as subsidiary, while the economic was all-important. When distress was at its worst, political agitation assumed its most dangerous character. As material conditions improved the demand for reform became less vocal and not so urgent.

A review of the distress in which the labouring poor found themselves during the decades of 1816 to 1850 must not be regarded as unimportant in this connexion. A report from Birmingham in the third week of June, 1816, avows that 'the number of hands out of employ, in this once thriving town, is greater than ever was known'.[1] The distress is so great in Staffordshire that three gangs of colliers decide to advertise their sufferings by drawing three wagons of coal on the way to London. A placard on one of the conveyances said the miners would 'rather work than beg'. The Westminster meeting in September was ostensibly called for the purpose of taking 'into consideration the distressed state of the labouring and manufacturing classes'.[2] At Leeds the condition of the lower classes is so depressed that the Mayor appeals to the various ministers of religion to come to their aid. 'The number of labouring persons', he says, 'now wanting employment in this township, and in deep distress, was never before equalled.'[3] Meetings to consider the distress of the poor were held at Sheffield, Liverpool, and London. It was the greatness of the 'privation and suffering', as well as the increasing 'distress and misery' which impelled the Lord Mayor, Aldermen and Commons of the City of London to approach the Prince Regent with a remedy for the same.

Similar conditions appeared to be prevalent during the next year. The rector of Broseley, writing to the Home Secretary in February 1817, speaks of the condition of the 30,000 colliers and furnace men residing in his district, and 'all of whom', he says, 'are in the utmost distress from the pressure of the times'. Yet he triumphantly announces that he caused 'two men to be apprehended for distributing Cobbett's Pamphlets, and had them well flogged at the whipping post'.[4] A very strange way to relieve distress. Dr. Grey of Sunderland reports 'some hundreds of the starving population', who were forming a plot to kill him.[5] Some of the Leicester workmen protest against the low wages in the hosiery trade and declare that more than 100 per cent rise could be afforded without danger to the trade.[6] The reports of the Secret Committee to the Houses of Parliament admit 'the pressure of the times' and 'the distress' of the labouring classes, but regard such conditions 'rather as the instrument than as the cause of disaffection'.[7] Toward the end of the year an improvement of trade was manifest in some quarters. General Sir

[1] *Leeds Mercury*, June 22, 1816.
[2] *Morning Post*, Sept. 12, 1816. Also *The Times*, Sept. 12, 1816.
[3] *Leeds Mercury*, Sept. 21, 1816.
[4] H.O. 42. 159, 1817.
[5] *ibid.*, 42. 159, 1817.
[6] *ibid.*, 42. 166, 1817.
[7] *Hansard's Parliamentary Debates*, 1817, Vol. xxxvi, p. 950.

James Lyon expresses with satisfaction concerning Leicestershire that 'the increasing prosperity of the county has in a great measure banished discontent'.[1]

During the spinners' strike of 1818 in the Manchester area, an address by the strikers to the public lays stress upon the fact that for a considerable time the cotton spinners had been working on 'prices very inadequate to procure even the coarsest necessaries of life for ourselves and families'. The employers in their estimate of the spinners' wages argue that the weavers were in a worse condition, their wages being 'only a half or even a third of the spinners'.[2]

In the following year general distress was more manifest. At a delegate meeting of reformers in Oldham held in the early part of June, emphasis was placed on the 'scarcity' and 'high price of provisions', and on the 'low wages and deepest distress'. During the same month, J. Norris tells of a reform meeting at which 12,000 people had assembled, and adds, 'The distress of the labouring classes is great beyond all expression'.[3] Another magistrate of the same district also speaks of the 'deep distress of the manufacturing classes'.[4] When the Boroughreeve and Constables of Manchester were seeking advice from the Law Officer concerning the spirit of insubordination and disaffection, they also refer to 'the low state of wages'.[5] Speaking at a meeting in the vicinity, a Mr. Smeetham (a sort of local preacher) is reported to have said that 'the condition of the people in this country was much worse than that of the Israelites in Egypt', and that 'not one cottager in that assembly had spent a shilling for animal food during the last twelve months'.[6] A letter from a poor weaver to the *Manchester Observer* (Jan. 2, 1819), confesses that 'the condition of the labouring classes in the manufacturing districts beggars all description. They are deprived of almost everything that can render life desirable, or even endurable'. Another letter a few months later (May 29, 1819) asks 'what is our country to us now, but a burying ground?' 'Death stares us in the face,' he exclaims, 'and death by hunger, too! And in

[1] H.O. 42. 172, 1817.
[2] *The Skilled Labourer*, J. L. & Barbara Hammond, p. 97.
[3] H.O. 42. 188, 1819.
[4] *ibid.*, 42. 189, 1819.
[5] *ibid.*, 42. 191, 1819.
[6] *ibid.*, 42, 192, 1819.

the land of plenty.' The reason for holding the demonstration in Manchester on August 16 was 'to consider the best, most loyal, and most efficient means of alleviating their present unparalleled sufferings'.[1]

Distress apparently was at the root of the Cato Street Conspiracy in 1820. According to the *Leeds Mercury* (March 11, 1820), which was usually well-informed, when Ings and Thistlewood, two of the chief conspirators, appeared before the Privy Council, the former suddenly cried in a loud voice, 'It is want of food that has brought us here. Death! death would be a pleasure to me. I would sooner be hanged this instant, than turned into the street there; for I should not know where to get a bit of bread for my family; and if I had fifty necks, I'd rather have them all broken, one after the other, than see my children starve'.

In the later agitation of 1831 to 1835, the economic factor was again prominent. When the final rules were adopted for the National Union of Working Classes, the members were asked to endeavour to procure for every working man 'the full value of his labour, and the free disposal of the produce of his labour'. They were also requested to resist by all 'just and fair means' any 'unjust combination seeking to reduce wages'.[2] At one of the early meetings in the Rotunda, 'The General State of the British Nation' was publicly considered.[3] A fortnight later the meeting at Castle Street decided that the 'distress and starvation now existing among great numbers of the working classes are mainly due to the land being held in the hands of a few, instead of being cultivated for the benefit of the community at large'.[4] Toward the end of 1831 a notice appears in the *Poor Man's Guardian* (Dec. 3), inviting all the members of the National Union of Working Classes to join a society for renting land and purchasing stock with a view to mutual support when out of work. When the Select Committee inquired into the conduct of Policeman Popay, one of the witnesses avowed it was poverty that brought them together. A correspondent, writing to the *Poor Man's Guardian* (March 1, 1834) about the same time, seeks to show 'that high rents, high tithes, high tolls, high usury, high profits, and low wages amongst useful working people are the cause of their poverty'. In the days when the Union is on the

[1] H.O. 42. 193, 1819.
[2] Place MSS. 27835, p. 251.
[3] *Poor Man's Guardian*, July 9, 1831.
[4] *ibid.*, July 23, 1831.

wane, the working classes are advised 'to establish Unions in every town in the United Kingdom, on the principles of the National Union of the Working Classes in London; and meet frequently together, to enquire, to consult and consider your grievances'.[1]

When faced with a decrease of members and a smaller income, the General Committee find consolation in the assurance that most of those who had seceded 'were still active in endeavouring to procure an amelioration of the sufferings of the labouring classes'.[2] Francis Place (Place MSS. 27797, P. 290), regarded the 'nonsensical doctrines preached by Robert Owen and others', and 'the rights of labour' which they had emphasized as the real cause of their decreasing influence and membership. Yet almost with their last breath the 92nd Class of the Union appeals to 'the friends desirous of redeeming the human race from bondage' to come along and join them.[3] Whatever success the agitation achieved can be partly explained by the economic appeal which was made to the distressed classes. A review of the Government reports published about this time on the condition of the hand loom weavers leaves no doubt about the poverty and distress of this portion of the community. Other sections of the labouring poor lived in a similarly precarious condition.

Irrespective of the stress laid by the Chartists upon the 'People's Charter', the economic factor was more important. The vision of an economic regeneration produced by the establishment of the Charter drew large numbers into the Chartist ranks. They saw in its programme the possibility of relief from their material distress. Working men in their despair were glad to accept any form of alleviation. 'A great mass of our unskilled and but little skilled labourers,' says Francis Place (Place MSS. 27819, P. 9), 'and a very considerable number of our skilled labourers are in poverty and great privation all their lives, they are neither ignorant of their condition nor reconciled to it, they are amongst others who are better off than themselves, with whom they compare themselves and they cannot understand why there should be so great a difference . . . and they come to the conclusion that the difference is solely caused by oppression, oppression of bad laws and avaricious employers. To escape from this state is with them of paramount importance.' When the

[1] *Poor Man's Guardian*, Jan. 31, 1835.
[2] *ibid.*, Feb. 14, 1835.
[3] *ibid.*, March 28, 1835.

Birmingham Political Union came to new life in 1837, a public meeting was held at Newhall Hill, and at this gathering the conditions of the people were considered. The first resolution passed at the meeting concluded 'that the present sufferings of the industrious classes are general and extreme, and require the immediate interference of the legislature for their relief'. The second resolution stated 'that nearly the whole of these sufferings are undoubtedly to be attributed to the cruel and oppressive laws which have made food dear and scarce, and money dear and scarce'.[1] In the May of 1838, P. H. Muntz, presiding at another public meeting, made the assertion that 'there were thousands of mothers and children who were crying for bread and could not obtain it'. 'He had taken the trouble to investigate the amount of distress which existed in Birmingham and he found it was enormous. He found that the wages of the working men were reduced a third generally and in many cases one half, yet vast numbers could not obtain work at any price.'[2] The National Petition, published in 1838, voices the same feeling when it says: 'We find ourselves overwhelmed with public and private suffering.' Notwithstanding the skill of merchants, 'our workmen are starving'.[3]

In the April of 1839, D. Maude reports from Manchester 'a very large unemployed population thrown out of work by the total or partial stoppage of mills to an unusual extent'. The Manchester Working Men's Association in a published address refer to the smallness of their earnings and the high price of food. 'We are compelled by the Government', they proclaim, 'to purchase coffee at two shillings per pound instead of sixpence, to buy sugar at sevenpence or eightpence per pound instead of threepence, tea at four or five shillings which we could purchase at one shilling or one shilling and threepence.' 'Bread, too, we are compelled to buy somewhat about double its value; the consequence of these things is that we endure hunger, and thirst, and nakedness, which is unchristian, and inhuman to make us endure.'[4] A similar report comes from Bolton in the August of the same year. A handbill contains the following appeal: 'Men of Bolton—think of mourning England, and suffering Englishmen. Think of your own wretchedness and your own wrongs. Think

[1] Place MSS. 27819, p. 108.
[2] *ibid.*, 27820, p. 87.
[3] *Birmingham Journal*, May 19, 1838.
[4] H.O. 40, 43, 1839.

of the iniquities which Government is daily perpetrating.'[1] The situation seemed to be no better in Leicester. Writing from Sheepshed, C. M. Phillips declares that 'this village is full of poverty and ignorance'.[2] Later in the year, Wemys from Manchester expressed his alarm by saying, 'want of employment and consequent distress amongst the labouring population, occasioned by the depressed state of trade, may, I fear, lead to disturbances during the winter'.[3] An unusual appeal is published in Colne. It comes from the hand of a special constable. He tells his fellow constables 'of the appalling sufferings and privations of the working classes', and asks them to sympathize 'with their deeply oppressed countrymen' and to take 'the side of equity, justice, and mercy'.[4] Another report comes from Sheepshed stating that 'many of the people in despair at not getting work, have joined the Chartists, as their only hope of a change for the better. . . . In short, we, like our neighbours, are in a pitiable state.'[5]

Conditions were no better in the early part of 1840. John Skevington, writing to Lord Normandy from Loughborough, says 'many families that have even work or part work have to live the last three days in a week on stolen turnips or on potatoes. Others, they cannot rest at night through hunger. This, my Lord, is not an exaggerated statement'.[6]

The National Petition of 1842 also refers to the prevailing distress and suffering. After commenting on the Archbishop's income of £52 10*s*. 0*d*. a day, it exclaims 'thousands of the poor have to maintain their families upon an income, not exceeding two pence per head per day'.[7] Chartism at the moment was exceedingly popular with the lower classes of the community, and it was just at this time that their sufferings were most acute.

An examination of the Home Office Papers for 1841 to 1850 leaves no doubt about the distress of the labouring poor. From Burnley comes the message of the Town Clerk that 'the state of distress experienced by the lower orders in this densely populous manufacturing district from an almost total want of employment is alarming'. He adds a further confession, when he asserts, 'it is most difficult and almost impossible to alleviate that distress'. At Oldham, a largely attended meeting of shopkeepers sym-

[1] H.O., 40. 44, 1839.
[2] *ibid.*, 40. 44, 1839.
[3] *ibid.*, 40. 43, 1839.
[4] *ibid.*, 40. 52, 1839.
[5] *ibid.*, 40. 53, 1839.
[6] *ibid.*, 40. 57, 1840.
[7] Place MSS. 27835, p. 188.

pathized with 'the labouring classes on account of their low rate of wages', and pledged itself 'to render all the pecuniary assistance in its power'.[1] About the same time, a petition to Sir James Graham from the power loom weavers at Manchester, says that many of their number are 'at this moment suffering under circumstances which are beyond human endurance'. They are 'perishing for lack of the necessities of life'.[2] Col. Wemys, reporting from the same place, admits that there is 'much distress amongst the working classes'. At Bolton 'inflammatory placards' announce that the people want 'Justice not charity', 'bread not barracks'. He says in regard to the area round Colne, 'the Chartist ranks are swollen by the unfortunate people . . . that are literally starving, and who attend meetings in despair of receiving help from legitimate sources'.[3]

Similar stories are received from other counties. In Leicester, under the influence of Thomas Cooper, the unemployed invade a Dissenting chapel. After the service is finished, they stand on both sides of the street, hold out their hats, and ask for help as the members of the congregation pass along. At another church they repeat the process and say 'Remember the poor'.[4] Birmingham reports both masters and workmen 'in a state of unprecedented suffering'. In Yorkshire men were sent to prison, it was said, 'for giving their honest opinions upon the cause of the sufferings of the labouring class together with the remedy for removing the same'.[5] Lieutenant-General Sir Thomas Arbuthnot, in his report for October, admits that, though the men are back to work in the Potteries, they are 'not working more than at the rate of three days in a week'.[6]

From 1843 to 1847 conditions in all districts, apart from the mining areas, showed signs of improvement. In 1845 Arbuthnot reports the 'working classes in general in full employment'.[7] Coincident with this change, or perhaps as a consequence, Chartist activity became less lively for a time. The year 1847 saw the beginning of another depression. F. Forster, in October, speaks of great distress and unemployment at Manchester. The total number of mills in the vicinity engaged at full time was 84 out of 175. In Preston, Bolton, and Ashton, only 28 mills out of

[1] H.O. 45. OS. 249, 1842.
[2] *ibid.*, 45. OS. 249C, 1842.
[3] *ibid.*, 45. OS. 269, 1842.
[4] *ibid.*, 45. OS. 250, 1842.
[5] H.O. 45. OS. 264, 1842.
[6] *ibid.*, 45. OS. 268, 1842.
[7] *ibid.*, 45. OS. 1125, 1845.

153 employed all their workmen.[1] Throughout the whole of the year unemployment in Lancashire caused a great deal of distress. From Arbuthnot's monthly report the tragic fact was revealed that 50 per cent of the mill hands were out of work.[2]

The distress continued for another year. In the early part of 1848, E. Armitage, the Mayor of Manchester, tells the Home Secretary that 'during a long period the trade of this district has, from a variety of causes, been exceedingly depressed. All classes have suffered, but the pressure has fallen most heavily upon those who depend upon the wages of their continued labour for the supply of their continually recurring needs. Numbers, unable to find employment, have to endure with their families severe deprivations'. The traders of Liverpool believed 'that the existing discontent arises not from disloyalty, but from the necessities of the people. Independently of the general suffering, through want of employment, the people labour under the impression that the Government have no sympathy with their distressed condition'.[3] From Birmingham comes the news that 'upwards of ten thousand individuals' are 'receiving Parish Relief'.[4] The situation seemed worse in the Bradford area. One report says: 'We are cognizant of the fact that thousands of our fellow countrymen are absolutely starving for want of the common necessities of life.' Conditions are no better in Staffordshire. Colonel Arbuthnot reports '20,000 men out of work at Dudley with little prospect of the majority getting employment'.[5] When conditions improved Chartist agitation died down.

Reviewing the whole period it can be asserted with a considerable amount of confidence that the real motive in the mind of the working classes, when seeking independently or in association with the Whigs for Parliamentary Reform, was purely economic. Sedition and insurrection were never ulterior motives. Violence was either accidental or due to the natural annoyance created by the reactionary measures of masters, magistrates, and Government officials. Deprivation and distress more than philosophic discussion compelled working men to agitate for a change in the political system. To escape from their sufferings was a perfectly natural desire, and because so many believed that political reform offered a necessary panacea they accepted it with a kind of religious fervour.

[1] H.O. 45. OS. 1797, 1847.
[2] *ibid.*, 45. OS. 1802, 1847.
[3] *ibid.*, 45. OS. 2410A, 1848.
[4] *ibid.*, 45. OS. 2410B–Z, 1848.
[5] *ibid.*, 45. OS. 2410AB–AC, 1848.

CHAPTER V

THE METHODIST NEUTRALITY

In the first fifty years of its history Methodism had succeeded in maintaining an attitude of strict neutrality in regard to politics. This was made possible by three circumstances. 'A measure of freedom,' had been inherited from the struggles of Dissenters. Working men, generally speaking, had not as yet entered the arena of political agitation. Through their love for the Established Church and their kinship with Dissenters, the Methodist people had taken up a middle position between the two. Political neutrality was an impossible position for the 'Older Denominations.' In the seventeenth and eighteenth centuries their very existence was bound up with civil liberty. Religious and civil freedom had been denied them by the passing of the Uniformity, Five Mile, and Conventicle Acts. By their continued opposition to these obnoxious measures a certain amount of toleration was granted to all Dissenters. When the Methodists began their crusade, they obtained without conflict the benefits of this toleration. They could therefore continue their work without insisting on the recognition of civil rights. While many of their pioneers had to face persecution from the various mobs, it was not because of their political opinions. In fact they had no political view. They had adopted the 'no politics rule'. This was made more easy by regarding their position in the State as one of privilege. Although their original purpose was 'to reform the Church and the nation', this objective never had any political reference. They did not wish to change the institutions of the State, nor alter the framework of society. Seeking to establish 'a purely spiritual system', they wished to avoid interfering 'with any public ecclesiastical or political institution'. They were mainly concerned with 'the spiritual state and the moral conduct' of their disciples.

The establishment of the 'no politics rule' was rendered less difficult by the absence of a reform agitation before 1791. Consequently the disciples of John Wesley were never in his lifetime called upon to take sides in political conflict. When working men began to form political societies in 1792, the matter was different. Some of the leading Methodists tried to walk the 'tight rope' of political neutrality and naturally failed.

Although the middle position between the Establishment and Dissent was an anomaly and only temporary, it enabled the Methodists to assume an attitude of 'quietism' in both religious and political conflicts. 'To be the friends of all and the enemies of none' was the command of John Wesley to all his followers, and on the whole they loyally responded. After his decease in 1791 his successors in office endeavoured to continue his policy, but the attitude of the Bishops pushed them further from the Church. In the course of time circumstances brought them nearer to Dissent, and political neutrality became an impossibility.

Signs of the impossibility are manifest during the years 1792 to 1815. On the one hand some of the rank and file of Methodist societies began to dabble in politics. On the other hand official Methodism went over to the side of Toryism. An example of the former is provided by the *Leeds Mercury* of May 2, 1807, when a Methodist, confessing that his fellow Methodists are not in the habit of 'taking part in political broils', strongly advises all the Methodist freeholders of Yorkshire to vote for the opponent of Lord Lascelles. Examples of the latter are supplied by the repeated injunctions of Conference to support the King, Constitution, and Government, and by the activity of certain Methodist preachers in the localities where disorder broke out.

With the formation of political societies in the winter of 1816–17, Methodism as practised by the Wesleyans openly abandoned its neutrality. Until the middle of the century opposition to working-class societies became a leading feature of Methodist activity among the Wesleyan preachers. On February 6, 1817, the London members of their 'Committee for Guarding the Privileges of the People called Methodists', under the chairmanship of Joseph Entwisle, adopted an address and ordered it to be sent to all the Methodist societies. They speak with pleasure of 'the uniform attachment shown by the Methodist Societies at large, to the person of the Monarch, and the Constitution of the country, and they recollect how, at different critical periods, they have maintained a peaceable demeanour'. Their hostility to the reformers is clearly evident by the confessed desire 'to prevent every member of the Methodist Society from being misled by the delusive acts of designing men, and to guard them, in the most solemn manner, against attending tumultuous assemblies, joining themselves by oath, or otherwise, to illegal political associations, and in any projects contrary to the duties of true Christians and loyal subjects'. Adopting the language of the 1812 Conference, they 'look at the principles which have given birth to this state of things with the utmost horror', and feel assured that 'the Societies are uncontaminated with that spirit of insubordination, violence, and cruelty, which has caused so much distress and misery'. Therefore they proclaim 'loudly and earnestly: "Fear the Lord and the King, and meddle not with them that are given to change". Avoid them, come not near them'. The address ends with a solemn exhortation to the richer brethren to assist those who are poor. In a footnote the Conference pronouncements of 1792, 1793, 1798, 1800, 1803, and 1814 are taken as an endorsement of the sentiments expressed in the address. It is noteworthy to remember that the Committee was composed of both laymen and ministers.[1]

At the Conference of 1817, in a message to the Irish Assembly, reference is made to the 'agitations of a political nature . . . in various parts of the country'. It is asserted that 'some evil-minded men, disciples of infidelity, have taken advantage of the distresses of the poor, to foment and increase those agitations by the circulation of seditious and blasphemous publications under ensnaring titles, and in cheap forms'. But the danger having been seen, the 'people were admonished; and they heard the voice of pastoral affection and caution'. 'In this time of trial, the Methodist Connexion has been steady to the principles of the Bible, so zealously maintained and exemplified by our Venerable Founder . . . and has given new proof of attachment to the person and family of our beloved Monarch, of obedience to the laws, of gratitude for unexampled civil and religious privileges, and of zeal for the support of our unrivalled constitution.' Gladness was expressed at the fact that these were also the sentiments of the Irish Brethren and that they were resolved 'to fear the Lord and the King, and to meddle not with them that are given to change'.[2]

The only published reference of the 1818 Conference to the prevailing political situation voiced the satisfaction of the preachers

[1] *Methodist Magazine*, 1817, pp. 301–3. [2] Wesleyan Conference Minutes, 1817.

that the Irish were still loyal to 'Constitution', 'Church', and 'State'.[1]

At the 1819 Conference the assembled preachers once more refer to the political agitation of the period. Sympathy is expressed to the 'dear Brethren, who, from the pressure of the times, and the suspension of active commerce, are, in common with thousands of your countrymen, involved in various and deep afflictions'. Condemnation is meted out to those 'unreasonable and wicked men' who 'render the privations of the poor the instruments of their own designs against the peace and the government of our beloved country'. The members of the Connexion are therefore reminded that they are 'Christians and are called . . . to exemplify' their religion by 'patience in suffering, and by living peaceably with all men'. They are called upon to remember that they belong to 'a Religious Society, which has, from the beginning, explicitly recognized as high and essential parts of the Christian duty, to "Fear God, and honour the King, to submit to magistrates for conscience sake, and not to speak evil of dignitaries".' They are warned against those who would deceive them into joining 'political parties and associations' and exhorted to follow their 'occupations and duties in life in peaceful seclusion from all strife and tumults'.[2]

The Committee of Privileges, at its meeting in City Road on November 12, goes farther than the Conference. Its views are clearly expressed in eleven resolutions to be sent to the societies of the Connexion. Reference is made to 'the alarming progress which Infidelity and Sedition have recently made in several parts of the country'. The members of the Committee therefore feel it their duty to declare 'their utter abhorrence of those principles which have been industriously disseminated for the purpose of alienating the people from their Christian Faith, and from the Laws, Authorities and Constitution of the Realm'. Methodist people are reminded of 'the undisturbed and legalized enjoyment of their Religious Liberties', granted 'at the hands of the Civil Government'. Hence they 'are bound to evince by their loyalty, that they deserve the privileges which they claim'. They are informed that 'the Holy Scriptures explicitly state it to be the indispensable duty of Christians, to be subject to the higher

[1] Wesleyan Conference Minutes, 1818.
[2] *ibid.*, 1819. Also *Methodist Magazine*, 1819, pp. 709–10.

powers, to obey magistrates . . . to submit themselves to every ordinance of man for the Lord's sake'. Christian duty demands they should 'unite with their fellow subjects in every proper and lawful demonstration of attachment to our free Constitution'. Resolution six expresses 'strong and decided disapprobation of certain tumultuous assemblies which have lately been witnessed in several parts of the country; in which large masses of people have been irregularly collected (often under Banners bearing the most shocking and impious Inscriptions)'. In the next resolution the Committee 'strongly exhort the members of the Methodist Societies most conscientiously to abstain from such public meetings'. This is regarded as 'a duty which they owe to God and to their country, and to the Government, from which we as a Body have received so many instances of protection'. Members of society are warned against the 'Private Political Associations, illegally organized', and the preachers are advised to expel all those 'who shall be found to persist, after due admonition, in identifying themselves with the factious and disloyal, either in public meetings or Private Associations, described in the previous resolution'. Finally, the Committee heartily approves 'of the conduct of those ministers, and other official members of our Societies resident in the Disturbed Districts, who, by their firm and decided measures, have supported the principles of Christian, and social order, notwithstanding the opposition and calumny which they have incurred from men of infidel and factious minds'.[1] As these resolutions were printed in circular form, there can be no doubt that through the medium of the travelling preachers they would reach their destination. According to one critic, 'the Methodist pulpits everywhere resounded with the murderous doctrines of passive obedience and non-resistance'.[2]

At the Conference of 1820, reference is made once more to the political quietism of the Methodist people. The King is told of their 'undeviating attachment' to him and to the 'unrivalled Constitution of our Country'. This attachment is derived 'from early instruction, from principle, and from choice'. They also promise to use their influence 'to discountenance sedition and disorder in all forms, and strongly to enforce subjection to the laws, and to all civil authorities constituted by the State'.[3]

[1] *Methodist Magazine*, 1819, pp. 942–5. [2] *Wooler's British Gazette*, Jan. 21, 1821.
[3] Wesleyan Conference Minutes, 1820. Also *Methodist Magazine*, 1820, pp. 862–3.

Dr. Adam Clarke, writing from Liverpool on July 26, informs Lord Sidmouth of the unanimous decision of the assembled preachers and adds, 'it will afford your Lordship great pleasure to find that His Majesty's Person and His Government are so highly venerated and loyally supported by such a large number of deeply religious people, who hold everything in abhorrence disrespectful to the Throne and subversive to the laws'.[1] As the vehicle of such a loyal message, Dr. Clarke would find a peculiar delight. Unlike his fellow Irishmen he had a special love for the King and Constitution. According to the *Birmingham Advertiser* (Jan. 5, 1837), which had for its motto, 'It is good not to try experiments in States', Adam Clarke believed that 'of all the civil constitutions under Heaven the British is demonstrably the best. . . . It is an honour to be born under it; a blessing to live under it; and a glory to defend and support it. . . . God alone can destroy it; but he will not destroy the work of his own hands'. While the Wesleyan Conference was composed of men with such sentiments, it was natural to commend, as was done in 1821, 'the firmness, prudence and Christian loyalty evinced by Mr. Stephens, Mr. Thomas Jackson, and the other preachers of the Manchester Circuit, during the last three years, in reference to the agitations which occurred in that town'.[2]

From the evidence available it appears that these Conferential pronouncements were not mere platitudes. Some of the preachers who took a prominent part in the public utterances of the yearly assembly went back to their circuits to carry out the mandates so earnestly given. Thomas Jackson, one of this number, was stationed at Manchester during the turbulent period of 1818 to 1821. He and his fellow preachers took the side of law and order, and manifested 'opposition to the revolutionary changes which many wished to introduce'. On one occasion he was forced by the magistrates 'even after the public services of the Sabbath-day, to walk the streets through the night, in company with others for the purpose of reporting any suspicious movements that might appear'.[3] Dr. H. Taft, another Methodist preacher who resided in Manchester about the same time as Thomas Jackson, confessed that he used his influence to counteract 'the dangerous nature of

[1] H.O. 44. 2, 1820.
[2] Wesleyan Conference Minutes, 1821.
[3] *Recollections of My Own Life and Times*, Thomas Jackson, p. 173.

radical politics'. He also warned as many as he could 'to stand apart from those who feared not to speak evil of dignities'. For this purpose he visited house to house, and in addition to this self-imposed task, he distributed 20,000 tracts with the same object.[1]

It may seem rather strange to the admirers of the Rev. J. R. Stephens to be told that his father, the Rev. J. Stephens, revealed a great deal of antagonism to the Radicalism of Manchester during 1819 and 1820. In speech, sermon, and attitude he expressed his hostility to its aims and methods. As a consequence, he was constantly exposed to ridicule by the local Radical press. On one occasion the *Manchester Observer* charged him with 'frequently and so violently inveighing against what he calls political madmen of Jacobins'.[2] The same paper widely proclaims the fact that at a Methodist meeting, over which the Rev. J. S. presided, a local preacher was expelled from the Connexion because he signed the 'Manchester Declaration' against the magistrates. At this meeting the chairman is reported to have said 'it was monstrous for anyone to find fault with the civil officers of the town'.[3]

The Rev. John Rigg of Newcastle is another Methodist preacher who opposed the Radicals where he laboured.[4] According to a Methodist correspondent to *The Black Dwarf* (March 29, 1820), Mr. Rigg, just a few days before the Radical meeting on the Newcastle Town Moor in the early part of October, 1819, strongly advised the members of the Newcastle Methodist Society to keep away from the demonstration. 'I earnestly entreat you,' he is reported to have said, 'and sincerely hope, that none of you who are here present, will go among that squabble.' 'This very loyal minister,' says the correspondent, 'next took occasion to enforce the doctrine of passive obedience.' In order to give a Divine authority to his advice, the minister read to his audience the thirteenth chapter of Romans.

Richard Watson, hiding away in one of the confines of a city office, as one of the Secretaries of the Wesleyan Missionary Society, takes the safer and the more secret course in his opposition to the Radical agitation. Writing to Lord Sidmouth on August 20, 1819, he tells his Lordship with the utmost confidence 'that no

[1] *Memoirs of the Life, Character and Death of the Rev. H. Taft, M.D.*, p. 124.
[2] H.O. 42. 190, 1819.
[3] *ibid.*, 42. 201, 1819.
[4] John Rigg was father of the well-known Dr. John Harrison Rigg.

man would be tolerated as a member of our Societies who should make himself a member of a political club, or take any part in such meetings as have recently disturbed the country'. 'Veneration for the reigning family,' he says, 'love for the Constitution and respect for the laws, are sentiments we proclaim in every part of the land; and during the prevalence of Luddism and the more recent spread of disaffection, several of our ministers who had publicly warned their congregations, were, and continue to be, the objects of sanguinary menaces of desperate and violent men.' Enclosed with the letter he sends a copy of the 1819 Conference Address to the Societies. His Lordship expressed his pleasure on the receipt of this assurance by appending a note to it in his own handwriting, saying, 'Lord Sidmouth has read with great satisfaction his assurance of the loyalty of this class of H.M. subjects'.[1] Watson's avowal 'that no man would be tolerated as a member of our Societies who should make himself a member of a political club' seemed strangely inconsistent with his conduct a few years later when he departed from the professed neutrality of the Wesleyans in regard to politics and interfered in the Leeds election of September, 1831. Writing to the Rev. Sanderson, he asked him 'to do as much for Macaulay as is consistent for us as ministers'. As a result of this action, a long correspondence took place in the Leeds papers. He was denounced by the *Patriot* (Sept. 24, 1831) as a 'blasphemer', while his letter was described as 'the officious interference of a Methodist parson', 'in every sense only deserving of the most profound contempt'. The *Intelligencer* (Nov. 30, 1831) regarded his conduct as 'a prostitution of religion in the cause of party politics', and setting an 'example, which, if followed up, would convert the religious and moral influence of the Methodist ministers into a social evil, a public wrong, and a political nuisance'.

Another letter that reached the Home Office shortly after Watson's came from the pen of J. Briggs Holroyd, a Methodist preacher at Haslingdon. Not knowing which was the best course to adopt to oppose the Radical activities in his locality, he sends a long letter to his namesake, Judge Holroyd. The famous judge, believing the letter contained important information, sent it to the Home Secretary. In this letter the Methodist preacher declares that 'this neighbourhood . . . may be considered the

[1] H.O. 42. 192, 1819.

hotbed of Radicalism. In no part of the Kingdom that I have heard have they assumed a more hostile spirit'. He maintained that although he preached nothing but 'Christian politics', he was 'one of the five in this town who are marked to be killed'. 'On the 13th Nov. last, about 7 in the evening a great concourse of people assembled in front of my house. . . . Not judging it prudent to attempt forcing my way through the crowd, I stopped inside the garden gate. They gave three horrible groans. With each groan, a young man brandished a pike within three feet of my heart accompanied with dreadful imprecations.' 'I have heard it repeatedly hinted,' he adds, 'that should His Majesty object to the Queen's Coronation, the Radicals will immediately rise to espouse her cause.' The writing of this letter had cost him 'many hours' anxiety', for he believes if it were known, he would 'soon be a dead man'.[1]

The effect of all this political teaching and practice is estimated by a Radical writer in 1831. Looking back upon the conduct of the Methodists, he maintains that 'in 1819 their pulpits were turned into political rostrums, while their preachers, who profess to have nothing to do with this world, instead of letting politics alone, absolutely came forward to support Lord Castlereagh in passing the Odious Six Acts against the Liberty of the press'.[2] A more friendly writer avows that 'no ministers have enforced the duties of patriotism and loyalty more than the Methodist preachers, and no people have been more observant of these duties than the Methodist people'.[3] Examples of enforcement can easily be supplied. Disobedience to Conference injunctions was often met with expulsion. During the excitement of 1819 several scholars of the Wesleyan Sunday School at Manchester were expelled for wearing the Radical badges, while some of the teachers were warned that if they did not discard their colours they would suffer the same penalty.[4] In the summer of 1820, according to the *Leeds Mercury* (Aug. 19 and 26), a Mr. Monkton was 'excluded from the Methodist pulpits for having had the temerity to pray publicly for the Queen'. When the matter was reported in the local press, the Rev. Richard Reece, who had 'by a kind of ecclesiastical bull fulminated against Mr. Monkton', strongly denied the charge. He admitted that the complaint

[1] H.O. 40. 11, 1820.
[2] *Leeds Patriot*, Sept. 24, 1831.
[3] *Methodist Magazine*, 1820, p. 828.
[4] H.O. 42. 197 and 198, 1819.

against Monkton was not 'that he prayed "for the Queen", but that he used improper expressions in praying for the Queen, which were offensive to many respectable people in the congregations. He was admonished, and advised to go home and read his Bible more carefully and learn his politics from that book'. Another case of expulsion was reported by the *Manchester Observer* in 1821 (Oct. 27 and Nov. 24). One report says that Mr. Brickill was expelled for preaching in the Union Rooms, but Brickill himself affirmed that he was suspended from preaching 'for putting on a drab hat, to testify my disapprobation of the proceedings on the awful 16th of August'.

All this hostility against the Radicalism of that time shows how easily the doctrines of 'passive obedience and non-resistance', as well as the exhortations to submission and loyalty can become the active agencies of reaction and repression. The policy of calling the Radicals 'evil disposed persons', 'factious and disloyal', 'designing', 'unreasonable and wicked men', 'disciples of infidelity' was entirely misleading and exceedingly mischievous. It was equally mischievous to imply that the reform movement always synchronised with 'insubordination, violence, and cruelty', and usually produced 'infidelity and sedition'. A belief of this sort tended to make reaction and repression an imperative Christian duty, while opposition to reform and a defence of political injustice were transformed into patriotic virtues. Under the influence of the Methodist preachers a large number of the labouring poor were persuaded or compelled to remain outside the political movements of that time. But others repudiated the Toryism of the Methodist leaders and severed their relationship with the Wesleyan Connexion. Thus for the first time in its history Wesleyanism had to acknowledge a decrease of members, the number being over 5,000 for the year 1819.[1] That many of the working class people of Methodist persuasion suffered through unemployment and material scarcity cannot be gainsaid. They were, however, advised to cultivate patience and to endure with hope till better days arrived.

The traditional hostility of the Wesleyan Connexion in regard to political agitation was steadily maintained during the years 1833 to 1835. At the Conference of 1826 the preachers were 'happy to notice the absence of all political strife or disaffection',

[1] Wesleyan Conference Minutes, 1820.

although 'unexampled distress' had 'plunged so many thousands of the labouring classes into penury and want'.[1] Sentiments like these did not exempt the body from charges of disloyalty and of 'adopting practices dangerous to the State'. The editor of the *Methodist Magazine* for 1828 repudiates with indignation this false charge published in the pages of the *Christian Guardian* and claims that certain Methodist ministers 'have openly inculcated subjection to "the powers that be" in populous neighbourhoods which have been in a state of incipient rebellion. They have done this among a people exasperated by hunger, and by the harangues of demagogues; and they have done this with the certain knowledge that they were marked out for assassination by incendiaries'.[2]

A less hostile attitude seemed to be momentarily apparent in 1831, for the injunction to the members of society among other things, said, 'Let not worldly politics engross too much of your time and attention'.[3] Methodists had been committed to political action by their opposition to increased facilities being granted to Roman Catholics, and by Conference resolution advising them to petition for the abolition of slavery.[4] In harmony with this recommendation many petitions were sent to the House of Commons. The Trustees at Brunswick Chapel in Leeds objected on one occasion to a petition being signed at their place of worship against the Roman Catholics. 'To their immortal honour,' said the *Leeds Patriot* (March 21, 1829), 'the Trustees have decided that no party politics should be allowed and preached there.' The editor congratulates them and concludes 'that they have arisen and quitted themselves like men'. Reference has already been made to the political activity of Rev. R. Watson. During the reform agitation of 1831, the Wesleyan schoolroom at Elland, in Yorkshire, was lent to the reformers. At this meeting it was decided 'to petition the House of Lords to pass the Reform Bill without delay'. The petition was ultimately signed by 1,400 persons.[5] Breaking through the traditional attitude of the Wesleyan Connexion, the Rev. B. Godwin addressed a reform meeting at Bradford in the October of 1831.[6]

With examples of this kind in memory, the Conference of

[1] *Methodist Magazine*, 1826, p. 689.
[2] *ibid.*, 1828, p. 399.
[3] Wesleyan Conference Minutes, 1831.
[4] *ibid.*, 1829.
[5] *Leeds Mercury*, Oct. 8, 1831.
[6] *ibid.*

1832 continues its milder attitude. The Annual Address refers to the agitation caused by 'political questions', and confesses that into these 'it has seemed more allowable for Christians to enter than into the common topics originating in some party feeling'.[1] Nevertheless, the Methodist people were affectionately advised to guard against every solicitation urging them 'to become party politicians', being reminded that it was impossible for them to preserve their peace if they became 'the ardent agents of political parties'.[2] The old time opposition was clearly apparent at the next Conference. All the Methodist members are warned against the 'Associations which are subversive to the principles of true and proper liberty, employing unlawful oaths, and threats, and force to acquire new members, and to accomplish purposes which would tend to destroy the very framework of society'.[3] In the address to the Irish Conference, the 'demoralizing state of society' is said to be 'greatly increased by political agitation', but gladness is expressed because 'our people, as a body, have been happily preserved from all interference with political matters'.[4]

At the Conference of 1834 'grateful satisfaction' is found at 'the peaceable spirit and conduct of the great majority of our Preachers and people, in reference to certain questions of national policy, which have been agitated during the past year'; and the societies are exhorted 'to a steadfast perseverance in the same course'. 'Surprise and deep regret' were revealed at the confession 'that in two or three cases, our Chapels have been used for the purpose of public meetings having more or less a political object and character' and the 'strongest disapprobation' was shown to this 'appropriation of our places of worship'.[5] A similar course was pursued at the next Conference. The original purpose of Methodism 'to spread scriptural holiness through the land' received new endorsement, and the Methodist people are advised 'to keep aloof from all party-purposes, from all party spirit'.[6] The 1836 Conference continued in the same strain. Members are warned against the danger caused by 'the turbulent

[1] Wesleyan Conference Minutes, 1832.
[2] *ibid.*
[3] Dr. Rattenbury believes this refers to Trade Unions. See *Wesley's Legacy to the World*, p. 216.
[4] Wesleyan Conference Minutes, 1833.
[5] *ibid.*, 1834.
[6] *ibid.*, 1835.

excitement of political and party feeling'. They are therefore advised to guard 'against all associations' which carry them 'unnecessarily into the fields of political emulation and strife'.[1] The subject is again discussed in 1837. Confession is made that prayer has been frequently made in order to save the Connexion 'from becoming a political association', 'mere party politics' having been avoided by 'the public acts of the body'.[2]

During the years 1837 to 1850 official Wesleyanism maintained its hostility to reform societies. The Conference still under the influence of Jabez Bunting, made no secret of its Toryism.[3] In the early part of 1837 the *Birmingham Advertiser* (Jan. 5) asserted 'that the Conference, as at present constituted, as well as the vast majority of lay hands of the Connexion throughout the kingdom, espouse Conservative principles'. A correspondent of the *Leicestershire, Nottinghamshire and Derbyshire Telegraph* (Oct. 29, 1842) refers in a cynical manner to 'Bunting and Company'. 'Not content with patching up Toryism,' they throw the blame on Divine Providence for the widespread depression. 'At the Manchester election of 1839,' according to this correspondent, 'Mr. Jabez Bunting repaired thither to move heaven and earth for the return of Sir George Murray, the Tory.' An anonymous writer in the *Bradford Observer* (Jan. 29, 1841) sincerely desires 'the Wesleyan Connexion emancipated from the sinister influence of Dr. Bunting and other dictatorial patrons of the *Watchman*'. The *Leeds Mercury* (June 26, 1841) opens its columns to the same kind of criticism. An observer describes the *Watchman* as 'that truly Conservative cesspool, which is under the surveillance of Dr. Bunting, and readily receives the contribution of his satellites and toad-eaters'. He roundly condemns the endeavour of 'some of the preachers and their contemptible organ, the *Watchman*, to Toryise and enslave the body of Wesleyans'. He is convinced that there are so many laymen of 'decidedly Liberal' views, 'that if these reverend Tory meddlers with politics do not take care, the Connexion will soon run away from the Conference, in spite of all the Conservative cunning of the latter'. The prediction of this writer was almost fulfilled a few years later, when one third of the people left the Connexion.

[1] Wesleyan Conference Minutes, 1836.
[2] *ibid.*, 1837.
[3] Maldwyn Edwards in his *After Wesley* contributes a whole chapter on 'The Dominant Toryism of Methodism', pp. 13-36.

While the Wesleyan Conference was dominated by a Toryism both religious and political it was only natural that it should be hostile to Chartist agitation. An evidence of that hostility is supplied by the reported decision of the Wesleyan Preachers in the Bath District. At a meeting comprised of thirty to forty of them 'it was unanimously resolved that any member of the Methodist Connexion, who should join himself with the Chartists, should be excluded from their body'.[1] At the Conference of 1842 the activity of 'infidels and irreligious men', who 'are charging all the sufferings of the community upon the selfish policy of rulers', is openly condemned.[2] Six years later it speaks of the 'disloyal and disaffected men', who are 'endeavouring to allure the humbler of our fellow countrymen to take part in their schemes', and who 'have sought to excite them against their rulers'. But there is cause for gladness because the Methodist people have always been 'so entirely on the side of order and attachment to the throne'. They are therefore advised not to run needlessly 'into the arena of political controversy'.[3] While some of the ministers kept out of the controversy, others went into it on the Tory side. The Rev. Samuel Dunn, one of the expelled of 1849, may be taken as an example of the former. Writing in the *Wesley Banner* (Vol. i, 1849, 68–9) he says, 'I have never meddled with party politics, never voted for a member of parliament, never took such a prominent part in any state of affairs as to afford even a clue to the friends in the circuits in which I have travelled as to whether I am a Radical, Whig or Conservative'. 'Our readers are witnesses that we have never advocated . . . triennial or annual parliaments; the vote by ballot; universal or all but universal suffrage, and the separation of Church and State.' The Rev. W. J. Shrewsbury is an example of the latter class. Because of his well-known hostility to Chartism while at Longholme, Rawtenstall, Lancashire, he received a visit one night from a few enraged reformers. After parading in front of his house for a time, they entered his home in order to menace him. But adopting the methods of the Chartists, he forced them outside before they were able to do any damage.[4]

The more democratic sects of Methodism were never hostile

[1] *Halifax Express*, May 25, 1839. (Quoted from the *Bath Post.*)
[2] Wesleyan Conference Minutes, 1842.
[3] *ibid.*, 1848.
[4] *Memorials of the Rev. W. J. Shrewsbury.* By his Son, p. 452.

unite with Radicalism disaster would have been certain. Apart from creating disunity within, such a policy would have brought all the forces of Government against it. On various occasions people in high quarters had the suspicion that Methodism was seditious. That suspicion might have been confirmed by a hasty alliance with Radicalism. The attempt of Lord Sidmouth to limit lay preaching in 1811, together with the expressed wish by certain magistrates to suppress Primitive Methodist Camp Meetings, shows how ready the authorities were to act. Self-preservation demanded neutrality, though hostility to reformers was unnecessary. John Wesley and his successors were acting more prudentially than they knew when they advocated the 'no politics rule' for Methodists. In later days when reform societies were exempt from the charge of sedition, the Methodists could adopt a more liberal policy and express their mind more freely on matters concerning the framework of society. That may be one of the reasons why Methodism, as E. R. Taylor admits, became more Liberal in the second half of the nineteenth century.[1]

[1] *Methodism and Politics*, p. 215.

CHAPTER VI

THE METHODIST LEADERSHIP

BEFORE the advent of the working-class political societies Methodism had already organized a new form of democratic fellowship. Although religious in its nature and practice, it afforded an example and encouragement to other pioneers of reform movements. In this Methodist democracy ordinary men and women were given the religious franchise and learnt the art of local government. Approximately one in every five became a member of the governing bodies, such as the Leaders' and Circuit Quarterly Meetings. Among those who had no office there was always an opportunity to exercise their talents and to take some share in the management. Local affairs, under the guidance of a travelling preacher, usually were administered by the lay officials. This indeed was a new kind of religious democracy. Its friends and critics thought otherwise. John Wesley, for example, has been described as a High Churchman and a Tory, while the organization that he created has been designated as 'far from being democratic'.[1] A successor to the office of paternal autocracy, and later depicted as the 'Pope of Methodism', once avowed that 'Methodism was as much opposed to democracy as it was to sin'.[2] In a book recently published on Methodism and Politics, the author contends that the Methodist approach toward Liberalism in the later nineteenth century was a deviation from Wesley's plan.[3] Contemporaneous Radicals often criticized its Tory leadership, while sections of the Press repeatedly condemned its reactionary attitude to politics. Present day social historians have inherited this tendency to criticize, Methodism being conceived by some as a cross current to Radicalism and a rival flag to Trade Unionism.[4]

In some respects these charges may be true of Wesleyanism,

[1] *Methodism and Politics*, E. R. Taylor, pp. 24 and 43. Also *John Wesley*, Maldwyn Edwards, p. 13.

[2] A statement by Jabez Bunting reported in *Nottingham Review*, Dec. 14, 1827.

[3] *Methodism and Politics*, E. R. Taylor, pp. 196–216.

[4] *The Town Labourer*, J. L. & B. Hammond, p. 286.

though not of Methodism. But if applied to Wesleyanism one must distinguish between the lay and the official attitude to politics. The two attitudes were not always identical. Moreover, Methodism was always greater than its annual assemblies and more democratic than its political professions. To understand the real nature of Methodism, one must not exaggerate the influence of its yearly Conference, or underestimate the importance of local administration. An examination of the latter reveals much more than a 'potential democracy'. Although the founder of the Methodist New Connexion might be charged with having his 'historical sense' 'twisted by the French Revolution's ideas of Liberty, Equality, and Fraternity', and thus getting 'a perhaps distorted view of John Wesley's work', which was 'an unhistoric view', he nevertheless saw without coloured spectacles something more than mere 'democratic elements' in the sytem.[1] It matters not if they 'formed no part of Wesley's intention'. Wesley did not intend to establish the system of local preachers, neither did he intend to form a separate Church. He certainly never purposed the introduction of a democratic order. But Wesley often succeeded in doing what he never intended to do. As a friendly critic puts it, 'Wesley, like a strong and skilful rower, looked one way, while every stroke of his oar took him in an opposite direction'.

Whether Alexander Kilham had his 'historical sense' twisted or not, he saw further than most of his fellow preachers. He saw in Methodism the basis of a democratic society. Later events have proved the correctness of Kilham's view. Without departing from Methodist practice or teaching, religious democratic bodies were ultimately created. They came into being by a natural interpretation of Wesley's teaching on personal and social virtues.

Although Methodism taught the corruption of human nature, it always emphasized the possibility of a sudden transformation. Theologians described this as 'regeneration'. Methodists called it 'conversion'. The Apostle Paul said it was a passing 'from death unto life'. 'Old things,' he declared, 'are passed away . . . all things are become new.'[2] In daily life it meant the creation of

[1] *Methodism and Politics*. E. R. Taylor thinks Alexander Kilham overlooked 'the essentially autocratic character of Methodist organization', p. 77.

[2] 2 Corinthians v, 17.

new thoughts, nobler ambitions, and higher ideals. All who entered into this experience came into new relationships. It produced a vivid sense of kinship with God. The old relation was described as 'alienation' and 'enmity'. Sinful mortals who lived 'afar off' were reckoned to be 'strangers to the commonwealth of Israel'. But by a miracle of Divine grace they were brought nigh unto God and adopted into His family. God's spirit could witness with their spirit that they were the children of God. Every 'new born man' came into this kinship, and he was taught to sing by the Methodists:

My God is reconciled,
His pardoning voice I hear;
He owns me for His child,
I can no longer fear;
With confidence I now draw nigh,
And, Father, Abba, Father! cry.

'He that loves God,' said John Wesley, 'that delights and rejoices in Him with an humble joy, and holy delight: and an obedient love, is a child of God.'[1]

This relationship brought with it a new sense of vocation. The common people were taught that 'life was more than meat, and the body than raiment'. They had talents to be used and not to be destroyed. In reality man was a steward. He was not a proprietor, but only a trustee. The time would arrive when his Lord should require an account of his stewardship. Till that day came he must be faithful to his calling. A steward 'has no right', says John Wesley, 'to dispose of anything which is in his hands but according to the will of his Lord'. 'On this condition he hath entrusted us with our souls, our bodies, our goods, and whatever other talents we have received.' 'God has entrusted us with our soul, an immortal spirit . . . together with all the powers and faculties thereof, understanding, imagination, memory, will, and a train of affections, either included in it or closely dependent upon it.' 'God has . . . entrusted us with our bodies.' 'He has entrusted us with the organs of sense, of sight, hearing and the rest.' 'None of these are lent us in such a sense as to leave us at liberty to use them as we please for a season.' 'It is on the same terms that He hath imparted to us that most excellent talent of

[1] *Fifty-Three Sermons*, John Wesley, p. 129.

speech.' 'To Him we are equally accountable for the use of our hands and feet, and all the members of our body.'[1] Though we are told 'not to lay up treasure upon earth', we are not forbidden 'the providing for ourselves such things as are needful for the body; a sufficiency of plain, wholesome food to eat, and clean raiment to put on'. 'Yea, it is our duty, so far as God puts it into our power, to provide these things also.'[2] 'We ought not to gain money at the expense of our health. Therefore, no gain whatsoever should induce us to enter into, or to continue in, any employ, which is of such a kind, or is attended with so hard or so long labour, as to impair our constitution.' 'But whatever it is which reason or experience shows to be destructive of health or strength, that we may not submit to, and, if we are already engaged in such an employ, we should exchange it, as soon as possible, for some which, if it lessen our gain, will, however, not lessen our health.'[3]

While regarding man as a kind of steward who was responsible to his Lord for the way in which he exercised his talents, John Wesley never neglected to emphasize the social duties of the individual. 'To serve the present age, My calling to fulfil,' was a duty incumbent upon every Methodist. When giving a definition of an 'altogether Christian', he affirmed, 'it means among other things the love of our neighbour'. And lest anybody should be in doubt as to 'who is my neighbour?' he adds, 'Every man in the world'. 'Nor may we in any wise except our enemies.'[4] In his sermon on 'The Way to the Kingdom', he contends that righteousness is the way. 'Righteousness' consists of 'Thou shalt love the Lord thy God', and 'thou shalt love thy neighbour as thyself'.[5] When speaking on the marks of a new birth, he argues that the love of God must be seen in 'the love of our neighbour; of every soul which God hath made, not excepting our enemies'.[6] He comes back to the same theme when talking about 'the right use of money'. His followers are advised to gain all they can. In doing this, he says, 'we must not hurt our neighbour'. 'This we may not, cannot do, if we love our neighbour as ourselves. We cannot, if we love every one as ourselves, hurt anyone in his substance.'[7] 'We cannot consistently with brotherly love, sell our goods below the market-price; we cannot study to ruin our

[1] *Fifty-Three Sermons*, John Wesley, pp. 717–8.
[2] *ibid.*, p. 407.
[3] *ibid.*, p. 705.
[4] *ibid.*, p. 23.
[5] *ibid.*, pp. 86–7.
[6] *ibid.*, p. 243.
[7] *ibid.*, p. 706.

neighbour's trade, in order to advance our own; much less can we entice away, or receive, any of his servants or workmen whom he has need of. None can gain by swallowing up his neighbour's substance without gaining the damnation of hell.'[1]

Upon this foundation laid down by Wesley, the whole fabric of social duties devolving upon Methodists seems to rest. 'I shall endeavour to show,' he said when preaching about the 'Sermon on the Mount', 'that Christianity is essentially a social religion; and that to turn it into a solitary religion is indeed to destroy it.'[2] In harmony with this conception of religion, he organized his followers and gave them suitable rules of conduct. When they became members of his class meetings, they were exhorted to practise the social virtues. The class itself was not only a religious meeting, it was also a social gathering. All who attended were taught their inter-dependence, and were encouraged to assist one another.

Their social duty extended to all the members of other classes which comprised the local society, even to those in other societies. They had a duty to the whole Connexion. By the establishment of the 'Contingent Fund' in 1763 (now called the Home Mission Fund), Methodists were taught their duty to the poorer circuits. In 1771 it was ordained that 'every Methodist in England, Scotland, and Ireland' should 'give, for one year, a penny a week', for the support of this fund. Because of the unequal ability of members to subscribe, it was decided that 'those who are not poor in each society, pay for those that are'.[3] Other Connexional Funds were established in later years, and the yearly collections for these constantly reminded them of their duty to those of their own persuasion.

The Methodists were taught to practise the social duties not only to those inside their own religious community, but also to those outside. John Wesley led the way in this duty. At his London headquarters he repeatedly provided for the poor. In 1763 'great numbers of poor people had pease and pottage and barley broth given them at the Foundery at the expense of Mr. Wesley'.[4] In one period he had twelve persons visiting the sick

[1] *Fifty-Three Sermons*, John Wesley, p. 707.
[2] *ibid.*, p. 329.
[3] Conference Minutes quoted by William Pierce in his *Ecclesiastical Principles of Wesleyan Methodism*, p. 538.
[4] *Early Methodist Philanthropy*, E. M. North, p. 66.

of the neighbourhood. He opened a dispensary in order to help the needy. As early as 1746 he says, 'I took into my assistance an apothecary, and an experienced surgeon'.[1] He established a poor house at the Foundery, and in 1748 he had there 'nine widows, one blind woman, two poor children, and two upper servants, a maid and a man'.[2] His followers in many places were inspired to follow his example. At Tetney he found the best society in England. When examining the class papers, which gave an account of the contribution to the poor, he found that 'one gave eightpence, often tenpence a week; another thirteen, fifteen, or eighteen-pence; another sometimes one, sometimes two shillings'. Enquiring the reason of such generosity, Wesley was told they did it gladly so that they could 'from time to time entertain all the strangers that come to Tetney, who often have no food to eat, nor any friend to give them a lodging'.[3] As a result of Wesley's teaching and example, the 'Strangers' Friend Society' was established in many places. By the year 1800 this philanthropic institution had been set in operation at Bristol, Manchester, Birmingham, Sheffield, Leeds, York, Hull, and London.[4] Its declared purpose was to provide for the poor who were not definitely connected with Methodism.

Wesley's desire to help the poor led him to form the 'Christian Community' at the Foundery in 1772. Through this society he secured a body of workers who regularly visited the workhouses in several of the London parishes, and sought to 'improve and elevate the moral and social condition of the poor inmates'.[5] This society is still in existence. For the same reason he instituted a loan fund at his London headquarters. Writing about this fund, he says, 'I went from one end of the town to the other, and exhorted those who had this world's goods, to assist their needy brethren'.[6] James Lackington was one of those helped by this fund, and he afterwards acknowledged his obligation to the Methodists.[7]

Wesley was greatly distressed at this time because of the condition of the poor. Writing to *Lloyd's Evening Post*, he asks,

[1] *John Wesley's Works*, Vol. viii, p. 264.
[2] *ibid.*, p. 256.
[3] *John Wesley's Journal*, Vol. ii, p. 8 (Everyman Ed.).
[4] *Early Methodist Philanthropy*, E. M. North, p. 51.
[5] *Historical Sketch of the Christian Community*, p. 2.
[6] *Wesley's Works*, Vol. viii, p. 267.
[7] *The Confessions of James Lackington*, p. 181.

'Why are thousands of people starving, perishing for want, in every part of England?' He declared he had seen one woman 'picking up stinking sprats from a dunghill, and carrying them home for herself and her children'. He had seen another 'gathering the bones which the dogs had left in the streets, and making broth of them to prolong a wretched life'. The reason for this is because they have nothing to do. 'They have no meat, because they have no work.' 'But why have they no work?' 'Why are so many thousand people in London, in Bristol, in Norwich, in every county from one end of England to the other, utterly destitute of employment? Because the persons who used to employ them cannot afford to do it any longer.' They cannot employ them because 'they have no vent for their goods'. 'Why is bread so dear? Because such immense quantities of it are continually consumed by distilling.' 'Why are oats so dear? Because there are four times the horses kept.' 'Why are beef and mutton so dear? Because most of the considerable farmers . . . who used to breed large numbers of sheep or horned cattle, and frequently both, no longer trouble themselves with either sheep, or cows, or oxen, as they can turn their land to far better account, by breeding horses alone.' 'But why are pork, poultry, eggs, so dear? Because of the monopolizing of farms, as mischievous a monopoly as was ever yet introduced into these kingdoms.' 'Why is land so dear? Because . . . gentlemen cannot live as they have been accustomed to do, without increasing their income, which most of them cannot do but by raising their rents.' 'But why is it, that not only provisions and land, but well-nigh everything else is so dear? Because of the enormous taxes which are laid on almost everything that can be named.' 'But why are taxes so high? Because of the national debt.' As a remedy for all these evils, Wesley recommends the provision of work by increasing the sale of commodities, and 'by sinking the price of provisions'. This could be done, he believed, by prohibiting distilling and by reducing the number of horses. He also advises an increase in the number of cattle that could be bred, and at the same time desires to limit the size of the farms.[1]

John Wesley's social instinct was so active that at one time he desired to establish a kind of religious communism. 'He told me,' says Mr. Viney in his diary for Wednesday, February 22, 1744,

[1] *Life of John Wesley,* Rev. L. Tyerman, Vol. iii, pp. 130–4.

'of an intention he and some few have of beginning a Community of goods, but on a plan which I told him I doubted could not succeed. Tis this; each is to bring what cash they have and put it together. If any owe shall debts, they are first to be paid. Then each abiding in their Dwellings and following their Business as they do now, are to bring weekly, what they earn and put it into the common box, out of which they are again to receive weekly, as much as is thought necessary to maintain their Families, without Reflecting whether they put much or little into Ye Box.'[1]

Coupled with these conceptions of personal and social duties John Wesley provided some useful machinery for the exercise of individual talents. Local administration, with all the offices of class leader, trustee, steward, and local preacher were open to all without any financial qualification. Even females could attain to the position of a leader. With such opportunities for service and leadership there was much more in Methodism than an 'Underlying Liberalism'.[2] Here indeed were some of the foundations upon which a new religious democracy could be built. Some of the builders, like John Wesley, made their contribution to the new structure unintentionally. Others contributed deliberately.

Among the pioneers of this latter group a few could be found in the days of John Wesley. Being dissatisfied with every kind of autocracy, no matter how paternal it might appear to be, they were not quite happy with the Toryism of their leader, and less happy still with his yearly Conference.

Only once during his life did this dissatisfaction declare itself. It had been kept underground through genuine respect for his character. Directly after his death it became articulate. Its exponents began to complain that 'the people had no voice in making the laws, no control over public monies, nor any participation in the Government whatever. The Conference was one high court of parliament; and it consisted but of one house; all preachers and none of the people'.[3] They declared publicly that 'in the Church, therefore, as well as in relation to civil Government, it became a subject of important inquiry, whether

[1] *Wesley Historical Society Proceedings*, Vol. xiv, pp. 29–30.

[2] Edwards has a whole chapter on this 'Underlying Liberalism'. See *After Wesley*, pp. 37–59.

[3] *An Apology for the Methodists of the New Connexion*. By a Trustee and a Layman.

the order and prosperity of the community cannot be better secured, without absolute power being placed in the hands of any one class'. 'To this question the attention of the founders of the Methodist New Connexion was specially directed.'[1] Influenced perhaps by reports from France the pioneers of this democratic movement emphasized the equalitarian ideas of Methodism. 'The members of our community,' they contended, 'are all equal in Christ Jesus.'[2] Because of these sentiments they were called 'the disciples of Paine', instead of the followers of Jesus Christ.[3]

These religious reformers, not content with expressing their disapproval of ecclesiastical and civil autocracy, passed over from the ideas of duty (so often emphasized by the Wesleyan Conference) to those of right and justice. Whether they were influenced by Tom Paine's *Rights of Man* or whether their attitude was the natural outcome of their religious development, opinions may differ. Nevertheless they did insist on certain rights. Their newly-formed organization was based on 'the right of the people to hold their public religious worship at such hours as were most convenient', 'the right of the people to receive the ordinances of Baptism and the Lord's Supper from the hands of their own ministers, and in their own places of worship'; 'the right of the people to a representation in the District Meetings, and in the Annual Conference'; and 'the right of the Church to have a voice . . . in the expulsion of members, the choice of local officers, and in the calling of candidates for the ministry'.[4] The Primitive Methodist Connexion originated because its founders insisted on the right to hold camp meetings. The Bible Christians came into being because W. O'Bryan persisted in exercising the right to preach outside the prescribed circle determined by the Wesleyan circuit. The reformers of 1848 emphasized the rights of representation in the various Church courts.

These various types of religious reformers were not restricted in the statement of their demands by any affection for the Established Church, nor by any particular reverence for the officials of the State. Many of them had no love whatever for the Church. Hence John Wesley's 'Twelve reasons for not

[1] *The Jubilee History of the New Connexion,* W. Cooke, &c., p. 141.
[2] *Outlines of a Constitution.* By Thom and Alexander Kilham, p. 43.
[3] *ibid.*, p. 43.
[4] *The Jubilee History of the New Connexion,* W. Cooke, &c., pp. 56–7.

leaving the Church' left them untouched. Some of them had never belonged to the Church and had no desire to be connected with it. They were Dissenters. Their parents before them had been Dissenters. Most of them had suffered at the hands of the Church. A large number of their leaders had been persecuted by its clergymen. William Clowes at Newark had the fire engine turned out against him by the order of a clergyman.[1] Thomas Waller, described by the *Leeds Mercury* (October 20, 1821) as 'the Rev. Waller', was at Ashton-under-Lyne sentenced to three months' imprisonment by a court of justice over which a clerical magistrate presided, and his only crime was, preaching the Gospel in the streets.[2] Sometimes a resolute Methodist lost all share in the village charities largely because he was a Methodist.[3]

Moreover, many of these Methodists had slight cause for gratitude to the State. They had some reason for bitterness. Some of them found it difficult to imagine what privileges they got from its paternal care. They could easily remember their disabilities. Along with other Dissenters they were treated as rebels of the State. Their religion was a nuisance and not a benediction. What freedom they possessed had been grudgingly granted them, but only after a fierce struggle with the 'powers that be'. Certain offices of local government were closed against them. In the realm of industrial affairs they suffered with their fellow workmen the application of unjust laws. Industrial combinations were forbidden them. As members of a working-class fraternity they could not take an oath of fidelity to one another. Their position as victims of economic oppression and depression had been prolonged and aggravated sometimes by the reactionary measures, and at other times by the inaction of Government officials. In political matters the franchise was denied them. How difficult therefore it must have been for them to count the blessings which came from the State. Reverence for State officials might be a latent quality, but distress and disadvantage made it almost impossible to become an active virtue. It was natural for such people to emphasize rights instead of privileges and duties.

Having learnt to value their talents and exercise their rights in the Methodist community, it was not easy for some of them to

[1] *Journal of William Clowes*, p. 125.
[2] *The Romance of Primitive Methodism*, Joseph Ritson, p. 172.
[3] *Life of Joseph Arch*, pp. 15, 21.

remain quiescent concerning the problems of industrial and political life. Indeed, it has been admitted that a 'Liberalism' was eventually developed within the Methodist Church and that it was 'a laymen's movement'.[1] So while there were those inside Methodism who wanted to make it an adjunct of the State and subservient to the Established Church, there were others who desired to abide by its original purpose—'to reform the Church and the nation'. To this purpose they gave their own interpretation. They wished to transform the framework of society, as well as its members.

Evidence of their activity is not lacking. Sometimes they disobeyed their preachers and criticized reactionary measures. An old Methodist adopts this role toward the end of 1807, when Samuel Bradburn, an ex-President of the Wesleyan Conference, writes to the *Leeds Intelligencer* and condemns the Alverthorpe 'peace petition'. Bradburn's conduct is described as 'unnecessary', 'officious', 'obtrusive', and an 'hostile interference'. 'The right of petition,' says his critic, 'is secured by the Constitution to every British subject; it is an integral part of the compact, or the covenant by which the King holds his Crown.' 'Methodism does not destroy,' he contends, 'or impair the civil rights of its members.' 'The Methodists have an unquestionable right to petition the Throne for Peace.'[2] Another Methodist layman, writing a few months earlier to the *Leeds Mercury* (May 16, 1807), criticizes the Lascelles family for their hostile attitude to the local Methodists. He claims in his letter that 'neither Slavery nor Dealers in Blood can find Supporters among those Methodists who sincerely believe what Inspiration hath declared —that God had marked Men Stealers with Infamy'. Even the official circular emanating from the Committee of Privileges in 1817 is severely attacked in a long letter from a correspondent in the *Leeds Mercury* (March 8, 1817). The critic avows that the chief aim of the circular is 'to operate as a gag to the mouths of all Methodists who make any complaint about national grievances, and who think it right to petition for a reform respecting evils and abuses which no man can defend and which few have face to deny'. The same committee is once more criticized because of the document which it published in 1819 expressing opposition

[1] *Methodism and Politics*, E. R. Taylor, p. 212.
[2] *Leeds Mercury*, Dec. 12, 1807.

to the Radical agitation. A number of 'Radical Reformers in the Methodist Connexion' described the document as 'a base, sneaking, time serving Hypocrisy'. Methodists, they say, have no rights but 'hungry bellies, naked backs, empty pockets, and insults added to distress'.[1] According to *Wooler's British Gazette* (Jan. 21, 1821), one of the adverse results of this circular was the formation of 'a new community' under the denomination of 'Independent Methodists'. The Wesleyan Conference was not exempt from criticism. A cynical reference was made in the *Manchester Observer* in 1820 (Oct. 21) to the re-appointment of the Revs. T. Jackson and J. Stephens to Manchester for their 'Yeomanry approving notoriety'. In the discussion that followed the letter of Richard Watson, advising the Rev. J. Sanderson in 1831 to vote for Macaulay in Leeds, one of the critics cynically referred to Watson as a once 'flaming democrat'. Another correspondent advises the readers of the *Leeds Patriot* (Oct. 1, 1831) to join the New Connexion Methodists, 'whose members', he says 'are greatly tinctured with Radicalism'.

While the Wesleyan Connexion was not without its 'potential democracy', the younger sections of the Methodist movement were entirely democratic in their constitution and practice. The Primitive Methodists in particular can be described as a working-class association. Its polity, which was drawn up in an anti-clerical atmosphere and amid the political agitation of 1819–20, bears the impress of the age to which it belongs. To guard against any possibility of ministerial dominance, it is ordained that in every Church court there should be two laymen to every minister. By this provision legislation and administration, both locally and centrally, came under the control of the laity. The great success achieved by this section of Methodism can no doubt be largely ascribed to this arrangement. An almost equal Radicalism prevailed in the other sections of the Methodist movement.

Evidence of these facts might explain the purpose of certain local authorities in seeking to suppress particular forms of Methodist propaganda. The attempt of the Government to control the activities of the Methodist preachers in 1811 had a special significance. More significant still was the attempt of some of the Derbyshire and Nottingham magistrates to suppress the Camp Meetings of the Primitive Methodist Connexion. In the

[1] *Manchester Observer*, Jan. 1, 1820.

June of 1817, T. Beaumont, a magistrate of Burton, informs the Home Office that application had been made to him 'from several respectable gentlemen relative to the expediency of suppressing certain meetings which have recently been held by a religious Sect, who call themselves (and not inapplicably) the Ranters. These meetings are held in the open air, in the streets and lanes of the villages, on Commons or other Wastes, are attended by thousands of the lower orders of the people, and lately so much increased that we cannot but be apprehensive of the consequences'. The magistrate inquires whether 'they cannot legally be suppressed under any existing Act of Parliament'. He also suggests it would be 'expedient to amend the 52nd of the King by the introduction of a clause to confine all religious assemblies to some tolerated place of worship and to punish any Preacher or Hearer by fine, who shall be present at any meeting in the open air'.[1]

In less than a fortnight after this letter was written the High Sheriff of Nottingham informs the Home Secretary that he had dispersed between 2 and 3,000 people who had assembled in his neighbourhood 'for the purpose of hearing the discourse of persons calling themselves Ranters'. 'The different villages,' he says, 'in the vicinity have lately been *much disturbed* by this *new sect*, and their followers by praying, singing and making other noises (till near midnight) to the great annoyance of the peaceable inhabitants.'[2] Litchfield, writing from Lincoln's Inn on July 5, acknowledges that he has submitted to the Solicitor-General the case of suppressing 'certain meetings of a Religious sect called Ranters'. The latter with the Attorney-General announced that 'unless the persons assembled together are guilty of some acts of disturbance so as to amount to an unlawful or riotous assembly, we do not think any proceedings can be instituted against them'. They also express their doubts about 'the expediency in the present temper of the times of introducing any legislative measure on the subject'. In a second letter the High Sheriff reports that 'the ground on which the meeting was held is not licensed', and although no more meetings have been held at this place, 'they have been carried on in other Parishes in the neighbourhood'.[3]

[1] H.O. 42. 166, 1817.
[2] *ibid.*, 42. 166, 1817.
[3] *ibid.*, 42. 168, 1817.

It is rather significant that Derby and Nottingham were the only counties in which official attempts to suppress the Methodist Camp Meetings were ever made. Perhaps the local authorities connected these meetings with the foolish attempts at insurrection which took place in the vicinity about this time. Two years later the clerical magistrate of Woodstock Rectory also wants to limit the activities of itinerant preachers. Writing to the Home Office he asks for some Parliamentary measure to prevent '*religious*, as well as *Political* Itinerants, from exercising their vocation out of their proper sphere . . . For', he observes, 'we have many Parson Harrisons at this time'.[1]

There can be no doubt that a rather close connexion existed between the Methodists and the Radicals. The Curate of Holmfirth (a place where Methodism was very active) reports in February, 1817, that in a declaration of loyalty 'to our Sovereign and the Constitution', prepared for public signature by the Huddersfield magistrates, 'not a single individual of the Body of Methodists signed it'.[2] At Barnsley the Radical union was said to be 'identified or nearly so with a Religious sect called Kilhamites or sort of Dissenters from Methodism, but who with their Preachers are of the lowest description of ignorant and gross Methodists'. Another clerical magistrate, writing from Wakefield, expressed his opinion 'that the greater part of the people called Methodists are united with the *Radicals;* they assemble', he says, 'in the evenings in certain cottages in the country, under the pretence of religious worship, but their real intention is to promote the work of sedition'.[3] An anonymous writer informs the Home Office that only one reform meeting had been held in Staffordshire, 'and that was at Hanley, in the Staffordshire Potteries. Yates . . . was one of the speakers'. He 'is a tailor, and a Methodist Preacher; the other was Ridgeway, whom they called to the chair and is a Methodist, and I believe is father-in-law to Yates; the company that attended were most of them Methodists'.[4] Further information concerning these Hanley Methodists was sent to the Home Secretary a few months later. At a public meeting called to express loyalty to the Government, certain employers 'who belong to the New Connexion of Methodists' adopted an hostile attitude to the resolution, in

[1] H.O. 42. 200, 1819.
[2] *ibid.*, 42. 159, 1817.
[3] *ibid.*, 42. 200, 1819.
[4] *ibid.*, 42. 201, 1819.

consequence of which seventeen gentlemen withdrew from the gathering. These gentlemen were also annoyed because the employers in question had permitted their workmen to attend the meeting, and had paid their wages for doing so.[1] An informer, writing from London about this time, affirms that 'the disaffected . . . are turning their thoughts to the *Religious* world'. 'Great numbers of Methodists have separated from the orderly and regular Wesleyan body', and to these, he says, 'the Seditious are directing their attention'.[2] Among the disaffected engaged in the work of reform, the informer mentions the name of Robert Gunn, 'a Methodist Preacher'. He also reports with alarm the entry into London of the Bryanite Methodists and their women preachers.

This close relation between the Methodists and the Radicals never received any official sanction, though the Primitive Methodist Conference of 1821 came perilously near it. During one of the sessions, Hugh Bourne, who was not a member of the Conference, went into the chapel and disapproved of the proceedings. Pointing to one of the delegates, he said, 'That man shall not be in this chapel'. 'That man is a speeching Radical, a man who is employed in speaking against the Government, and he must not sit in this place.' 'They then opened out against me,' he adds, 'against the King (George IV), and against the Government. But I told them that the Scriptures required us to be subject to the Government under which we lived; that the King was favourable to liberty of conscience and had conferred a favour on us, for, when Prince Regent, in June, 1812, he signed an Act which opened our way to hold camp meetings, and which gave us more liberty of conscience and worship than we had before enjoyed; that up to the present time, we had stood well with the Government; and that, if on that occasion the Conference set up against the Government, as the Government had an eye upon us, measures might be taken to stop our camp meetings, and the Connexion might receive an injury from which it would never recover. The opposite party attempted reply after reply. But I got into strong and even peremptory language. After a time the speeches against the Government slackened and the more thoughtful began to intervene.' 'Such was the effect that, during the

[1] H.O. 40. 15, 1820. Ridgeway was one of the employers.
[2] *ibid.*, 40. 16, 1821.

meeting, no one lifted up a finger against the Government.'[1] Hugh Bourne's interruption of the Conference proceedings would never have been tolerated had not the chapel been his own private property. Writing about the incident in his Diary, he rejoiced in the fact that the chapel did belong to him. His action, though autocratic, saved the Connexion from an official alliance with political Radicalism.

The exact measure of Methodist support in the political agitation of 1829 to 1835 is rather difficult to estimate. It can, however, be affirmed with certainty that the traditional hostility of the Wesleyan Conference to political reform was greatly modified in 1831 and 1832. In several cases both Wesleyan and Primitive Methodist chapels had been used for reform meetings, and in each Connexion the practice was forbidden. One can assume that a considerable number of Methodists must have been on the side of reform, when the Wesleyan Conference confessed it was more allowable for Christians to take part in political affairs, and when the Primitive Methodist Conference warned its ministers against taking part in political meetings. Methodist local preachers were busy in the Potteries and also in the Newcastle area. Thomas Hepburn in the North, and W. Ridgeway, Yates and Capper in the Staffordshire district were prominent among the reformers. The biographer of Joseph Capper described him as 'a considerable figure in this agitation. . . . His tongue was like the sledge-hammer he used in his shop'.[2]

Methodist kinship with reformers becomes more pronounced in the Chartist period. In many districts the Methodist people supported Chartist principles and opened their chapels for Chartist meetings. Among the places that provided for Chartist gatherings the following can be definitely identified; Shefford and Wolsingham among the Wesleyans; Glossop, Thornley, Unsworth, Morley, Huddersfield, Bloxham, Gateshead, Byker Hill, and Newcastle among the Primitive Methodists; Dunston of the New Connexion; Oldham, Rochdale, and West Auckland of the Wesleyan Association; and Mirfield with Kingston Deveral among the Independent Methodists.[3]

While Methodism remained the most successful example of a

[1] *The Life of Hugh Bourne*, Dr. S. Antliff, pp. 180–1.
[2] *When I was a Child*, by An Old Potter, pp. 147, 149.
[3] *Northern Star*, *Northern Liberator*, *Birmingham Journal*, and *Manchester and Salford Advertiser*, 1839–48.

religious democracy, it was easy and natural for the movement to provide agents for the pioneer work of a political democracy. The Rev. Joseph Harrison, who called himself 'Chaplain to the poor and needy' and was founder of the Stockport Union Society in 1818, has been described as a Methodist preacher. Robert Pilkington of Bury, and J. Grundy of Manchester were local preachers among the Methodists, and both of them exercised their talents as political speakers among the Radicals of Middleton during 1817 and 1818.[1] Samuel Bamford, brought up in a Methodist home, trained by a Methodist schoolmaster on the weekdays and in a Methodist Sunday School on the Sunday, and afterwards becoming a Methodist adherent, was at one time secretary of the Middleton Radical Union. Because of his association with the political demonstration at Manchester on August 16, 1819, he suffered a term of imprisonment in Lincoln Gaol.[2] Local preachers were so active among the Political Protestants along Tyneside during 1819 that they were threatened with expulsion. Both men and women among the Methodist leaders were associated with the October demonstration at Newcastle. As a consequence some of them were expelled from the Wesleyan Connexion. The feeling was so bitter against the Methodist Preacher that a number of sympathizers left the parent body and called themselves Independent Methodists.

As already seen, a number of Methodist ministers were closely associated with the Chartist agitation of 1839–48, some of them having suffered imprisonment for their activity. Several local preachers were also prominent. According to one authority, Thomas Cooper, an ex-Wesleyan local preacher, 'gained such an ascendancy over the pale-faced operatives of Leicester as to be familiarly known amongst them as "the General"'. 'An ex-Primitive Methodist travelling preacher acquired similar ascendancy over the operatives of Loughborough, and, by virtue of the display of similar qualities. Thomas Cooper and John Skevington were the two most noted and trusted Leicestershire Chartists.' Writing of the Chartist Convention begun in 1839, Gamage in his *History of the Chartist Movement* records the fact that 'the democrats of Loughborough sent John Skevington, another veteran in the Radical cause, to represent them'. For his services

[1] H.O. 40. 5, 1816–18.
[2] *Passages in the Life of a Radical*, Bamford, Vol. i, pp. 29, 33.

in the district his portrait in oils was publicly presented to him in 1848 by Thomas Cooper.[1] 'Staffordshire, as well as Leicestershire, had its sturdy Primitive Methodist Chartist.' Joseph Capper was converted at the first Primitive Methodist Camp Meeting in 1807, and soon after became a local preacher with that body. As a prominent Chartist he was arrested in 1842, and had to stand two trials for 'sedition, conspiracy and rioting', and although 'no purer and more loyal patriot lived in the Queen's realms' he was sentenced to two years' imprisonment.[2] John Richards, another local preacher, 'the man who forsook the Bible for the Black Book', together with Thomas Cooper, was arrested at the same time, and suffered twelve months in gaol. Several other local preachers were associated with the Chartists of Leicestershire, Nottingham, and Staffordshire. J. Markham of Leicester, though not so influential as Thomas Cooper, had a longer association with the Chartists and for a time was the most prominent figure among them. John Black, J. Barratt, and J. Harrison were so active as lecturers among the Nottingham group that a local paper gave them the dignified title of 'reverend'.[3] Because of the activity of certain Methodists in the Potteries one paper throws all the blame on them for the disturbances in 1842. Through their influence, avows this critic, the working classes had been 'regularly trained up in Radicalism'. The neighbourhood was described as being 'steeped to the very neck in Radical dissent'.[4] Local preachers were also conspicuous in Lancashire, Yorkshire, and the North East. According to the *Manchester Guardian*, several Methodists were imprisoned for their association with the disturbances round Manchester in 1842. A Government Commissioner blames the Methodist local preachers for the violence in Northumberland during 1839. When the Chartists decided to inaugurate Camp Meetings like the Methodists, the chief speaker at the first gathering was a Primitive Methodist local preacher from Bradford. In the late forties as the Chartist movement was gaining new life through the revolutionary example on the Continent, Joseph Barker, an ex-Methodist minister, became a travelling lecturer in Yorkshire and Lancashire.

[1] *The History of the Primitive Methodist Church*, H. B. Kendall, Vol, i, pp. 336–7.
[2] *ibid.*, Vol. i, p. 341. Also *North Staffordshire Mercury*, March 25, 1843.
[3] *Nottingham and Newark Mercury*, Feb. 7, 21, March 6, 13, 1840.
[4] *The Bolton Chronicle*, Aug. 20, 1842.

With examples of this kind, it is perfectly clear that the pathway from Methodist passion to reforming zeal was not a very difficult one. As Methodism invariably created in the human mind a threefold sense of dignity, vocation, and responsibility, it was easy for those who came under its influence to rebel against political and social injustice. According to one historian, it gave to the democratic movement some of its leading personalities. They 'derived from Methodism that sense of right, that love of justice, and that feeling of pity and compassion, which, with religious conviction, turned some of them into never-to-be-forgotten social reformers'.[1] It was 'in the chapel-life working men first learnt to speak and organize, to persuade and trust their fellows. It was in the Little Bethel that many of the working-class leaders were trained'.[2]

Perhaps the clearest example of Methodist leadership was provided by its organization. As a religious democracy practically the whole of its technique was taken over by the political societies. A prominent Methodist in 1819 told Jabez Bunting that this was being done. Its Connexionalism, its large-scale finance and enterprise, its division into districts, circuits, and societies, its propaganda methods of itinerant preaching and Sunday open-air meetings, its society class and weekly penny subscription were all copied at some time or other by the political reformers.

The weekly class and the Sunday open-air meeting were the most important parts of the Methodist organization copied by the working-class political societies. As already seen, the political class was formed in July, 1818, and after various lapses and revivals it was finally abandoned in the October of 1848. In none of the periods when the political class existed was there any attempt to conceal its origin. Among the local newspapers, the Home Office records, and the Government reports numerous references are to be found of Methodist paternity. The first public avowal of Methodist influence was made in 1831, when the National Union of Working Classes adopted the class system. On several other occasions the same obligation was acknowledged. When the Chartists desired to organize themselves more thoroughly in 1839, they decided at a conference in Rochdale 'that the country should be formed into districts, and that the system of classes pursued by the Methodists should be adopted

[1] *Wesley Historical Society Proceedings*, Vol. xv, p. 220. [2] *ibid.*, p. 140.

by the Chartists in every district'.[1] The *Manchester Guardian* (June 29, 1839) described the discussion as 'one of no general interest', which was closed 'by the adoption of regulations similar to those of the Wesleyans—each town to have its districts, and the latter to be divided into classes, for the greater convenience of weekly meetings, and more regular and certain collection of the rent. The plan of the Methodists was pronounced to be an admirable one, and by far the best that could be adopted; local preachers and class leaders were to be appointed: and camp meetings for political purposes were recommended'. When the political classes were introduced among the Chartists of Sheffield, a placard on the walls announcing the fact, said they were 'similar to the Methodist Class Meetings', while the *Sheffield Independent* (Aug. 24, 1839) designated them as an 'imitation of the class meetings of the Methodists'. The *Sheffield Mercury* (Aug. 24, 1839) calls them a 'practical parody of private religious assemblies, which have so long been known among our Wesleyan friends'. 'As, however,' observes the editor, 'there are some renegade Methodists among the Chartists in this town, we should not be much surprised even to hear that some of the forms of religion to which they have been accustomed, were prostituted to give colour to their proceedings, the more so as they proclaim their purpose to be "holy".' The Mayor of Nottingham admits that the Chartists in his area have 'adopted a plan similar to the Wesleyans, dividing themselves into classes'.[2] At the Manchester Conference of Chartists in 1840, when the classes were officially endorsed, the Methodists were held up as an example by one of the delegates.[3] Because of the similarity between the Methodist and the Chartist systems, J. Begnon, writing from the Custom House in Liverpool to the Home Office, advises the abolition of the Wesleyan Conference. Commenting on its secrecy, he fears that its power may be used for political purposes. 'The Socialists and Chartists', he observes, 'have adopted the mode of weekly class meetings, such as are practised by some religious sects of the present time.'[4]

The political camp meeting was another form of Methodist organization adopted by the working-class reformers. From 1839 to 1850 Chartist Camp Meetings in imitation of the Methodists

[1] *Manchester and Salford Advertiser*, June 29, 1839.
[2] H.O. 40. 55, 1840.
[3] *Northern Star*, July 25, 1840.
[4] H.O. 44. 38, 1840.

were held in the summer months. Processions to these gatherings like the Methodists were also extremely common. Following the custom of the Methodists, hymns and prayers often served as an introduction to the speech, and in many cases texts from the Bible were freely expounded. Even before the beginning of Camp Meetings political meetings were sometimes held on Sundays in the open air. Several took place in Nottingham and Leicester, and political sermons published by the Rev. J. R. Stephens were read at these demonstrations. To provide suitable singing for such meetings the Wesleyan Hymn Book was sometimes used.[1]

Had Methodism been, as its critics avow, 'a cross current' to political Radicalism, such plagiarism as that which has been described would have been well nigh impossible. It is nearer the mark to say that the two movements were supplementary to each other. Methodism was a kind of Radicalism in the religious world, while Radicalism was a sort of Methodism in the political sphere.

[1] *Nottingham Review*, Aug. 16, 1839.

PART III

METHODISM AND THE TRADE UNIONS

CHAPTER I

THE MINERS' TRADE UNIONS

TRADE UNIONS are part of the fruit (either for good or for evil) of the Industrial Revolution. Their highest development belongs to the nineteenth century. They provide a striking example of working-class achievement. Nothing exactly like them is to be seen in any previous age. There had been 'trade clubs', 'trade societies', and 'associations' in the early days of industrial activity, but no evidence of their continuity to the modern period can be found. Neither is there any evidence that the Trade Union leaders had in front of them a model of some other union, or had copied the rules and regulations of an extinct association.

The unions of our period were born because of the circumstances of the time, and were not the offspring of earlier generations. Their main object was economic and not political. The political was an afterthought, something tacked on. In the later years it was a means (some folk believed it to be the best means) to achieve an economic purpose. This purpose has been variously described. Sometimes it was 'to protect' the wage-earners, at other times 'to advance their wages', and occasionally 'to shorten their hours'.

Such united action as these objects required naturally created suspicion. Conduct of this kind was regarded as 'seditious' and 'rebellious', and at least 'a restraint of trade'. Regulation of trade and industry had hitherto belonged to the central government as a necessary prerogative. For working men to suggest what remuneration should be given them created a precedent which could not be permitted. Hence the one-sided application of the Combination Acts of 1799. While associations of workmen were forbidden, the combinations of employers were allowed to continue. '*Laissez faire*' as a principle was not popular, but eventually it supplanted the unequal laws.

The Miners' Trade Unions bear the mark of the arduous nature of the work underground. Such work demanded strength, tenacity and endurance. These characteristics were equally necessary in the formation of their societies. Their combinations were born in conflict, and while they existed they remained in conflict. The law was against them. Local authorities usually opposed them. The mining proprietors always objected to them. Only one ally came to the help of the miners, and that was an important one, the development of the mining industry.

According to Clapham the coal mining industry of Great Britain yielded in 1816 an output of 16,000,000 tons of coal. Ten years later it had risen to 21,000,000 tons. In 1836 the increase was greater still, the total output being 30,000,000. By 1856 the grand total amounted to 65,000,000 tons.[1] While coal was produced in Yorkshire, Lancashire, Somerset and the Midlands, together with Scotland and Wales, the main sources of production to the middle of the century lay in Northumberland and Durham. It is mainly in these areas that the strongest unions were formed, and where the information about them is most complete.

In the period under review the miners of Northumberland and Durham made three desperate attempts to improve their position by collective action. The first occurred in 1810 through a dispute over the bond system. According to the 'bond' the colliers were obliged to work under stated conditions, for a given period, and at an agreed price. As these particulars, together with a number of regulations concerning deductions and penalties, were put into writing, many of the untutored workers were unable to understand them. Owing to difficulties in working the agreement a great deal of dissatisfaction ultimately ensued. Eventually the miners demanded an alteration in the system of agreement, and in the conflict that followed the pitmen were finally defeated.

Another struggle took place in 1831 and 1832. Once again the bond system was the main cause of the trouble. The miners, this time under the leadership of Tommy Hepburn, a working miner, fought a desperately hard battle. In the unequal fight only one result was possible. The masters, aided by many of the resources of the State, gained a complete victory and the new union was destroyed.

In 1844 a longer conflict eventuated. Encouraged by the sympathy and support of many people outside their ranks, practically the whole of the miners round the Tyne and Wear remained on strike from the early part of April to the middle of September.

[1] *Economic History*, Clapham, Chap. X.

Once again the colliers were beaten, and many of their number were boycotted by their masters and banished from their native village. But, thanks to the expanding industry, most of the homeless workers got employment in the new areas, and the formation of a permanent union was postponed to a later date.

Similar experience, though of a less violent nature, came to the miners of other districts. Repeated efforts were made in Yorkshire and Lancashire, and also in the Midlands, to obtain improvements by collective action, but usually with little benefit to the colliers. The forces against them were always too powerful.

Sectional efforts having failed, an endeavour was made on a larger scale in the forties to achieve their purpose. In the November of 1842 the Miners' Association of Great Britain and Ireland was formally organized at Wakefield. Its main object was to unite 'the Coal, Lead, and Ironstone Workers' into one great union, and by this means 'to equalize and diminish the hours of labour and to attain the highest possible amount of wages for the labour of the miner'. The association was to be governed by an executive elected at a Conference of delegates representing all the areas. The country was divided into districts, and the members of the local unions had to contribute a penny a week to the union funds.[1]

That such an association was necessary, the condition of the miner's life as revealed in the Government Reports of 1842 to 1850 can leave no doubt. A digest of the evidence in the 1842 Report on the Employment of Children (*Parliamentary Papers*, Vol. xv, pp. 255–9) reveals the following facts. A large proportion of the persons employed in coal mines were under the age of thirteen. Children began to work at the age of four. Female children were employed under the same conditions as males. Parish apprentices were often employed without pay. Ventilation and drainage were lamentably defective. Some of the work meant solitary confinement. Both sexes were usually employed together, even in places where men worked almost naked. The hours of labour were never less than eleven, and often fourteen and upwards. Accidents were numerous and of a fearful nature. The main cause was lack of superintendence. A large number of young people received fatal injuries.

[1] H.O. 45. OS. 434, 1843. H.O. 45. OS. 649, 1844.

G

The evidence given by a number of witnesses made the conditions appear more dreadful. In the West Riding district the case was reported of a man who took his child to work at the age of three. 'When the child was exhausted it was carried home, stripped and put to bed.' Another case of a similar nature was reported from Halifax. A child of three years was made to follow its father into the workings 'to hold the candle, and when exhausted with fatigue was cradled upon the coals until his return at night'. A Sub-Commissioner tells of meeting a small boy who usually got up at 3 a.m., went down the mine at 4, returned home between 4.30 and 5 p.m., and went to bed before 7 o'clock. In some of the Yorkshire mines men worked 'in a state of perfect nakedness', and were 'in this state assisted in their labour by females of all ages, from girls of six years to women of twenty-one, these females being themselves quite naked down to the waist'. Girls were often employed at pulling or 'hurrying', that is pulling the baskets or wagons of coal along the ground by means of a chain. Like a four-legged animal, these half-naked girls, creeping on their hands and feet with the chain between their legs, were compelled to go hither and thither for many hours on their burdensome track. When the road was wet, they often had to pass through dirty water and filthy clay. Two girls at one place had worn large holes in their trousers. One woman confessed that she worked in the mine while 'in the family way'. Two of her children were born in the pit. One of the unfortunates was brought up the pit shaft in her dirty skirt.[1]

The report of 1842 shocked the conscience of the nation and an Act of Parliament was immediately passed in order to prevent the employment of women and children in the coal mines. A minimum age was fixed for the employment of boys, together with a maximum of hours. Further reports were published in the following years for the purpose of showing how the new legislation operated. In South Staffordshire, conditions, on the whole, showed a slight improvement; but truck still continued to annoy the miners.[2] In Lancashire the application of the Acts was made more difficult because of the attitude of certain magistrates. At

[1] First Report of Commissioners on the Employment of Children in Mines. *Parliamentary Papers*, 1842, Vol. xv, pp. 12–24.

[2] The State of the Population in the Mining Districts. *Parliamentary Papers*, 1844, Vol. xvi, p. 55.

one colliery, which belonged to a magistrate, ladders had been placed at the entrance to the shaft to enable the women to descend if they desired. There were still 200 women working in the coal mines in 1845. Laxity existed also in regard to the employment of boys under age.[1]

It was amongst the people working under these conditions that Methodism exercised its most beneficent influence. The influence of John Wesley among the colliers of Kingswood and Newcastle was exceeded by that of his followers. Methodism came to the miners not merely as a form of religious dissent, but also as a welcome ameliorative, bringing a ray of sunshine into their dark and dismal environment.

To the miners of the Tyne and Wear it came as a civilizing influence. The Methodist chapel gave the collier a homely and joyous religion. It also provided a happy fellowship and a means of education. 'An educated pitman in the year 1800 was an exception.' There were, of course, exceptions, but 'they were very rare indeed'.[2] 'The typical miner was drunken, dissolute, and brutalized, tyrannized over by his employers and their underlings.'[3] The majority had never received any education whatever. To these people the Methodist class leader or preacher brought the Bible and the Methodist Hymn Book. They were eventually taught to read and reflect. There came to them a desire for learning and for improvement which had to be gratified. They sent their children to the Sunday School, and not content with that, they often accompanied them. 'Men who had grown up and had children to go to school, have been sitting side by side on a form learning the very rudiments of reading and writing.' The miner not only went to school, 'he took to going to Chapel, and, finding it necessary to appear decent there, he got new clothes and became what is termed respectable'.[4] In this way the Methodists improved the amenities of the underground toiler. 'They took away his gun, his dog, and his fighting cock. They gave him a frock coat for his posy jacket, hymns for his public house ditties, prayer meetings for his pay-night frolics. They drove into the minds of the naturally improvident race that extravagance was in itself

[1] The State of the Population in the Mining Districts. *Parliamentary Papers*, 1845, Vol. xxvii, p. 5.

[2] *The Miners of Northumberland and Durham*, Richard Fynes, p. 12.

[3] *The Story of the Durham Miners*, Sidney Webb, p. 20.

[4] *The Miners of Northumberland and Durham*, Richard Fynes, pp. 282–3.

a sin.'[1] Self-respect and a desire for social and material improvement were only part of the effects of the Methodist influence. These benign results were seen in many ways and especially in the endeavour to form Trade Unions. During the strike of 1831 a letter was sent to the resident viewer at Cowpen Colliery saying, among other things, 'Noo I naw some at wor colliery that has three or fower lads and lasses, and they live in won room not half as gud as yor cellar. . . . I don't pretend to naw very much, but I naw there shouldn't be that much differenc'.[2] In one village where the Methodists had entered, it was said, 'There hasn't been a fight all the week-end', and 'when the place came on the Sunderland Plan, none of the dwellers in Lambton had even seen its name in print, and they flocked to look at the strange sight'.[3]

It was the men whose interests and faculties had been stirred that became the leaders of the Trade Unions. In the Methodist Society, they learnt 'earnestness, sobriety, industry and regularity of conduct'. They stood out 'as men of character gaining the respect of their fellows'. 'From the very beginning of the Trade Union movement among all sections of the wage-earners, of the formation of Friendly Societies and of the later attempts at Adult Education, it is men who are Methodists and in Durham County especially, local preachers of the Primitive Methodists, whom we find taking the lead and filling the posts of influence. From their ranks have come an astonishingly large proportion of Trade Union leaders, from checkweighers and lodge chairmen up to County officials and committee men.'[4]

The Methodists were often prominent in the time of dispute. As early as 1831, they began to make their presence felt. The miners at that time not only objected to the bond, but complained about excessive hours which their children had to work, some of them being seventeen hours away from home. One of the local newspapers (*Durham Chronicle*, April 16, 1831) declared that the cause of the agitation was really due to 'the wild and frenzied declamations of Ranter Preachers who, on these occasions, play the orator'. A correspondent from Sunderland, writing to the *Sunderland Herald, Shields and Stockton Observer* (June 4, 1831),

[1] *The Miners of Northumberland and Durham*, E. Welbourne, pp. 56–9.
[2] *The Miners of Northumberland and Durham*, Richard Fynes, p. 21.
[3] *True Stories of Durham Pit Life*, George Parkinson, of Sherburn, p. 12.
[4] *The Story of the Durham Miners*, Sidney Webb, pp. 22–4.

discusses the question whether the Methodists are really to blame for the 'turn out', because 'several of the leading speakers and delegates of the pitmen are Methodists or Ranters'. He seems certain about one thing, namely, that the quietness and order which have characterized the strike are largely due to the influence of religion. That the leaders carried their religion into the conflict, the following is an illustration. At one of the conferences arranged between the miners and the Marquis of Londonderry, 'Hepburn, the leader of the pitmen in this conflict with the coal owners, and . . . a Ranter Preacher, observed that he never entered upon the consideration of important matters like that in dispute, without first praying to God to give him right direction; and he insisted upon their offering up a supplication to the Deity, for safe guidance before the conference began. The noble Marquis, it is added, piously joined in the act of prayer'.[1]

The religion of these men evidently gave them tenacity, patience, and tranquillity, even when their homes were being broken up and their work taken by others. One of the marvels of the strike was the way in which they stood in solemn and sullen silence while their 'young and weeping infants' were cast into the streets to spend 'the night in cold and wet, under temporary cover in the open air'.[2] At the same time they were compelled to witness the degrading spectacle of imported blacklegs taking their homes and getting their jobs. The surprising feature was not the extent of the violence, but the widespread tranquillity. In all this the influence of their leaders was manifest. Hepburn, the leader of the union, and a Methodist local preacher, always advised patience, peace, and order. He continued to do this even after 'the employers had turned 1,000 families into the streets'.[3] His advice was generally followed, though there were exceptions. For example, at one of the periodic ejections of the miners' families, one of the women refused to move from her house. She was therefore 'carried to the door by two men'. When she got outside, 'She seized the hat of a policeman, flourished it over her head, and cheered on the mob to onslaught'.[4] It was inevitable that the miners should be beaten. They were faced with a huge combination of magistrates, policemen, military, newspapers, and coal owners. Hunger was the

[1] *Durham Chronicle,* May 14, 1831.
[2] *ibid.,* May 4, 1832.
[3] *Newcastle Journal,* June 2, 1832.
[4] *ibid.,* May 12, 1832.

greatest weapon in working their defeat, but they clung to the belief that ultimately they would be delivered from their bondage.

Evidence from religious sources shows that many of the leaders in this conflict belonged to the Primitive Methodist denomination. They had learnt from Methodism 'the method of organizing men, and the art of public speaking'.[1] 'The leader *par excellence* was Thomas Hepburn, or as he was known, Tommy Hepburn. When the struggle was entered upon he was a Primitive Methodist, but subsequently ceased to be one. It was when with them that he received his aspirations and training.' 'He could be heard at one time by forty thousand people, and always carried the multitude with him.' 'A Sunderland man showed his likeness in a "penny peep show" for years.' 'On one occasion at Shadings Hill meeting, a blackleg was put into a pond.' Within a week three Primitive Methodist local preachers, who had attended the meeting, 'were arrested for conspiracy and lodged in Durham gaol'. 'The first night, and every night they were there, they held a prayer meeting. Mr. John Iley was an excellent singer, and was generally a leader of a choir or a singing pew. He organized a choir in gaol, and they made the prison vocal. The chaplain . . . . used the choir at his services, and was very kind to them. When they were liberated, he made them each a present, and expressed a wish there were more Primitive Methodists.' About the same time 'Seven young men were transported from Jarrow, and are known to history as the "Jarrow lads". . . . Five of them were Primitives, meeting in class. They were arrested, tried for conspiracy and transported for life to New South Wales or Botany Bay'. 'Twenty-eight years ago, finding myself within two hundred miles of them, I determined to pay them a visit. Those that had been Primitive Methodists I found had done well. One had become a Wesleyan local preacher; the others were members of the church.'[2] Among the strike leaders who can be definitely identified as Primitive Methodists are the following: Thomas Hepburn, Benjamin Embleton, Charles Parkinson,

[1] *Primitive Methodist Quarterly Review*, 1882, p. 393.

[2] *ibid.*, 1883. Article by the Honourable R. Richardson, member of the Victorian Legislative Assembly. Richardson was an eye-witness of some strike scenes in the county of Durham during 1831, 1832, and 1844. His father who lived at Tow Law was a strike leader in 1831–32 and was expelled from his house, pp. 264–6.

Ralf Atchinson, William Hammond, Ralf Heron, John Iley, George Charlton, James Wilson, and John Richardson.

Confirmation of the Methodist influence also comes from other sources. George Johnson, a viewer of the Wellington, Heaton, and Burdon Collieries, giving evidence before the Commissioner on April 16, 1841, confessed that 'the educated people, or the Methodists, are put forward to be the spokesmen on occasions of dispute with their masters'. 'These educated persons, or Methodists, are most decidedly the hardest to deal with.' Similar evidence was given by Thomas John Taylor, a coal owner. He tells of the causes of the conflicts and asserts that 'the men professing to be Methodists and Ranters are the spokesmen on these occasions, and the most difficult to deal with. These men may be superior men to the rest in intelligence and generally show great skill, and cunning, and circumvention'.[1]

The subsequent struggle of 1844 was conducted in a like manner, and had leaders of the same type. 'There were Mark Dent (brother of the Rev. W. Dent, a highly respected minister among the Primitives), Robert Archer, John Tulip, and Thomas Pratt. All these were Primitive Methodist local preachers.'[2] Mark Dent on one occasion was sarcastically described in the pages of the *Newcastle Journal* (May 18, 1844) as 'one of the "navvies" or "blacklegs" that was set to work in defiance of the regular pitmen last strike'. During the course of the stoppage 'twelve men were selected to go direct to the Metropolis—London—to inform public men and the public what was their complaint and what they asked for. The twelve were known as the Apostles. They appeared in Exeter Hall, and made a profound impression. Of the twelve . . . nine were Primitive Methodist Local Preachers, when they went, if not afterwards'.[3]

When the colliers were evicted from their homes, the leaders were the first to suffer, and Lord Londonderry, Lord Lieutenant of the county, writing to the Home Office, adds 'the men we have ejected are good riddance'.[4] At Bishop Auckland among the Primitive Methodists 'several of the trustees and members were evicted from their dwellings and their furniture thrust into the

[1] First Report of the Commissioners on the Employment of Children in Mines, 1842. *Parliamentary Papers*, Vol. xv, pp. 568 and 608.
[2] *Primitive Methodist Quarterly Review*, 1882. Article by T. Burt, p. 393.
[3] *ibid.*, 1883. Article by Richardson, p. 268.
[4] H.O. 45. OS. 644, 1844.

street'. The Durham Circuit was so affected by this callous method of dealing with the miners that their numbers were reduced from 1,500 reported in 1843 to 520 in 1844. The societies situated between the Tyne and Blyth were reduced 'to mere skeletons of their former selves' by the same cause.[1] Many of the 'sacrificed men' held official position in the local Methodist society. So while Methodism gave men and organization to the Trade Unions, many of the societies suffered in consequence by enforced removals of their leading members.

The Commissioners' Reports, which must be accepted with a certain amount of reserve, because of the sources from which they got their evidence, also reveal something of the Methodist influence. While the Wesleyan Methodists are praised for 'having brought about a great change in the respectability of dress and general good behaviour of the miners',[2] the Ranters are blamed for leading them astray. Commissioner Tremenheere, referring to the strike of 1844, says, 'A religious feeling was mixed up in a strange and striking manner with this movement'. 'Frequent meetings were held in their chapels (in general those of the Primitive Methodists or "Ranters" as they are commonly called in that part of the country), when prayers were publicly offered up for the successful result of the strike.' 'They attended the prayer meetings "to get their faith strengthened", i.e. to encourage each other in the confidence that the strike would succeed.' 'The local preachers, the chief speakers at their prayer meetings, were the men who, by a certain command of language and energetic tone and manner, had acquired an influence over their fellow workmen and were invariably the chief promoters and abettors of the strike. They were consequently among the first, at most of the works, to be dismissed by the masters as soon as the strike was over.' One of Lord Londonderry's agents expressed a similar view. This witness stated that many of the pitmen 'were . . . intimidated to form the strike, and many were led to it by the "Ranter preachers" who made a religious question of it to induce the men to stick to their pledge, and stand out. Some few also of the local Wesleyan Preachers, who are working men principally, lectured on behalf of the union'. 'During the

[1] *Northern Primitive Methodism*, Patterson, pp. 95, 294, 337.
[2] Commissioners' Report on the Employment of Children in Mines, 1842. *Parliamentary Papers*, Vol. xv, p. 166.

strike they had regularly once a week prayer meetings at the chapels in the colliery villages, to pray to God to give them success.' 'Everything that could be collected in the Bible about slavery and tyranny, such as Pharaoh ordering bricks to be made without straw', was utilized. The Earl of Durham's manager avows that 'in these strikes there is a class of self-sufficient leaders, who are generally local preachers, and who are most decidedly the most difficult to control, and who urge the others to acts of very great insubordination'. Similar news comes from the Evenwood Colliery manager. 'The Ranters,' he asserts, 'were the worst agitators at the time of the strike. The Wesleyans were quite the other way.' In the parish of Earsdon according to the Commissioner, 'the people were entirely under the influence of Chartist leaders, delegates from the Colliers' Union, and their local preachers chiefly of the Primitive Methodists'. At the Seaton Delaval Colliery, 'the three leading men in the strikes were William Dawson, William Richardson, and John Nicholson; they were pitmen. They were Primitive Methodists and local preachers. They frequently assembled the people, from 100 to 400 together in the roadside, and offered up prayers for the success of the strike, and also that the men who were brought from a distance to work in a colliery, the "blacklegs", as they were called, might be injured, either lamed or killed, and they rejoiced when anything did happen to them'. 'These three men were of course discharged. About one third of the whole number of our hewers (heads of families) belong to the Primitive Methodists. The Wesleyans were very quiet and were among the first to go to work.' A Wesleyan Methodist witness asserted that 'the Ranters used their influence to disaffect' the members of the Wesleyan society. 'Some of their local preachers . . . were obliged to leave their own body because they would not join and encourage the strike.'[1] Thomas Burt, while recognizing the influence of the Methodist local preacher, repudiates the charge of incitement to violence and lawlessness made against this class of workmen. Such a charge, he says, 'is certainly a gross libel'. He criticizes the statement of Tremenheere, who said in reference to Earsdon Parish, 'there is no mining parish within these two

[1] The State of the Population in Mining Districts, 1846. *Parliamentary Papers*, Vol. xxiv, pp. 8–26. The statement that local preachers prayed for blacklegs to be injured must be an exaggeration. It is foreign to their general behaviour.

counties the people of which have given so much trouble to their employers, or have broken out in such violence as this. The people were under the influence of Chartist leaders, delegates from the colliers' unions, and their local preachers, chiefly of the Primitive Methodists'. 'In 1839 there were great disturbances in this parish (meaning Earsdon in Northumberland) from the assemblage of the Chartists and their threats of physical force. During the strike of 1844, the colliers, under the instigation of Chartist delegates and local preachers, chiefly of the Primitive Methodists or "Ranters", showed so strong a disposition to violence that a force of half a company of infantry, some cavalry, several mounted policemen, and from eighty to ninety special constables, was established at and near this colliery' (Seaton Delaval Colliery) 'for two months (from 18th of July to 24th of September) at a cost to this and two neighbouring collieries of £400.'[1]

Whatever violence was shown may be pardoned when the nature and the number of the incitements to violence are remembered. Though the military were called into action against the miners, some of the officers reported unfavourably of the employers. Major-General Brotherton, the Officer commanding the North Eastern District, reports his attendance at a meeting of five magistrates, 'four of whom', he says, 'are individuals more or less interested in the coal trade'. According to his opinion, 'the coal owners seem to rely solely upon the expedient of starving the colliers into submission to their own terms'. He admits 'that the colliers are much more disposed to conciliation and accommodation than the owners'. 'The latter must, in a great many cases, be the gainers by the continuance of the strike.' Eventually he offers mediation, but this is rejected by the owners. Major-General Sir T. Arbuthnot, when he hears of this, expresses regret 'that there is cause to conclude that the masters, from interested motives, are not likely to extend themselves, to put an end to the present strike, as soon as could be wished'. Lieutenant-Colonel Bradshaw disapproves of the intention to eject the strikers from their cottages, 'the custom rarely being resorted to', he contends, and 'unprecedently so to the extent that was proposed'. He expresses reluctance when called upon to use 'the military force

[1] *Primitive Methodist Quarterly Review*, 1882. Article by Thomas Burt, p. 394. Also the State of the Population in Mining Districts, 1846. *Parliamentary Papers*, Vol. xxiv, p. 25, and The State of the Population in Mining Districts. *Parliamentary Papers*, 1850, Vol. xxiii, p. 46.

under such circumstances'. He feels sure that 'by kindness and good temper on the part of the master and a few concessions on the subject of fines and a guarantee of work or wages during the month they are engaged by the owners' new bond . . . the whole of the pitmen will return to work'. When Mr. Surtees, a local magistrate, took some of the military to the Tantobie meeting of miners, Colonel Bradshaw objected to them being there and ordered them away.[1]

The connexion between Methodism and the Miners' Unions in the other coal areas of the country is difficult to trace because the references are so few. In the Midland district, where Methodism was strong, a little information is forthcoming. The utility of the Methodist Sunday Schools is definitely recognized in the Mining Reports. In most of the colliery villages, a Methodist Sunday School is to be found. As 'the children of the colliers go to work at a very early age', they must 'chiefly depend for what little education they receive on the Sunday Schools'.[2] Methodism therefore by means of its Sunday Schools exercised an intellectual as well as a moral influence. Edward Oakley, who had served as an apprentice for thirteen years without receiving any wages, tells of the effect of religion in the South Staffordshire mines. 'There are pits,' he says, 'in which there are prayer meetings every day after dinner, and all are obliged to attend, as the butties and the men will not work with any who do not. We have had preaching down in the pits. . . . Many a one goes down the pit to hear the preaching. When there is any prayer or preaching, the master allows five minutes beyond the hour.'[3] Hearing of these strange customs of having preaching and prayer meetings in the mines, the Commissioner attended one of the services. He found a very reverent congregation. John Wesley's Hymn Book was used for the singing. When the leader prayed, the others knelt. The Government official was apparently much impressed by what he saw and heard. Sometimes a single individual exercised a very extensive influence. Evidence of this is given by a Wesleyan minister of West Bromwich. 'John Thorn,' he says, 'has produced quite a revolution since the

[1] H.O. 45. OS. 650, 1844.

[2] Report from Commissioners, Children's Employment (Mines). *Parliamentary Papers*, 1842, Vol. xvi, p. 40.

[3] *ibid.*, pp. 27, 66.

strike in the pits, where he now is. His master is quite delighted with it. He tells all the men they must obey John or leave the pits. He insists upon their having prayers and reading the Scriptures in the dinner hour, and having rules against swearing and drinking, &c.'[1] According to the same minister, Wesleyan Methodist butties are not allowed to keep beer shops or they would be dismissed from the Connexion.[2] This Wesleyan Methodist influence did not prevent the cessation of work, for strikes took place in 1842 and 1844. The Commissioner believes these revolts 'from the legitimate influence and authority of their masters', to be due to 'the excitement applied to them by the formation . . . of the Miners' Association which established itself at Newcastle-on-Tyne'.[3]

In Yorkshire and Lancashire repeated attempts were made to organize unions, but the efforts were too isolated and the forces against them were too powerful to guarantee success. The usual methods were adopted by the authorities in conjunction with the coal owners. Most of the leaders became marked men and were usually penalized. The most successful Trade Union effort took place in the forties, when the Miners' Association of Great Britain and Ireland was formed. Lancashire had a thirteen weeks' strike in 1844, while some parts of Yorkshire also had a stoppage. The result was the same in each case. All endeavours to improve their position were finally crushed, and the desired amelioration was postponed till a later date.

Though Methodism was numerously represented in both counties, very little evidence can be found to show its direct influence on the Miners' Union. The good work done by the Wesleyan and Primitive Methodist Sunday Schools is mentioned in the Report of 1842. One of the Commissioners confessed that 'the boys at the Primitive Methodist school were the best instructed' he had 'met with at Silkstone, and it was evident that superior pains had been taken with them'.[4] At a colliery near Wakefield, 'nearly all the men were Wesleyan Methodists'.[5]

[1] First Report of Commissioners on Midland Mining (South Staffordshire). *Parliamentary Papers*, 1843, Vol. xiii, p. cxxxvii.

[2] *ibid.*, p. 16.

[3] *ibid. Parliamentary Papers*, 1844, Vol. xvi, p. 67.

[4] Report of Commissioners on Employment of Children in Mines. *Parliamentary Papers*, Vol. xv, 1842, p. 200.

[5] Report of Commissioners, State of Population in Mining Districts, 1845. *Parliamentary Papers*, Vol. xxvii, p. 29.

A few scattered references to Methodist influence can be found among the Home Office Papers. On July 10, 1843, the Rev. Thomas Mills, J.P., reports a miners' 'turn out' at Oldham. 'Harris,' he says, 'is appointed delegate for the colliers of Oldham, and is a leader amongst the Ranters and Primitive Methodists.' A few days later the clergyman could lay aside his clerical duties and attend the local pit. He was there 'before the men went down, they were preparing to go down', he says, 'when I got there, and I am glad to say that this man Harris was the first man I saw in his working dress, seemingly with no other intention but working; I shall, however, see if he stops at his work all day; he has no knowledge of my being at the pit this morning to look after him in particular, therefore if he intends going to the meeting he will do so notwithstanding my visit to the pit this morning'.[1] Perhaps the reverend gentleman was not aware of the destitute state of the folk he was seeking to drive to work for a mere pittance. An appeal by the workers to W. F. Hulton, Coal Proprietor and County Justice of the Peace, reveals their desperate condition. It speaks of 'the very scanty pittance we receive as remuneration for our labour', and then refers to the great danger of their vocation. 'We ask the advance in the name of that God who has declared that the labourer is worthy of his hire, we ask it on behalf of our once blooming wives, but now hunger stricken and emaciated wives and children, we ask it on behalf of ourselves who in many instances have to descend into the pit without a breakfast, for no other purpose but that ye be enabled to grow rich while we hunger and sink by slow degrees into a premature grave, victims to over-exertion, nauseous gases, and starvation.'[2] Whether Mills knew of this or not, it did not prevent him reporting that the colliers were joining the 'Miners' Association of Great Britain and Ireland, Established at Wakefield, November 7, 1842', based on the sentiment expressed in the words 'Let Unity, Peace, Law, and Order, be your motto. United we stand, Divided we fall'. Such a union as this he thought 'might become extensively dangerous and more especially should it hereafter be connected with Chartist Agitation'.[3] Towards the end of 1844, Mills informs the Home Office of the presence in Lancashire of Hembleton and

[1] H.O. 45. OS. 350, 1843.
[2] *ibid.*, 45. OS. 350, 1843.
[3] *ibid.*, 45. OS. 350, 1843.

Parkinson from the Northern Counties.[1] Apparently these two delegates were among the 'Twelve Apostles' sent from the North East to instruct the country of the real condition of the miners on the Tyne and the Wear. The magistrates and the coal owners succeeded in their joint purposes. All the miners were driven back to work on the masters' terms, and the infant National Union died a premature death, only to be resurrected in later days.

[1] H.O. 45. OS. 645, 1844. Hembleton, whose proper name was Embleton, and Parkinson were Methodist local preachers.

CHAPTER II

THE INDUSTRIAL TRADE UNIONS

THE Industrial Trade Unions, like the Miners' Trade Unions in the first half of the nineteenth century, had to fight for a precarious existence. They were popular nowhere. The Government by its legislative enactments of 1799 had declared against them. The local magistrates, many of whom were employers of labour, were almost unanimous in their dislike of them. 'The lords of industry' could not be expected to favour them. What was true in the legal and political sphere was equally true of the economic realm, that 'the common people had nothing to do with the laws but to obey them'. The working classes had nothing to do with the economic laws. They were compelled to obey them. When they tried by combined action to alter them, they were threatened by their rulers with boycott or imprisonment.

Industrial life at that time was organized in some senses according to the military pattern. The first and the final duty of the common soldier was instant obedience. 'His not to reason why. His but to do or die.' In a similar manner the common people had to learn obedience. They were servants only. In all things they had to practise submission. For working men to suggest how a master should conduct his business constituted an unforgivable impertinence. They had neither the training nor the intelligence for such an important undertaking. On no account must they be permitted to interfere with the prerogatives of those ordained to rule over them. The right of the employer to do what he liked with his business and workmen could not be questioned. By most of the authorities it was regarded as a kind of Divine Right. The ordinary man had no rights. Thomas Paine and his crazy followers might prate about such rights, but they were only visionary. Besides, it was expressly laid down in Scripture that servants should obey their masters in all things and always be subject to the higher powers. Moreover, that new doctrine called '*laissez faire*' provided for the '*status quo*'. The only right granted to a workman was the right to dispose of his labour at whatever price he cared to accept, without any dictatorial interference from other workmen. Of course, it was never recognized that distress and poverty on the one hand, and the arbitrary will of the employer on the other hand, might compel him to sell his labour at less than cost value. That really didn't matter very much so long as no combinations were permitted to exist. All the machinery of an oligarchic Government was used for many years to prevent that eventuality.

Conditions of this kind made it extremely difficult for under-fed and untutored men to unite together with much certainty of success. Failure was evident from the onset. That becomes more apparent when the nature and the scope of the first associations are discerned. As a rule, they were small and weak, often independent of each other, and at best a kind of small-scale enterprise. The difficulties of any other sort of united enterprise were manifold. A clear class consciousness had not yet been sufficiently evolved. The segregation of manual workers had just begun. Lack of elementary education constituted a severe handicap. The facility of transport and communication was not yet even imagined. The want of leadership was constantly apparent, while the necessary motive power to establish and sustain a big organization was so far not generated. Circumstances therefore appear to have compelled the unions at first to organize themselves on a small scale. The geographical as well as the trade factor often decided the dimensions of a union. Examples of the former can be seen in the Cotton Spinners Unions formed at various places, yet independent of each other. The Weavers Associations, the Woolcombers Societies, and the Framework Knitters provide another illustration of the same thing. Examples of the latter are to be found among those unions described according to the nature of their trade, such as Builders, Carpenters and Smiths Unions, &c.

Scattered references to both kinds of union are not difficult to find in the Home Office Papers. One report in 1801 mentions the fact that 'numerous associations of Woolcombers' are operating in the areas covered by Wellington, Taunton, and Honiton.[1] In 1804 the activities of the Journeymen Mechanics Society, the Journeymen Shoemakers Society, and the Cordwainers Society are briefly described; one of them is said to be somewhat like

[1] H.O. 42. 61, 1801.

the corresponding society.[1] At Loughborough in 1811, the unions endeavour to raise wages and the attempt is immediately designated as illegal.[2] Many of the Woolcombers Societies are still operating in 1812.[3] The Rev. W. R. Hay of Manchester tries his best to put down the Printers, Cutters, and Drawers Combination in 1814.[4] During the same year, the Town Clerk of Nottingham seeks to achieve a similar object with the Framework Knitters Societies.[5] In 1818, the Weavers of Bolton organize themselves like a Methodist class meeting and subscribe to their funds a penny a week.[6] About the same time, the Cotton Spinners Committee at Manchester are committed to take their trial for a conspiracy to raise wages. On the day of their trial they are let off on the promise of good behaviour, but not before the judge tells them they are going headlong into destruction.[7] A few years later, the Fustian Cutters Union at Manchester imitates the Methodists by forming classes and adopting the penny a week subscription.[8] In 1826 the Spinners and Miners Unions at Oldham unite and effect a 'turn out',[9] while at Trowbridge the societies are organized into clubs and endeavour to prevent the practice of truck and seek to raise wages.[10]

After the Trade Unions had been legalized,[11] they were compelled to fight not only for the rights of labour, but also for the right of collective action. Examples of the latter conflict are not very difficult to find. There was some truth in the comment made by Edward Baines (*Leeds Mercury*, July 25) during the Cotton Spinners strike in 1818. 'Combinations amongst workmen,' he declared, 'are always attended with danger, and the greatest sufferers by them are generally the workmen themselves.' Strike action by workmen has always meant self-inflicted suffering. The suffering, however, has usually been aggravated by the callous conduct of the masters. During the six months' strike of the Woolcombers and Stuff Weavers at Bradford in 1825, the employers determined not to employ children whose parents belonged to the union. The wives of men connected with the union were also refused employment. Finding that the

[1] H.O. 42. 79, 1804.
[2] *ibid.*, 42. 118, 1811.
[3] *ibid.*, 42. 130, 1812.
[4] *ibid.*, 42. 138, 1814.
[5] *ibid.*, 42. 140, 1814.
[6] *ibid.*, 42. 179, 1818.
[7] *ibid.*, 42. 186, 1819. Also 42. 179, 1818.
[8] *ibid.*, 40. 18, 1825.
[9] *ibid.*, 40. 21, 1826.
[10] *ibid.*, 40. 23, 1829.
[11] This was done in 1824 by the repeal of the Combination Laws.

strikers were getting support from other workmen, the masters decided to discharge all the members of the 'Combers and Weavers Union' and all who supported them.[1] Finally, the workmen agreed that the employers couldn't pay more, so they went back to work again.[2]

Reference will later be made to the attempt to break the National Association for the Protection of Labour during the strike at Ashton and Stalybridge in 1831. Similar action was taken against the Builders Union in 1833. It was reported in the *Leeds Mercury* (July 13) of that year that 'the Master Tradesmen of Liverpool, Manchester, Bolton, Blackburn, and Preston have united to put an end to the Builders Trades Union, and have determined to employ no workman who is a member of the Union'. When the nine weeks' 'turn out' of the Dyers at Leeds terminated in September 1833, it was said that 'the Master Dyers generally have got their complement of men, at the old rate of wages, and under written engagements to abandon the Trades Union'.[3] More drastic action was taken by the Master Manufacturers in the West Riding district of Yorkshire. At a meeting held in Leeds for the purpose of resisting 'the encroachments of the Trades Union' of the 'Operative Woollen Manufacturers', they decide 'to enter into a bond, binding the subscribers in a heavy penalty not to employ any persons who were in the Trades Union, or who would not abandon that Union'.[4] Fortunately for the workers the bond remained dormant, not sufficient signatures having been attached. This indeed was the result in spite of the statement of Lord Melbourne concerning 'the strong opinion entertained by His Majesty's Ministers of the criminal character and the evil effects of the Unions'.[5] These constant conflicts, and the habit of mutual support adopted by the workmen, prepared the way for larger unions.

Attempts at large-scale enterprises in Trade Unionism commence approximately with the thirties. Although the Wool-

[1] At this time 'the Cabinet-Makers, Woolcombers, Sawyers, Weavers, Carpenters, Tailors, Plasterers, Blacksmiths, Cordwainers, and Shuttlemakers of Norwich' had formed themselves into 'a joint Union to act with the Combers and Weavers of Bradford', and were 'straining every nerve to afford them assistance'. *Leeds Mercury*, Aug. 20, 1825.

[2] *Leeds Mercury*, June 11, July 16, Aug. 20, Sept. 10, Nov. 12 and Nov. 26, 1825.

[3] *ibid.*, Sept. 21, 1833.

[4] *ibid.*, Oct. 5, 1833.

[5] *ibid.*, Sept. 7, 1833.

combers in 1812 ventured to organize a National Union, it apparently ceased to function after a very short existence. Signs of the endeavour to form larger unions can be seen in 1826 when the Miners and Spinners at Oldham associated for a time. But the first-fruits of large scale enterprise are clearly evident in 1830. During this year the Cotton Spinners organized themselves into 'The Grand General Union of all the Operative Spinners of the United Kingdom'. Their first meeting was held at the Isle of Man in 1829. Districts were formed and the customary penny a week subscription to the general fund was ordered. At this conference it was decided to ask the various districts to make a petition to Parliament concerning the hours of labour and the question of young people in factories. J. Doherty became the first secretary. A few months later, at a delegate meeting in Manchester, 'The National Association for the Protection of Labour' was formally instituted. A general committee took charge of the movement. Election to this committee was based upon the proportional system, one delegate being appointed by every 1,000 members.[1]

Evidence is available to show that the National Association represented up to that time the biggest thing in Trade Union Organization. By 1831 it had established its own weekly newspaper under the title of *The Voice of the People*. From its columns (Jan. to June, 1831) the fact can be ascertained that the union operated in Lancashire, Yorkshire, Staffordshire, Warwickshire, Leicestershire, Derbyshire, and Nottinghamshire. Branches were to be found at Birmingham, Nottingham, Derby, Mansfield, Sutton-in-Ashfield, Knaresborough, Rochdale, Oldham, Ashton, Bury, Bolton, Preston, Blackburn, Blackrod, Accrington, Clitheroe, Rossendale, and Macclesfield. Like all the Trade Unions of that period it had to fight for its continued existence. In the early part of 1831, at least 20,000 persons were on strike at Ashton and Stalybridge, Dukinfield and Mossley because of a reduction of wages. The action of the fifty-two employers who combined against the workmen was described by the latter as 'an attempt . . . to break up that powerful establishment—"The National Association for the Protection of Labour"'. After several weeks' struggle the men at Stalybridge yielded to the masters' price, and the strike ended in the usual way by a defeat of the workers. Although the Association did not exist for more

[1] H.O. 40. 27, 1830.

than three years, it served a useful purpose. It demonstrated the need of united action, and it afforded a good example for other unions to follow.

In addition to the National Association there existed in 1831 another union called the 'National Associated Smiths Union', otherwise known as the 'Derby Union'. A correspondent, writing to the *Voice of the People* (April 2) affirms that they are already 'joined in union with Derby, Nottingham, Leicester, Northampton, Huddersfield, Leeds, Sheffield, Liverpool, Worcester, Birmingham, Bilston, &c'.

Reference has been made in a previous chapter to the formation of the National Union of Working Classes which had its headquarters in London. According to Francis Place it began first as a Trade Union and was later turned into a Political Union through the influence of William Lovett. It continued its activity from the April of 1831 to the November of 1835. In 1834 'The Grand Consolidated Trades Union of Great Britain and Ireland' was finally instituted. This result was achieved by the amalgamation of several other unions. Robert Owen exercised a predominating influence at its formation. So extensive were its operations that it became possible to establish a workers' periodical called *The Pioneer* or 'Trades Union Magazine'.[1] Like previous Trade Unions the 'Grand Consolidated' had a rather short life, but the attempt at a big organization had been made and it served as a pattern for later days. In 1841 Colonel Wemys reports a meeting of five trades for the purpose of forming a big union in Manchester. At this conference the Mill Wrights, the Machine Makers, the Iron Moulders, the Smiths and the Turners were represented.[2] During the next year a violent demonstration of the strength of large-scale unions was given in Lancashire, Yorkshire, Staffordshire, Derbyshire, Warwickshire, Cheshire, and Cumberland. Never before had there been such a response to a demand for a united 'turn out'. The movement however got out of hand, and many of the leaders were arrested, some of them being sent to prison.[3]

Though the Chartist organization was distinct from the Trade Unions, a rather close relation existed between them in many

[1] H.O. 40. 32, 1834.
[2] *ibid.*, 45. OS. 41, 1841.
[3] *ibid.*, 45. OS. 242, 243, 249, 258, 260, 261A, 263, 264, 1842.

places. Chartism as a national institution presented an example to the pioneers of Trade Unionism. While many Trade Unions continued their activity on a small scale, the need of bigger unions was constantly demonstrated. In several cases an attempt was made to unite the smaller ones and thus make themselves more powerful. As already seen, the miners at this time were organizing their unions on a national scale, and though defeated for the moment, the achievement of large scale Trade Unionism was only postponed. In later days it became an accomplished fact.

Looked at from the standpoint of the working classes, some sort of large-scale enterprise in Trade Unionism was imperative at this time. Above all things it was necessary in order to resist the increasing pressure of economic and social circumstances. The lot of the lower classes had not improved in proportion to the increase of the national wealth. Local action, while not an absolute failure in every case, had not improved their condition very much. Parliament, instead of relieving, had further oppressed them. Salvation had to come from below and not from above. Working men must learn to get together and assist each other in the work of redemption. Hitherto they had been the victims of economic conditions. They must now learn to conquer these conditions, to regulate them, and even make them contribute to their own material well-being. Their customary share in the results of industry had been long hours and low wages, or part time and unemployment. The belief was continually pressed upon them that the employers of labour got more than their just share of the fruits of production. The latter could live in their mansions, while many of the former with their families had to reside in cellars and be fed with potatoes like the pigs in the pens.

The Government Reports of 1832 to 1850 provide a useful commentary on the social and economic conditions of the working classes. The Factory Reports make known the fact that one third of the people that worked in factories were young folk, many of them just boys and girls. Children of slender age were compelled to labour in circumstances detrimental even to adult workers. Apprentices were taken from the workhouses and enlisted against their will to engage in factory work. Cruel treatment instead of good wages was not infrequently meted out to them. Evidence was produced to show that children of two years of age had been compelled to assist their parents, while it was a common practice for children of five, six, seven and eight years of age to work long hours in the mills. All this enforced and cheap labour made the adult worker less valuable and more easily displaced. New-born children were welcomed in some families because they would increase in the near future the earning capacity of the home.

The social conditions of the time did not diminish but aggravated the evils of economic pressure. In some of the factory towns of Lancashire, the homes of the lower classes were little better than pigsties. Liverpool stood out pre-eminently in this respect. It was described by one doctor as 'the most unhealthy town of England'.[1] 'There are', said another witness, 'thousands of houses and hundreds of courts in this town without a single drain of any description.'[2] 39,000 persons, being one-fifth of the working classes, resided in 7,800 cellars. 'The great proportion of these inhabited cellars were dark, damp, confined, ill-ventilated and dirty.'[3] Manchester had 15,000 persons living in cellars, almost one-eighth of the working population. Among these cellar dwellings there were 1,500 cases in which three persons slept in one bed, 738 cases where four slept in one bed, 281 cases where five slept in one bed, 94 cases where six slept in one bed, 27 cases where seven slept in one bed, two cases where eight slept in one bed, and 31 cases where there were no beds.[4] In Preston, noted for its cesspools and filth, almost similar conditions prevailed.[5] Among many of the towns examined by the Commissioners drainage was 'decidedly bad'. Water supply was generally deficient. A large number of the courts and alleys had no privies and no covered drains. The average life of the labourer in consequence was extremely short. In Liverpool it was fifteen years, in Manchester seventeen, in Bolton eighteen, in Leeds nineteen, while in the Metropolis it was twenty-two.[6] The average life of those who attained the age of twenty-one or above was slightly more than double in each case. According to this reckoning it was better to be a pauper than a worker. The average life of the labourers in the Metropolis was twenty-two and

[1] State of Large Towns and Populous Districts, 1844. First Report, *Parliamentary Papers*, Vol. xvii, p. 483.
[2] *ibid.* Second Report. *Parliamentary Papers,* Vol. xviii, p. 26, 1845.
[3] Select Committee on Health of Towns, 1840. *Parliamentary Papers*, Vol. xi, p. 284.
[4] State of Large Towns and Populous Districts, Second Report, 1845. *Parliamentary Papers,* Vol. xviii, p. 328.
[5] *ibid.* Vol. xviii, p. 330.
[6] *ibid.*, p. 202.

that of the paupers forty-nine. The average life for those who reached the age of twenty-one or over for the labourers was forty-nine, and for the paupers sixty.[1] Add to all this the ravage of diseases, the lack of open spaces, the abject poverty and unexampled misery, and one cannot be surprised at the persistent endeavours of the working classes, sometimes accompanied by violence, to relieve the situation. The Factory Acts are a blot on English civilization. They should never have been needed. The same is true of the Mining Reports and the Reports on Health and Sanitation. Singly and unitedly they present a strong indictment of 'the powers that be', and a forceful justification for Trade Union action either on a small or a large scale.

The attitude of official Methodism to the Industrial Trade Unions can be described as non-committal or neutral. It was neither hostile nor sympathetic. In a sense it was '*laissez faire*'. This view is entirely at variance with that expressed by Dr. Rattenbury when he asserts that 'The Conference forbade Wesleyans to become members of the Trade Unions', and also that of the Hammonds who frankly state that 'the Methodist movement and the Trade Union movement were rival flags'.[2]

While the Methodist people were continually warned against associating themselves with political parties, no such warning was given against Trade Unions, unless the Wesleyan Conference address of 1833 be interpreted that way. Dr. Rattenbury believes that the advice to avoid 'Associations which are subversive to the principles of true and proper liberty, employing unlawful oaths, and threats, and force to acquire new members' clearly refers to Trade Unions.[3] Even if it does (which is very unlikely), it stands out as an isolated reference, and becomes part of the general attitude of the Wesleyan body to all associations believed to be inimical to law, peace, and order. It might indeed have reference to the societies that were operating in Staffordshire. Various lodges such as Druids, Loyal Britons, Knights of the Wood, Odd Fellows, and Friendly Odd had been established round Dudley. Most of them met in public houses, and members were initiated by means of an oath of secrecy. Several class

[1] Report on the Sanitary Condition of the Labouring Population of Great Britain, 1843. *Parliamentary Papers*, Vol. xii, p. 636.

[2] *Wesley's Legacy to the World*, J. E. Rattenbury, p. 216. Also *The Town Labourer*, J. L. & B. Hammond, p. 286.

[3] Wesleyan Conference Minutes, 1833. Also *Wesley's Legacy to the World*, p. 216.

leaders and local preachers had apparently joined some of these clubs and much contention was aroused on that account. A preachers' meeting in the Dudley, Birmingham, and Wednesbury area decided that separation from these lodges should henceforth be made an absolute condition of membership in their Connexion. 'From the time this evil was put away', says one of the preachers (*Methodist Magazine*, 1835, p. 167), 'the Societies prospered more abundantly.' Associations of the type indicated had spread into many districts, and Methodists were undoubtedly attracted by them.

Be that as it may, the Methodists were not indifferent to Trade Union activities. In many places they took a keen interest in them. As already indicated in the previous chapter, local preachers became leaders of the Miners' Unions and sometimes organized a cessation of work. They were not expelled from the Methodist Connexion on that account. They continued to retain their association with both. Dr. Rattenbury (*Wesley's Legacy to the World*, p. 227) admits that 'Methodists flocked to the flag of Trade Unionism without forsaking the flag of Methodism'. 'No body of people in England', he confesses, 'have been more conspicuous in their oneness with Labour aspirations and propaganda, than the Primitive Methodists.'

Unofficially and indirectly, Methodism became a powerful incentive to Trade Union activity. In its organization it presented an example of large-scale enterprise. Its connexional system gave supreme control to the central authority, while administration was relegated to districts, localities, and individual societies. On the administrative side a tremendously large number of posts were available for men and women of various standards of talent and intellect. The use of the lay agency, so favourably appraised by the Commissioner in the Religious Census of 1851, developed the abilities of an increasing number of people as the century advanced. Sometimes disreputable characters, coming under Methodist influence, had their lives transformed and finally became successful orators and useful citizens. Others, having been taught the art of organization in the Methodist community, showed great powers of administration and initiation. It was easy for these people to use their developed abilities in the improvement of their material circumstances and in the organization of Trade Unions. Innumerable ready-made agencies were in this manner provided by the Methodist movement. Some of the reformed characters remained in membership with the Methodist people, others for some reason or other separated and eventually devoted all their energies to the task of industrial improvement.

Evidence of Methodist influence in this direction is not entirely lost. The Home Office Papers bear witness to this fact. In the early part of the century, a Methodist named Wild is reported from Lancashire to be actively engaged in arranging for delegates to attend a workers' meeting in his district.[1] The Woolcombers Association had in 1801 been said to consist mostly of Dissenters, and when a National Union was formed in 1812, the adopted rules are said to be based on Scripture. Even the Divine sanction is claimed for their movement.[2] In 1818 the Weavers of Bolton decide 'that the most effectual means of attaining the object' they had in view would be 'by immediately dividing the Weaving neighbourhoods of Bolton and its vicinity, into classes'. They also agreed for each weaver 'to pay one penny per week to the head of his class in order to carry these resolutions into effect'. About the same time, Harrison, a Methodist preacher, preaches for the 'turn outs' in Manchester. Another man in Methodist fashion addresses the weavers 'with his Bible under his arm'.[3] In the Barnsley district, the Union Societies which were both political and economic are said to be identified 'with a Religious Sect called Kilhamites, or sort of Dissenters from Methodism'. They are charged with meeting together for the purpose of regulating wages.The Rev. F. Westmoreland, of Sandal Vicarage, Wakefield, reports similar activities in his neighbourhood. 'The greater part of the people called Methodists', he says, 'are united with the Radicals. They assemble in the evenings in certain cottages in the country under the pretence of religious worship. . . . At these meetings they form plans for advancing the wages of operative manufacturers by means of associations. Each of these meetings is under the direction of a class leader; and these class leaders assemble at stated periods to consult together and give directions to the whole association formed in the district.'[4] In 1824, the Society of United Fustian Cutters was formally organized because the system of reducing wages had been introduced by the masters. The sixth rule decided 'that the towns of Manchester and Salford

[1] H.O. 42. 62, 1801.
[2] *ibid.*, 42. 130, 1812.
[3] *ibid.*, 42. 179, 1818.
[4] *ibid.*, 42. 200, 1819.

be divided into districts, and that the members in each district be divided into classes, each class to consist of not less than twelve, nor more than twenty-four members; and to each district, or class, there shall be one collector, and that the members shall meet at a convenient house in their respective districts on the last Monday in every month, or oftener if required, for the purpose of appointing collectors and other officers that may be necessary; to inquire if the said officers duly perform their duty, and to examine the district accounts'. The next rule ordained 'that there shall be a collector for each district, and that every member (except females and apprentices) shall be liable to serve the office of collector for the district, or class in which he shall reside, and that the collectors shall be appointed monthly as their names shall successively appear on the list or class books'. It was further arranged that 'each collector shall call once a week upon the members of his class for their weekly payments'. 'The collectors shall also communicate to the members of their respective classes all such orders as the Committee, or representative of districts, may deem necessary for the immediate information of the trade.' 'And when any of the members shall remove, the collector shall inform the representative and district treasurer of such removal, and of the new place of residence of such members, respectively.' The tenth rule determines 'that when members change their place of residence, they shall acquaint the collectors of the class which they are leaving who shall give them certificates or transfers, on which shall be noted whether they are in arrears or not; and they shall acquaint the collectors of the classes to which they are transferred with their new place of residence within seven days after the time of their removing'. Members are to pay one penny per week towards the funds. Quarterly meetings have to be held and a governing committee is established, comprised of twelve elected representatives from the districts.[1] Many of the features of this organization are a replica of certain Methodist practices. At a later period the operatives of Rotherham got the loan of the New Connexion Methodist Chapel for the purpose of petitioning for the release of the five cotton spinners sentenced at Glasgow.[2] The religious aspect appears to be prominent in the Wood Sawyers Union, for in their lodge meetings they have hymns and prayers.[3] During the Weavers' turn out at Bacup in 1847,

[1] H.O. 40. 18, 1825. [2] *ibid.*, 40. 40, 1838. [3] *ibid.*, 45. OS. 40, 1841.

the strikers organize a Sunday camp meeting for the purpose of expounding their grievances.[1]

In the critical period of 1842, the Chartists and Trade Unionists at many places joined hands. Sometimes they were the same people trying first the political, then the Trade Union, and occasionally both methods to improve their condition. As the Chartist movement was infected by Methodist practices, it was impossible for the Trade Union movement to escape a similar infection. Some of the Methodist people were implicated in the 1842 disturbances, several of them being imprisoned for alleged participation. Though it is not so easy to identify the Methodist influence on the Industrial Trade Unions as one can do in regard to the Miners Trade Unions, the evidence that is available shows it to be, not a 'cross current', but an example and a spur to collective endeavour.

[1] *Northern Star*, Sept. 18, 1847.

CHAPTER III

THE AGRICULTURAL TRADE UNIONS

'THE years from 1814 to 1847 were gloomy years for agriculture.'[1] They were gloomier still for the agricultural labourer. During the Napoleonic Wars the price of cereals had greatly increased. The benefit of this increase had gone to the farmer, the tithe owner, and the landlord. The landed gentry got the most, while the farmer had the least. With this extra income, they could with ordinary prudence fortify themselves for the lean years that were sure to come. The labouring poor had no advantage of this sort. No unearned increment had come to them. As a matter of fact, part of their heritage had been taken away. While they were compelled to pay dearly for the common necessities of life, they lost, or were fast losing, their holding on the land. The rights and privileges which they had so long enjoyed, though undefined according to English Law, were by a conspiracy of the law rudely torn from their grasp. Enclosure 'assumed by the enlightened opinion of the day to be beneficial and progressive was more or less a gigantic disturbance'.[2] The Rev. Richard Jones, a Tithe Commissioner, reporting to the Committee on Enclosure in 1844 (*Parliamentary Papers*, Vol. v, P. 17), admitted that since 1800 'about 2,000 Inclosure Acts' had passed, 'and prior to that time, about 1,600 or 1,700 Inclosure Acts making something short of 4,000' had been sanctioned. He further admitted there were in the kingdom many parishes that consisted 'altogether of intermixed or commonable lands', while there were others which had 'a great intermixture of common land with the commonable and intermixed land'. He was astonished 'at the great extent of these intermixed and commonable lands'. Examples of this state of things could be found in Oxford, Berkshire, and Yorkshire. In certain areas every family had some sort of right on the land. For instance, at Walberswick, Suffolk, 'All persons belonging to the parish and residing therein'

[1] *History of English Agricultural Labourer*, Dr. W. Hasback, p. 242.
[2] *The Village Labourer*, J. L. & Barbara Hammond, p. 40.

were 'entitled to turn one head of stock on No. 1; and in the same parish can feed any number of stock or geese at all times on Nos. 2 and 3, and also cut turf or litter from off No. 3'. No. 1 piece of land consisted of over thirty-six acres and was described as the Town Marshes. No. 2, the Town Saltings, had over seventy-three acres. No. 3, called the Common possessed more than eighty-six acres.[1] Among the 6,000 inhabitants of Abingdon, every householder had a right connected with the land. In the parish of Newbury, there was a marsh measuring about fifteen acres upon which every inhabitant householder had 'the right to turn one horse, or two cows'.[2]

It was this system of common rights that Enclosures, mostly engineered by interested parties and sanctioned by Parliament, was gradually breaking up. In some instances, fierce resistance was shown by the common people. A case in point was found at Chinnor, Oxford, where it took several years to enforce the Enclosure Acts. The enraged commoners repeatedly pulled down the fences. At Nottingham, the people were 'very tenacious of the right', hoping by their resistance to get 'a greater share in the improved value of the land', and they resisted enclosure 'from year to year'.[3] In Cornwall, the 'commoners were never consulted', and one witness confessed that he assisted 'in pulling down the enclosures'. Naturally, 'there was a great deal of dissatisfaction in the neighbourhood upon the fact of enclosures'.[4] At Leicester, where the land was inclosed in 1803, and where some 3,000 freemen exercised certain customary rights, a piece of land to the extent of 140 acres was allotted to them in lieu of those rights.[5] Something similar was done in one or two instances for the poorer folk, but in the majority of cases, no provision whatever was made. Legislation and military force finally made enclosure a fact, and whether the common people willingly acquiesced or not, they were inevitably compelled to submit.

The village labourer therefore lost all his auxiliary resources. 'He was now a wage-earner and nothing more. Enclosure had robbed him of the strip that he tilled, of the cow that he kept

[1] Select Committee on Commons Inclosures. *Parliamentary Papers*, 1844, Vol. v, p. 60.
[2] *ibid.*, p. 308.
[3] *ibid.*, p. 224.
[4] *ibid.*, pp. 415–17.
[5] *ibid.*, p. 296.

on the village pasture, of the fuel that he picked up in the woods, and of the turf that he tore from the common.'[1] Being thus deprived of his ancient rights, and being compelled to rely on his labour for the maintenance of his wife and family, his condition became precarious. Although he lost his hold on the land by Enclosures, the Settlement Laws kept him bound to a particular parish. He was free to move from one parish to another under certain conditions, but in times of destitution he could be sent back to the place of his birth. His position was not improved by the enforcement of the Speenhamland system, which gave to the farmers cheap labour and to the labourers a paltry maintenance. Unhappily it made numerous wage-earners into miserable paupers. As a consequence, 'the Poor Law which had once been the hospital became now the prison of the poor. Designed to relieve his necessities, it was now his bondage'.[2] The cost to the parishes and the nation gradually rose each year until the amount reached a total of £8,000,000.

The rural poor—robbed of their ancient rights, fastened to the parish of their birth, held in bondage to the Poor Law system, dependent on wages implemented by relief for their sustenance, frightened into obedience to the landlord-made laws by the severity of the criminal code—could not by any stretch of the imagination be envied of their lot. From 1815 onwards the price of cereals fell somewhat, and the members of the Select Committee on Agriculture in 1833 (*Parliamentary Papers*, Vol. v, P. 7) expressed the view 'that the general condition of the Agricultural Labourer in full employment is better now than at any former period, his Money Wages giving him a greater command over the necessities and conveniences of life'. But the tragedy of the situation lay in the fact that the supply of labour in many districts was greater than the demand. One farmer admitted in his evidence that there were 'many able hands out of employment'. 'An increased abundance of hands,' and 'a decreased means of employing them', correctly described the conditions in many places. In Kent, 'a considerable surplus of labourers' was reported. One parish had fifteen to twenty out of work. The Committee apparently recognized the existence of this state of things and still believed 'that the agriculture of the Kingdom' was 'the first of all its concerns, the foundation of all its prosperity'.

[1] *The Village Labourer*, J. L. & Barbara Hammond, p. 106. [2] *ibid.*, p. 165.

They knew also that 'the produce of Great Britain' was 'in the average of years unequal to the consumption', and therefore in years of 'ordinary production partially dependent on the supply of wheat from Foreign Countries'. Nevertheless, they calmly and deliberately adopted a negative attitude by restating what Mr. Burke had once said, 'that it is a perilous thing to try experiments on the farmer'.[1] So the farmer was protected a few years longer, while experiments were tried on the labourers. The Poor Law system eventually was amended. In practice this brought a considerable saving of public money, but in reality it made a less demand on the pockets of the folk who had benefited through high prices and cheap labour.

Although the condition of the agricultural labourer might be officially described as 'better' in 1833 than any time before, the statement did not produce a feeling of jubilation among the common folk. They knew the real state of things. Ten years later, it was no consolation to be told that the wages in Wiltshire amounted to 8s. a week in winter and up to 10s. a week in summer. Whatever the wages were, their diet was very meagre. Their food, it appears, consisted of 'wheaten bread, potatoes, and a small quantity of beer, but only as a luxury, and a little butter or tea'. One woman asserted they rarely bought 'butchers fresh meat, certainly not oftener than once a week, and not more than sixpenny worth'. 'We could eat much more bread', she said, 'if we could get it.' Another witness declared 'our common drink' was nothing better than 'burnt crust tea'. 'We never know', she added, 'what it is to get enough to eat; at the end of the meal the children would always eat more.' A labourer from East Anglia confessed that the diet of his family consisted 'principally of bread and potatoes'. They never got any meat. At Dereham the usual diet for the wage earners was 'flour, potatoes, tea, meat, rarely'; in Tuttingham 'chiefly bread, some potatoes', while at Fakenham it was 'bread and swedish turnips'. A Dorset family was reported to be living on 16s. 6d. a week. There were eleven of them altogether and they lived in two rooms, each room having one window measuring fifteen square inches.[2] Three years later the wages in some parts amounted to no more than

[1] Select Committee on Agriculture. *Parliamentary Papers*, 1833, Vol. v, pp. 3–261.
[2] Report of the Poor Law Commissioners on the Employment of Women and Children in Agriculture, *Parliamentary Papers*, 1843, Vol. xii, pp. 13–242.

7s. a week.[1] In Lincolnshire and Yorkshire, the labourers were better off. On the whole the South was in a worse condition. Wages were usually higher in the North. According to Caird, wages of the Northern Labourers since 1770 had gone up 100 per cent, those of the Southern only 14 per cent. The number of paupers was in proportion of two to one, the South having the greater number.[2]

The condition of the rural labourers thus described demanded some kind of movement, not only to protect them from being the constant victim of economic depression, but also to improve their material position. The Government had failed to do this. From a kind of paternal interest in the rural poor they had gone over to an easy '*laissez faire*', a do-nothing attitude. It was too much to expect from human nature to think that landlords and tithe owners would voluntarily reduce their claims upon the returns of agriculture merely for the sake of improving or preserving the interests of their hired servants. No, the labourers must plan and work out their own salvation.

In view of these facts it might appear strange that no Trade Union movement was organized during the first half of the nineteenth century. An attempt, however, was made to establish a small union at Tolpuddle in Dorset, but it was immediately destroyed by the hostile attitude of Lord Melbourne. The failure to form a Trade Union among the agricultural labourers is mostly due to the fact that internally they were incompetent, and externally the opposition was too powerful. A Trade Union rightly understood is a piece of constructive machinery, and exists for constructive and not destructive purposes. In order to organize a movement of this kind, intelligent leadership is needed as well as courage and tenacity. Members of such a society must have facilities for fellowship and discussion. These conditions were absent in the life and circumstances of the rural workers. They had very little opportunity for fellowship. On the whole they were uneducated. They had to work in isolated places, and often had very little chance of contact. From early morn till late at night the daily round and common task required them. Hence they had practically no spare time for Trade Union activity. Yet it would not be true to say that the agricultural labourers were satisfied with their economic conditions.

[1] H.O. 45. OS. 1636, 1846. [2] Caird's *English Agriculture*, p. 513.

Indications of discontent can be seen at various times. In 1800 violent protests against the high price of food were made in many areas, and the Government had to institute an inquiry into the state of wheat crops. This was done through the medium of the bishops and the clergy.[1] Immediately after the conclusion of the Napoleonic Wars a depression of trade and industry began. So depressed became the state of things that the Annual Register confessed that 'peace was scarcely welcomed. . . . The triumphant sensations of national glory seem almost obliterated by general depression'.[2] The increase of poverty naturally gave birth to a furious discontent. As a result riots broke out during the year 1816 in Norfolk, Suffolk, Huntingdon, Cambridge and other places.[3] Many acts of violence were committed upon bakers, butchers, millers, and other dealers in the first necessities of life.[4] Threshing machines, mole ploughs, and mills were also destroyed, while 'houses, barns, and ricks were set on fire'.[5] The Rev. Edwards of Ashill, near Watton, is told in a threatening letter what the rioters believed to be the cause of their poverty. 'You do as you like', says the unknown writer. 'You rob the poor of their Commons Right, plough the grass up that God sent to grow, that a poor man may not feed a cow, a pig, horse, nor ass.'[6] The riots at Downham in Norfolk originated through a sudden rise in the price of flour.[7] Those at Ely were more disastrous.

Though the disturbances of 1830 have been aptly described as 'The Labourer's Last Revolt', the agrarian movement did not break up at that time. It only changed its tactics. Three years later it appeared in the garb of a Trade Union, but the political cloak appeared more attractive. Disappointed with the provisions in the Reform Bill of 1832, the working classes in the country joined the artisans of the towns in forming political unions. Although the immediate object of these societies was to extend the franchise and to reform Parliament, the final object was the relief of their unnecessary sufferings. In 1838 Working Men's Associations were reported in Dorset, missionaries being sent to

[1] H.O. 42. 49 & 55, 1800.
[2] *Annual Register*, 1815, p. 144.
[3] *ibid.*, 1816, *General History*, p. 93. *Chronicle*, pp. 64–74, 190–191.
[4] Cobbett's *Political Register*, Aug. 8, 1817, p. 548.
[5] *The Village Labourer*, J. L. & B. Hammond, p. 177.
[6] H.O. 42. 150, 1816.
[7] *ibid.*, 42. 151, 1816.

Tolpuddle. George Loveless, the pardoned convict, is elected to the National Convention as a representative for Dorset.[1] The Rev. W. P. Spencer, J.P., from Norfolk, informs the Home Office that 'a spirit of discontent and insubordination is fast spreading among the labouring classes in Harleston, and the surrounding villages, and the Chartist Association which has been formed is daily increasing in numbers'. He wants two of the Metropolitan Police to assist him in keeping the peace.[2] About the same time the Chartists are reported to be in the Warminster district.[3]

The agrarian movement in the late forties once more adopts the method of violence. In the parish of Axminster the workers' wages are said to average about 7*s.* a week, and the magistrates with a certain amount of understanding admit that this rate 'was inadequate to the support of a Labourer's family'. So they suggest 'that the Churchwardens and Overseers, shall set to work all persons married or unmarried having no means to maintain them'.[4] It was this condition of things that caused 'a considerable degree of discontent, and some disposition to insubordination' in Somerset during 1847. On May 19, in the same year, great alarm prevails at Bridgwater because of 'the necessities of the poor in consequence of the high price of provisions'. Instead of relieving the distress of the poor, special constables are appointed. Disturbances occur in Taunton, window smashing takes place at Shepton Mallet, and mob demonstrations are held at Wells.[5] Food riots break out at Cullompton, Honiton, Exeter, Exmouth, Axminster, Torquay, and Tiverton, but Providence instead of the economic mismanagement is blamed for the distress. The trouble spreads further West, and riots occur at Callington, Tavistock, Camelford, Holsworthy, and Launceston.[6] With the beginning of better times in 1849 discontent becomes less violent. In later days the agrarian movement adopts a more constructive policy when the Agricultural Trades Union is formed in 1872.

The influence of Methodism on the agrarian movements in general and on the Agricultural Unions in particular is very difficult to define. To a certain extent Methodism had neglected the country areas. It had always been the policy of the Methodist missionaries to go to the places where there were no spiritual

[1] H.O. 40. 36, 1838.
[2] *ibid.*, 40. 46, 1839.
[3] *ibid.*, 40. 48, 1839.
[4] *ibid.*, 45. OS. 1636, 1846.
[5] *ibid.*, 45. OS. 1796, 1847.
[6] *ibid.*, 45. OS. 1799 & 1801, 1847.

shepherds, and that meant to the towns mostly. The villages in many cases, until the advent of the Primitive Methodists, had been left entirely to the care of the Anglican clergy. As late as 1830 many of the agricultural areas could be correctly described as a 'Methodist wilderness'. For example, according to the returns published in 1824, the proportion of Methodists to the population in Berkshire was 1 in 111, Wiltshire 1 in 115, Hereford 1 in 119, Westmorland 1 in 121, Warwick 1 in 130, Buckinghamshire 1 in 134, Hampshire 1 in 143, Suffolk 1 in 151, Middlesex 1 in 152, Essex 1 in 189, Sussex 1 in 211, Surrey 1 in 249, and none in Rutland.[1] It may be just a coincidence, but it ought to be noted, that in several of these counties the agrarian movement adopted the method of violence in 1830. As already seen, the Methodist leaders were usually on the side of law, peace, and order. The violence of the riots in 1830 may have been partly due to the absence in the villages of a disciplinary movement like that provided by Methodism. In the counties where Methodism counted a bigger proportion of the population no disturbances of any note took place. Lincolnshire, for example, which was adjacent to Norfolk showed no sympathy for violence. In this county Methodism counted 1 in every 23 of the population. Cornwall averaged 1 in 27, Derby and Durham 1 in every 34, Staffordshire 1 in every 35, and Leicestershire 1 in every 40 of the population. Nottinghamshire had the same proportion as Leicestershire.[2] In none of these counties was there much violence shown by any of the rural labourers, though slight disturbances took place in Cornwall during 1847.

These facts may be accidental, but they must be taken into conjunction with other considerations. After 1820, and more especially after 1830, all the various sections of Methodism began to invade the rural areas, and in many cases came into conflict with the Anglican clergy. The Primitive Methodists entered into Wiltshire, Berkshire, and Norfolk. They spread very rapidly for a time in Norfolk and Wiltshire. In some of the villages fierce opposition was encountered, chiefly stirred up by the clergy and their supporters. The Bible Christians concentrated on Devon, Cornwall, and Kent, while the Wesleyans became more active in most of the counties. The other sects followed the same policy. The final result was to be seen in the existence of a Methodist

[1] *Annual Register*, 1824, *Chronicle*, Vol. lxvi, p. 180.

[2] *ibid.*, p. 180.

society in most of the villages by the middle of the century. In practically every case the formation of a village Methodist society meant the organization of a body of people independent of the squire, parson, and landlord. As a rule the advent of Methodism meant the end, or the beginning of the end, of the paramount influence of these sections of the nobility in the rural districts. The Methodists taught the labourers that they were precious in the sight of God, and that they had a soul to save and maintain equally with the richest in the land. In the Methodist society and at the communion altar, all were equal in the sight of Providence. At the class meeting, a special kind of fraternity was formed, and each member was encouraged to be frank and honest with the rest. His individual talents of speech and service were inspired by fellowship and opportunity. He was offered responsibility and office. He might become a class leader, a prayer leader, a steward, a local preacher and even a trustee of his place of worship. He thus became an administrator of Methodist law and property. He could exercise his vote in the Leaders' Meeting, in the Society Meeting, perhaps in the Trustees' Meeting, and maybe in the Preachers' Meeting and the Quarterly Meeting. All this opportunity and trust was offered to the poorest of the poor. Hence it happened that years before he was entrusted with the political vote he was offered in various ways the religious franchise. The effect upon his mind and personality must have been considerable. His outlook upon life and society was equally affected. The results were various with different individuals. Some became restless in their cramped material environment. Many endeavoured to be indifferent to it. Others tried to change or improve it. A village could no longer be the same after an independent society had been established. Short-time as well as long-time results were bound to follow.

How many Methodists took part in the agrarian movements it is impossible to say. No evidence appears to be available. There are signs that in Norfolk the Primitive Methodists opposed the violence of the agitated labourers. 'While the misguided emissaries of Capt. Swing were burning down farmsteads and destroying machinery, Robert Key and his coadjutors were among them, practically doing national police duty, and doing it without pay or recognition, and what is more, they often accomplished by their village evangelism what patrols and magistrates were unable to effect.'[1] Sometimes 'the whole character of a country parish has been changed for the better by the effects of these rustic missionaries'.[2]

The long-time results can be seen in the gradual development of a sturdy village independency. The emancipation of the rural population from the dominance of the landed gentry and the clergy had of necessity to come gradually. The least that can be said about Methodism is that it either began, or it co-operated with others in that work. Methodists did many things in the villages. They built a separate place of worship. They organized a separate religious community. They developed a communal and an individual life that remained outside the direct control of the clergyman and squire. In these ways they aided the labourer's march to freedom.

Evidence of that result is not entirely lost. The attempt of the Tolpuddle Labourers to form a Trade Union is a case in point. On January 30, 1834, James Frampton, a local magistrate, informs Lord Digby that 'nightly meetings have been for some time held by Agricultural Labourers in the parishes of Tolpuddle and Bere Regis—where Societies . . . or Unions are formed'. He consults his fellow justices and on their advice informs Lord Melbourne, the Home Secretary, 'that Societies are forming amongst the Agricultural Labourers in parts of these Divisions, in which the Labourers are induced to enter into combinations of a dangerous and alarming kind'. He reports that 'trusty persons in the neighbourhood' have been asked 'to trace the proceedings and identify the parties'. Lord Melbourne replies next day to say 'that the magistrates have acted wisely in employing trusty persons to endeavour to obtain information respecting the unlawful combinations'. His Lordship directs their attention to Section 25 of the 57 Geo. 3rd C19, but does not think it necessary 'to refer to the Statutable provisions relative to the administration of Secret Oaths'. Lord Digby replies to Frampton on February 5, and expresses the hope that 'the Secretary of State may enable you to stop the mischief'. Frampton sends another letter to Lord Digby on February 4, and states his belief that the Act of Parliament to which the Secretary of State refers 'certainly meets the case of these Combinations if we can but get sufficient information to enable us to act'.

[1] *History of the Primitive Methodist Church*, H. B. Kendall, Vol. ii, p. 241.
[2] *Six Centuries of Work and Wages*, T. Rogers, p. 516.

From the further correspondence it appears that the spies got to work. Several of the unionists were committed for trial. Lord Melbourne assents to the decision and advises the necessity of seeking further information in readiness for the Assizes. Six of the leaders had been arrested, and Frampton believed that he had sufficient 'information on Oath against some of the persons'. Notwithstanding the arrests, the unions continue their activity, and Lord Melbourne on March 3 expresses regret at this. He also requests that the depositions against the prisoners should be sent to him. Two days later Frampton forwards the necessary information and reports that meetings are held twice a week 'in the house of this George Romaine who I am told is a Methodist Preacher as are the two Lovelesses'. The magistrate assures his Lordship that the said house is watched by faithful guards. On March 6, Frampton asks Lord Digby 'how to proceed in discharging from their employ such labourers as are known to have joined the Union; as it would be extremely hard if the Secretary of State should throw all the responsibility of such a proceeding on the Justices'. On March 10, Lord Melbourne informs Mr. Frampton of 'his entire approbation of the course which you have pursued in committing the Individuals accused of administering unlawful Oaths for trial at the ensuing Assizes'.

The six men were eventually tried and received sentence of transportation for seven years. A storm of indignation among the working classes swept throughout the country. On March 27, Lord Melbourne asks the magistrate for the 'names, ages, callings, character, and habits of the Individuals in question, together with any other circumstances which may appear to you to be of importance'. His Lordship required this information for Parliamentary purposes. Frampton gladly sends him the desired material, making sure that he blackens the character of the men who had no chance of defending themselves. James Loveless, he says, has a wife and two children. 'He is a Methodist Preacher and was very active in the Riots in the winter of 1830.' George Loveless, aged thirty-seven, has a wife and three children. 'He is a Methodist Preacher.' 'He was the first person who set the Union on foot in this neighbourhood. He was also very active in the Riots of 1830.' Thomas Stanfield, aged forty-four, 'is brother-in-law of Loveless, and his son, Thomas, belonged to the union. He has a wife and three children. He is the owner of the house in Tolpuddle where the meetings of the union were held and also of the Methodist meeting house there, where he preaches occasionally. He is a labourer and a discontented man, and if any disturbance is going on, he is sure to be in it'. 'John Stanfield, aged twenty-one.' He is a 'son of the above, a Methodist, a single man, very saucy and ready for any disturbance'. 'James Hammet, aged twenty-two. A labourer—wife and one child. He was convicted of Felony in Stealing Iron at the Easter Sessions in 1829 and Sentenced to Four Months' Imprisonment with hard labour, always a very idle man and ready for mischief.' 'James Brine, aged twenty, a single man, a labourer, was about seventeen years of age at the time of the riots in 1830 when he behaved well and tried to keep out of them; but since that time has become very idle and kept company with James Hammet.' 'I ought to add that no doubt is entertained in this neighbourhood that the six men in question were the ringleaders of the whole; assisted very much afterwards by Romaine and others at Bere Regis. Romaine is a Methodist Preacher and owner of a meeting house at Bere Heath.'

Lord Melbourne was not quite satisfied with some of the statements in this report, so he wrote to Frampton on March 31, asking to be acquainted 'with the grounds on which it was stated that James and George Loveless were active in the Riots of 1830'. The only evidence that the magistrate could give was taken from 'a very respectable Farmer of the Parish of Tolpuddle'. This man apparently 'had recognized in the darkness the voice of George Loveless'. Lord Melbourne also desired evidence concerning the conviction of James Hammet for stealing, but no reply is found among the correspondence. The Home Secretary was no doubt greatly influenced by this uncorroborated information. When an urgent demand was made both in and out of Parliament for the release of the prisoners, he adopted for a long while an unbending attitude. Such was the insistence, however, for the unconditional pardon of these penalized Trade Unionists, that his Lordship was ultimately though reluctantly compelled to yield. All the men were brought home after serving approximately half of their sentence.

The apparent purpose of the conviction of these humble Trade Unionists is gathered from a letter to Lord Howick who had succeeded Lord Melbourne at the Home Office. Frampton in his letter admits that he and 'the other Justices . . . refused to order any parochial relief to the Wives and families of those convicts'. Two reasons were given for this callous attitude. The magistrates contended that the wives had supplied the prisoners with more food than they could eat while in gaol, the assumption being that the women were not in need. Another reason was because the leaders of the Union had promised to maintain all their families 'for so long a time as they were thrown out of work and deprived of their earnings and that therefore they ought to apply to these Leaders and require them to keep their promise. Our object in doing this was to prove to the Labourers that the Leaders of the Unions had deceived them if they did not support their families'.

This respectable magistrate supported by his fellow justices, 'directed the overseer not to allow any Parochial Relief to any persons *whose names appeared in the book which was proved at the Trial of the six men to contain a list of those who had taken the illegal Oath and had joined the Union*'. They did this for the reasons already named and because they concluded 'that no person could be considered entitled to receive Parochial Relief who could afford to pay a shilling on entering and a penny a week afterwards to the support of the Unions'. The same magistrates 'particularly recommended to the Farmers (who have expressed themselves most willing to follow our advice) that every encouragement should be given to those Labourers who did not join the Union by increasing their wages and placing them in all the most profitable work, so that they may feel the advantage of their good conduct, by making a marked difference between them and the Unionists; and on no account at present to make any addition to the wages of the latter'.[1]

This severe treatment of union members at Tolpuddle served its purpose for a time. Trade Unionism among agricultural labourers was destroyed in its infancy. The movement, however, received a fillip elsewhere. Stirred by disgust at Lord Melbourne and his supporters, working men in different parts of the country came together and expressed their discontent. They not only demanded the release of Loveless and his companions, but they supported the grief-stricken families and prepared for the reunion.

[1] Additional MSS. 41567L. Frampton-Melbourne Correspondence, British Museum.

George Loveless returned to England in June, 1837. Four of his companions arrived on March 17, 1838, but the other was delayed a few months longer. The London Committee which had been acting on behalf of the 'Dorset Labourers', decided to spend £1,200 to provide the liberated men with farms of their own. In 1839 the two Lovelesses and James Brine were in possession of the farms provided by this committee, having settled near Chipping Ongar, Essex. The two Stanfields had a farm in Harlow, but were in difficulties though £100 had been granted to each.[1]

Methodism cannot escape some share of the responsibility for the conduct that brought these men to prison and transportation. For several years they had been subject to its discipline and guidance. Its influence upon them may be seen by the place they occupied in its communion. Five of them were members, while three of them occupied the position of local preachers. Some of their companions, who escaped imprisonment, belonged to the same religious persuasion. George Romaine, the secretary of the Tolpuddle Trade Union, was the proprietor of a Methodist meeting house and a local preacher. Contact with the Methodist principles and practices such as these men experienced would naturally arouse their suppressed mental and moral powers. It would likewise quicken their sense of right and justice. It would give them a passionate desire for self-improvement, and it would make a prudent provision for the well-being of dependants appear to be a religious necessity. Trade Union action to such people could not be conceived as a crime, but rather as an imperative duty.

What Methodism did for other rural workers is not so clearly indicated. Nevertheless, it is no exaggeration to say that it taught the art of organizing, the worth of corporate action, and the joy of fellowship. Among the pioneers of Trade Unionism in East Anglia many were Methodist adherents and some were local preachers. Joseph Arch is an example of Methodist influence in the Midlands. Born in 1837, he became a Methodist and learnt among other things the skill of organizing men and moving them to action by his oratory. When he formed the Agricultural Labourers Union, 'half the speakers' at the Leamington Congress

[1] Place MSS. 27821, p. 360. Also *Northern Star*, March 31, May 5, and June 9, 1838.

in 1872 'were preachers of various denominations'. During the sessions 'the members were continually addressed as "my Christian friends", "beloved brethren" or "dear fellow Christians" in a manner suggestive rather of a Church than a social congress'.[1]

Although the Agricultural Trade Unions were ostensibly seeking a material benediction, the religious element was not absent. In motive power and organization, in idea and enthusiasm it was constantly expressed. The influence of Methodism can be seen in these respects. It also provided a discipline and a dynamic.

[1] *History of the English Agricultural Labourer*, Dr. W. Hasback, p. 278.

CONCLUSION

VIEWED from the religious standpoint, Methodism in the first half of the nineteenth century can be described as a very popular movement among the working classes of this country. That is one of the conclusions to be derived from a study of the available material. Taking the data of numbers alone the conclusion is inevitable. In spite of conflict and division within, together with opposition from various sources without, the registered members of 1850 were six times greater than in 1800. No other movement at the time showed such a continuous success. While it had practically no effect upon the upper portions of the community, its influence on the lower sections was almost phenomenal.

Another conclusion about which one can be certain is the main cause of its popularity. It captured the affections of the common people because of its religious appeal. Through its agency a panacea for all their troubles was gratuitously offered them, and they accepted it with whole-hearted enthusiasm. Having won so many by its religious appeal, it retained and utilized the majority of them by its collective and democratic customs. By offering opportunities for service it created a sense of individual and communal responsibility. That sense of accountability was never lost while the members had a share in the enterprise. Methodism indeed was much more a layman's movement than a minister's. The Wesleyan preachers might endeavour to appropriate to themselves all the power of legislation and administration, but in the long run they had to yield to the growing demands of the democratic elements within their borders.

Looked at from the sociological standpoint, Methodism presented a clear example of a dualistic tendency. On the one hand it emphasized the importance of the individual, and on the other it illustrated the utility of the collective enterprise. According to John Wesley's teaching, the individual and not society was accountable to the Divine Lord for the way in which personal powers and talents were used. No arbitrary or natural grouping of individuals into a community could obliterate that personal sense of responsibility. In that way Methodism may be described as an individualistic movement. But it was also social. John Wesley stoutly maintained that the religion which he propagated was a social religion. He would have nothing to do with the monastic type of religious exercises. In harmony with this view he organized his followers into groups, and called them classes. He formed the classes into societies, and the societies into circuits, which in turn were made into districts. All the districts were made into one whole and called the 'Connexion'. Methodism thus became a collective movement. Although John Wesley might be regarded by many as 'a benevolent autocrat', his greatest achievement was in the realm of collective activity. He taught his disciples the art of working together. Long before the days of industrial and political collectivity, Methodism developed a highly successful type of religious collectivism. The success becomes all the more astounding when the nature of human material to be utilized is truly visualized. Before the majority of the Methodist recruits could be used in a collective capacity they had to learn discipline, self-control, and even self-sacrifice.

A similar dualism is detected when the movement is regarded from the political standpoint. All the writers of Methodist history readily recognize the autocratic features of John Wesley's system. The Wesleyan Conference was exceedingly authoritative. By its pronouncements on politics it has rightly earned the name of 'reactionary' and 'conservative'. While the extent of its Tory influence may be over-estimated both by its friends and critics, one ought to remember that it did not always speak for the whole of Methodism. It did not represent the democratic elements inside Wesleyanism. Neither did it represent the democratic sections of the other Methodist sects. These sects could not belie their origin. They were formed on democratic principles, and as their numbers increased a religious democracy developed. Let it be said quite clearly that during our period the democratic elements were always more potent than the autocratic. This factor, associated with the religious appeal, attracted and retained within the Methodist borders large sections of the working-class community. Although Methodism always remained a religious movement, its influence could not be confined to the narrow limits created by its leading preachers. It went beyond the artificial restrictions and filtered to the industrial and political activities of its members. When no other example of collective endeavour presented itself to the working classes, Methodism became a pattern and parent for their democratic exercises and idealism. The Methodist leaders had planned otherwise. But the foolishness of some provideth wisdom for the many.

BIBLIOGRAPHY

Arch, Joseph.
The Story of his Life (London, 1898).
Arthur, William.
The Successful Merchant, Sketches of the Life of Samuel Budgett (London, 1852).
Ashworth, Jesse.
A Biography of Hugh Bourne (1888).
Barker, Joseph.
The Life of Joseph Barker (London, 1870).
Beaumont, Joseph.
The Life of the Rev. Joseph Beaumont, M.D. (London, 1856).
Beech, John H.
The Good Soldier, The Life Labours and Character of the Rev. Hugh Beech (London, 1856). *Outer Life of a Methodist Preacher* (London, 1884).
Begbie, Harold.
Life of William Booth. 2 Vols. (London, 1920).
Best, Mary Agnes.
Thomas Paine, Prophet and Martyr of Democracy (London, 1927).
Blanshard, Thomas W.
The Life of Samuel Bradburn (London, 1870).
Bourne, F. W.
A Memoir of Billy Bray or The King's Son (London, 1871). *The Life of James Thorne of Shebbear* (London, 1893).
Bowes, John.
Autobiography of the Life of John Bowes (Glasgow, 1872).
Brailsford, E. J.
Richard Watson, Theologian and Missionary Advocate (London).
Bruce, William N.
The Life of General Sir Charles Napier (London, 1885).
Bunting, Thomas P.
The Life of Jabez Bunting. 2 Vols. (1859).
Burdekin, Richard.
Memoirs of Robert Spence of York (York, 1827).
Carlyle, E. I.
William Cobbett, A Study of His Life as shown in His Writings (1904)
Cartwright, Frances D.
Life and Correspondence of Major Cartwright. 2 Vols. (1826).
Carvosso, William.
A Memoir of William Carvosso, Sixty Years a Class Leader in the Wesleyan Methodist Connexion. 2nd Ed. (London, 1836).
Clowes, William.
Journals of William Clowes (1844).
Cole, George D. H.
Robert Owen (London, 1925).
Cooper, Thomas.
The Life of Thomas Cooper (1879).
Corderoy, Edward.
Father Reeves, the Methodist Class Leader (London, 1853).
Coulson, John E.
The Peasant Preacher, Memorials of Charles Richardson, the Lincolnshire Thrasher. 2nd Ed. (London, 1866).
Croft, W. R.
Oastler and His Times (Huddersfield, 1888).

Dictionary of N.B.
John Fielden.
Dixon, Joseph.
A Memoir of Thomas Dixon of Grantham (London, 1871).
Dunckley, Henry.
Bamford's Passages in the Life of a Radical (London, 1893).
Edwards, Maldwyn.
John Wesley (London, 1933).
Entwisle, Joseph.
Memoir of the Rev. Joseph Entwisle (Bristol, 1848).
Etheridge, J. W.
The Life of the Rev. Thomas Coke (London, 1860). *The Life of the Rev. Adam Clarke* (London, 1858).
Everett, James.
The Wall's End Miner, or a Brief Memoir of William Crister (Newcastle, 1835).
Memoirs of the Life, Character, and Ministry of William Dawson (London, 1842).
The Village Blacksmith in a Memoir of the Life of Samuel Hick (London, 1845).
Fowler, Edith H.
The Life of Henry Hartley Fowler, First Viscount of Wolverhampton (London, 1912).
Forester, Matthew.
Miller Manning, or a Story of Cornish Life (London, 1881).
French, A. J.
The Life of John Birchenall (London, 1881).
Gregory, Benjamin.
The Thorough Business Man, Memoirs of Walter Powell (London, 1871). *From Cobbler's Bench to President's Chair, Samuel Bradburn* (London, 1895). *Autobiographical Recollections* (London, 1903).
Hardy, R. Spence.
Commerce and Christianity, Memorials of Jonas Sugden of Oakworth House (London, 1858).
Herod, G.
Biographical Sketches (No date).
Hodder, Edwin.
The Life and Work of the Seventh Earl of Shaftesbury (1887).
Holyoake, George J.
Life of Joseph Rayner Stephens, Preacher and Political Orator (1881).
Huish, Robert.
The History of the Private and Political Life of Henry Hunt, M.P. 2 Vols. (London, 1836).
Hunt, Henry.
Memoirs of Henry Hunt. 3 Vols. (London, 1820).
Jackson, Thomas.
Recollections of my own Life and Times (London, 1873). *The Life of the Rev. Robert Newton* (London, 1855).
Jewell, F.
Little Abe, or the Bishop of Berry Brow, being the Life of Abraham Lockwood (London, 1880).
Jones, Lloyd.
Life and Times of Robert Owen (London, 1895).
Kirkham, William.
Memorials of Thomas Crouch Hincksman of Lytham, Lancashire (London, 1885).
Lackington, James.
The Confession of James Lackington (London, 1804).
Longden, Henry.
The Life of Henry Longden, compiled from his Memoirs (Liverpool, 1813).
Luke, W. B.
Memorials of Frederick William Bourne (London, 1906).
Lovett, William.
The Life and Struggles of William Lovett (1876).

Lowe, T.
Memorials of the Rev. Robert Key (1881).
Lunn, Arnold.
John Wesley (1929).
Macdonald, James A.
Memorials of Mrs. M. A. C. Treffry of Maidenhead (London, 1866).
Mackintosh, Robert J.
Memoirs of the Life of Sir James Mackintosh. 2 Vols. (1835).
Maunder, George.
Eminent Christian Philanthropists, Brief Biographical Sketches (London, 1853).
McAllum, Daniel.
Memorials of the Life, Character, and Death of the Rev. H. Taft, M.D. (Newcastle, 1824).
Meech, Thomas Cox.
From Mine to Ministry, Life Story of the Right Hon. Thomas Burt, M.P. (Darlington, 1908).
Mitchell, William J.
Brief Biographical Sketches of Bible Christian Ministers and Laymen. 2 Vols. (Jersey, 1906).
Napier, Sir W.
The Life and Opinions of General Sir Charles James Napier. 4 Vols. (London, 1857).
Plummer, Robert.
The Successful Class Leader Exemplified in a Memorial of Mr. Benjamin Pollard (London, 1861).
Rattenbury, J. Ernest.
Wesley's Legacy to the World (London, 1928).
Richard, Henry.
Memoirs of Joseph Sturge (London, 1864).
Richmond, Legh.
The Dairyman's Daughter (London, 1814).
Rigg, James H.
Wesleyan Methodist Reminiscences, Sixty Years Ago (London, 1904).
Romilly, Samuel.
Memoirs of the Life of Sir Samuel Romilly. 3 Vols. (London, 1840).
Sadler, Michael T.
Memoirs of the Life and Writings of Michael Thomas Sadler (1842).
Shrewsbury, John V. B.
Memorials of the Rev. William J. Shrewsbury (London, 1868).
Sidney, Edwin.
Life of the Rev. Samuel Walker. 2nd Ed. (1838).
Simon, John S.
John Wesley and the Religious Societies (London, 1921). *John Wesley and the Methodist Societies* (London, 1923). *John Wesley and the Advance of Methodism* (London, 1925). *John Wesley the Master Builder* (London, 1927). *John Wesley, last Phase* (London, 1934).
Stacey, J.
A Prince of Israel, or Sketches of the Life of John Ridgeway (London, 1862).
Starr, R. W.
Life of the Rev. Peter Mackenzie (Leeds, 1896).
Steele, A.
Christianity in Earnest as Exemplified in the Life and Labours of the Rev. Hodgson Casson (London, 1853).
Stevenson, George J.
Methodist Worthies. 6 Vols. (London, 1884).
Taylor, John.
Reminiscences of Isaac Marsden (London, 1892).
Townsend, James S.
Reminiscences and Memorials (London, 1891).
Tracts Biographical.
The Life of Henry Hetherington. Abridged from the Eloge (London, 1841).

Treffry, Richard.
Memorials of the Rev. Joseph Benson (London, 1840).
Tyerman, Luke.
The Life and Times of John Wesley. 3 Vols. (London, 1870).
Walford, J.
Memoirs of Hugh Bourne (1857).
Walker, T. H.
Providence Row or The Successful Collier (London. No date).
Wallas, Graham.
The Life of Francis Place (London, 1918).
Watson, Richard.
A Sermon on the Death of Joseph Butterworth (London, 1826).
Watson, Aaron.
A Great Labour Leader, being the Life of the Right Hon. Thomas Burt, M.P. (London, 1908). *Thomas Burt, M.P., D.C.L., Pitman and Privy Councillor* (London, 1924).
Wesley, John.
Journal of John Wesley (Everyman Ed., London, 1921).
Whitehead, J.
Life of Wesley, with Life of Charles. 2 Vols. (London, 1805).
Wilberforce, R. I. and S.
Life of William Wilberforce. 5 Vols. (London, 1838).
Wilson, John.
Autobiography of Ald. John Wilson, J.P., M.P. (1909).
Wesleyan Preacher.
The Life of Adam Clarke, LL.D. (London, 1858).
West, Francis H.
Memorials of the Rev. Francis A. West (London, 1873).
Wood, Thomas.
A Biographical Sketch of the Life and Character of Mr. James Bundy (Bristol).
Woodcock, Henry.
The History of John Ellerthorpe. 2nd Ed. (London, 1880).

HISTORY

Allen, Richard. *History of Methodism in Preston and its Vicinity* (Preston, 1866).
Barratt, George. *Recollections of Methodism and Methodists in the City of Lincoln* (Lincoln, 1866).
Bebb, E. D. *Nonconformity and Social and Economic Life*, 1600–1800 (London, 1935).
Bretherton, Francis F. *Early Methodism in and around Chester* (Chester, 1903).
Brigden, Thos. E. *The Old Leek Sunday School, A Centenary Record* (Leek, 1897).
Caine, Caesar. *History of Wesleyan Methodism in the Crewe Circuit* (Crewe, 1883). *A Brief Chronicle of Wesleyan Methodism in Leyton*, 1750–1895 (Leyton, 1896).
Chick, Elijah. *A History of Methodism in Exeter and the Neighbourhood*, 1739–1907 (London, 1907).
Cole, G. D. H. *A Short History of the British Working Class Movement.* Vol. I, 1789–1848 (London, 1925–27).
Cooke, W., and Others. *The Jubilee of the Methodist New Connexion* (London, 1848).
Cornish, Francis W. *A History of the English Church in the Nineteenth Century* (1910).
Cotterell, Hannah. *Gate Pike, The Story of 80 Years of Methodism*, 1843–1923 (Bolton, 1924).
Court, Lewis H. *The Romance of a Country Circuit, Sketches of Village Methodism* (London, 1924).
Dyson, J. B. *History of Wesleyan Methodism in the Congleton Circuit* (London, 1856). *Methodism in the Isle of Wight* (Ventnor, 1865).
Eayrs, G. *A Short History of the United Methodist Church* (1913).
Edwards, Maldwyn. *After Wesley*, 1791–1849 (London, 1935).

MISCELLANEOUS

An Old Potter. *When I was a Child* (London, 1903).
Benbow, William. *Grand National Holiday of the Productive Classes* (London, 1832). *The Crimes of the Clergy, or the Pillars of Priestcraft Shaken* (London, 1823).
Caird, J. *English Agriculture in* 1850–1851.
Cole, G. D. H. *Cobbett's Rural Rides.* 3 Vols. (1930). *Social Theory* (1920).
Cooke, William. *The Lay Ministry* (London, 1858).
Darvall, F. O. *Popular Disturbances and Public Order in Regency England* (London, 1934).
Davis, Carless, H. W. *The Age of Grey and Peel* (Oxford, 1929).
Dicey, A. V. *Law and Opinion* (1914).
Engles, F. *Condition of the Working Classes,* 1844 (1845).
Fielden, John. *The Curse of the Factory System* (London, 1836).
Figgis, John N. *The Churches in the Modern State* (Glasgow, 1913).
Gibbons, H. de B. *English Social Reformers* (London, 1902).
Green, Richard. *Anti-Methodist Publications* (1902).
Grindrod, E. *A Compendium of Laws and Regulations of Wesleyan Methodism* (London, 1842).
Hobhouse, L. T. *Social Development. Its Nature and Conditions* (1924).
Kirkham, G. B. *Philanthropy and the State or Social Politics* (1908).
Luke, William. *The Village Chapel* (London, 1877).
Methodist New Connexion Minutes. 1843–1850.
Mullins, Edward. *The Magistracy of England.* 2nd Ed. (London, 1836).
Needham, R. *Religion in its Relation to Commerce and the Ordinary Associations of Life* (London, 1852).
North, Eric M. *Early Methodist Philanthropy* (New York, 1914).
Parkinson, G. *True Stories of Durham Pit Life* (London, 1912).
Pease, Howard. *Borderland Studies* (London, 1893).
Peirce, William. *The Ecclesiastical Principles and Polity of the Wesleyan Methodists.* 3rd Ed. (London, 1873).
Plummer, A. *The General Strike During One Hundred Years* (Article in *Economic Journal,* Sup. May, 1927).
Primitive Methodist Conference Minutes (1820–1850).
Prothero, R. E. *English Farming* (London, 1926).
Simon, John S. *A Summary of Methodist Law and Discipline* (1924).
Smith, Robert. *Rules, Regulations, and Reports of the Primitive Methodist Itinerant Preachers' Friendly Society.* 2 Vols. 1823–1850 (Leeds, 1854).
Taylor, Cooke W. *Notes of a Tour in the Manufacturing Districts of Lancashire.* 2nd Ed. (London, 1842).
Urwick, Edward J. *The Social Good* (1927).
Veitch, George G. *Genesis of Parliamentary Reform* (London, 1913).
Wallace, T. *British Slavery. Duty of Abolishing the Late Hour System* (1850).
Warner, Richard. *A Tour through Cornwall in the Autumn of* 1808 (Bath, 1809).
Warner, W. J. *The Wesleyan Movement and the Industrial Revolution* (London, 1930).
Wesley, John. *Fifty-Three Sermons* (London).
Wesley, John. *The Works of John Wesley* (London).
Wesleyan Conference Minutes, 1744–1850 (London).

MSS.

Frampton-Melbourne Correspondence, 1834. Additional MSS. 41567L at British Museum.
Holborn Collection (Primitive Methodist Papers) at City Road Methodist Book Room.
Home Office Papers:
H.O. 42. 49–203. 1800–20.
H.O. 40. 3–59. 1816–55.
H.O. 44. 1–39. 1820–61.
H.O. 45. O.S. 1841–50.
Place MSS.:
27808–27810. Political Societies.
27811–27817. London Corresponding Society.
27819–27822. Working Men's Associations, &c.
27823–27824. Schools and Institutions.
27835. Miscellaneous.
27789–27797. Political Narratives.
Vol. 47. Contains copies of the *Northern Star* (1848).
Vol. 64. Contains Chartist Circular (1839–41).
Vol. 66. Contains copies of the Charter (1839–40).

NEWSPAPERS

The Luddite Period, 1807–16

Leeds Intelligencer, 1807.
Leeds Mercury, 1807–16.
Nottingham Review, 1809 (1810–24 wanting).
Sheffield Iris, 1807.

The Radical Period, 1816–23

Birmingham Chronicle, 1819–21.
The Black Dwarf, 1817–24.
Cobbett's Weekly Register, 1818–22.
The Courier, 1818–21.
Derby Mercury, 1817–22.
Hull Advertiser and Exchange Gazette, 1818–23.
Hull Packet, 1818–23 (1820, 21, 22 wanting).
Lancaster Gazette, 1817–22.
Leeds Intelligencer, 1818–23.
Leeds Mercury, 1816–23.
Liverpool Courier, 1819 (one copy).
Liverpool Mercury, 1818–20.
Manchester Exchange Herald, 1819–22.
Manchester Gazette, 1819–22.
Manchester Guardian, 1821–22.
Manchester Mercury, 1818 (1819–26 wanting).
Manchester Observer, 1818–22 (becomes Wooler's *British Gazette and Manchester Observer* in 1821).
Morning Chronicle, 1818–20.
Morning Post, 1816–17.
Newcastle Chronicle, 1817–21.
Newcastle Courant, 1819–22.
Northampton Mercury, 1817–22.
Rockingham and Hull Weekly Advertiser, 1818–23 (1820, 21, 22 wanting).
Sherwin's Political Register, 1817–18.
The Times, 1816–22.
Tyne Mercury, 1818–22.
Wooler's British Gazette, 1819–23.
Worcester Journal, 1818–20.
York Chronicle, 1819.
York Herald and General Advertiser, 1818–23 (1821, 22 wanting).

The Political Unions Period, 1829–1836

Cobbett's Weekly Register, 1831–36.
Leeds Mercury, 1824–33.
Leeds Patriot, 1829–33.

Nottingham Review, 1825–30.
Poor Man's Guardian, 1831–35.
Sheffield Iris, 1828–30.
Trades Free Press, 1828.
True Sun, 1832–37.
Weekly Free Press, 1828–31.

THE CHARTIST PERIOD, 1836–50

Birmingham Advertiser, 1836–41.
Birmingham Gazette, 1836–40.
Birmingham Journal, 1836–47.
Bolton Chronicle, 1839–48.
Bolton Free Press, 1839–42.
Bradford Observer, 1839–48.
The Charter, 1839–40.
Halifax Express, 1839–41.
Halifax Guardian, 1839–48.
Leeds Mercury, 1839–48.
Leicester Chronicle, 1839–48.
Leicester Journal, 1839–48.
Leicester Mercury, 1839–48.
Leicester, Nottingham, and Derby Telegraph, 1839–42.
Liverpool Courier, 1839–42.
Manchester and Salford Advertiser, 1839–48.
Manchester Guardian, 1839–48.
Manchester Times, 1839–42.
Newcastle Courant, 1839–48.
Northern Liberator, 1837–40.
Northern Star, 1838–50.
Nottingham and Newark Mercury, 1839–48.
Nottingham Review, 1839–48.
Philanthropist, 1836–38.
Sheffield Independent, 1839–42.
Sheffield Iris, 1839–42.
Sheffield Patriot, 1839.
Sheffield Mercury, 1839–42.
Staffordshire Advertiser, 1839–42.
Staffordshire Examiner, 1839–42.
North Staffordshire Mercury, 1839–43.
Staffordshire Gazette, 1839.
Stockport Advertiser, 1839–48.
Stockport Chronicle, 1840–42.
York Herald, 1839–42.

TRADE UNIONS

Birmingham Journal, 1825–28.
Cobbett's Political Register, 1823–33.
Durham Advertiser, 1831–36.
Gateshead Observer, 1844.
Leeds Mercury, 1825–33.
Leeds Patriot, 1829–33.
Manchester Guardian, 1844.
Manchester Times, 1844.
Newcastle Advertiser, 1844.
Newcastle Chronicle, 1831–44.
Newcastle Courant, 1838–39.
Newcastle Standard, 1839.
Newcastle Journal, 1837–40.
Staffordshire Advertiser, 1844.
Sunderland Herald, Shields and Stockton Observer, 1831–36.
Ten Towns Messenger, 1844.
Tyne Mercury, 1831–44.
Trades Free Press, 1828.
Weekly Free Press, 1828–31.
The Voice of the People, 1831.

PAMPHLETS

Barker, Joseph. *Two Letters to the Church at Newcastle.*
Barker, J., and Others. *Who are the Cowards and Deceivers* (1844).
Beaumont, J. T. B. *Thoughts on the Causes and Cure of the Present Distress, with a Plan of Parliamentary Reform* (London, 1830).
Chartism. *The Chartist Mistake* (1870), *The Chartist's Friend*, by the Author of *Aids to Development* (1848).
Gilly, W. S. *Second Annual Report of the Committee of the Cottage Improvement Society for Northumberland* (1843). *The Peasantry of the Border, An Appeal on their behalf* (1841).
Hare, Edward. *Defence of the Scriptural Doctrine of Assurance* (Sheffield, 1809).
Hatton, William. *A Brief Account of the Rise and Progress of Local Preachers and of Local Preaching among the Methodists* (London, 1882).
History. *An Impartial History of Independent Methodism in the counties of Durham and Northumberland* (1819–24).
Hunt, Leigh. *An Attempt to shew the Folly and Danger of Methodism* (1809).
Kilham, A., and Thom. *Outlines of a Constitution Proposed for the Examination, Amendment and Acceptance of the Members of the Methodist New Itinerancy* (1797).

Larkin, E. R. *A Few Words on the Ten Hours Factory Question* (London, 1848). *Christian Sympathy*. A Sermon preached at Horbling, Lincolnshire on Obedience to the Queen's Letter on behalf of the distressed Manufacturers, July 24, 1842 (London, 1842).

A Layman. *An Apology for the Methodists of the New Connexion by a Trustee or a Layman* (1815).

A Minister's Wife. *Methodism and the Masses* (1858).

Strangers' Friend Society in Kingston-upon-Hull. Manchester Friend Society Annual Report of the Strangers' Friend Society in Manchester (1802–3).

Pamphlets, Anonymous.

Whig Radicalism v. Wesleyan Methodism (1841). *The Ecclesiastical Principles of Wesleyan Methodism. John Wesley Vindicated by Himself.* An Allegory (1839). *Report of Speeches delivered by Dr. Warren, Mr. Rowland and Mr. Graham in support of the Wesleyan Methodist Association at Darlington, Jan.* 21, 1836. *An Address to the Protestant Evangelical Churches of Great Britain and Ireland from Wesleyan Delegates* (1851). *Proposed Rules for the Temporary Government of the Branch Societies of Wesleyan Methodists. Temporary Rules of the Branch Societies of Wesleyan Methodists in the Eight London Circuits.*

Wawn, C. N. *The Benefit of Sunday Schools* (1818).

Webb, Samuel. *A Wesleyan Preacher's Thoughts on the Propriety of the Methodists attending Divine Service in the Church of England.*

Wesleyan Tracts. *A Collection of* 27 *Pamphlets on Methodism.*

Wesleyan Minister. *Prosperity for Members and Churches. Two Sermons* (1855).

Wood, Thomas. *Civil Government and Subjection and Obedience to the Higher Powers* (Wigan, 1796).

REPORTS

First Report of the Society for Bettering the Poor. 1797.

Report of the Society for Bettering the Poor. 1809.

The State of Children Employed in Manufactories of the United Kingdom. P.P.[1] Vol. iii. 1816.

The Employment of Boys in the Sweeping of Chimneys. P.P. Vol. vi. 1817.

Hansard's Parliamentary Debates. Vols. xxxv and xxxvi. 1817.

The Building of Additional Churches. Reports 1–30. 1821–50.

Artisans and Machinery. P.P. Vol. v. 1824.

The Laws Respecting Friendly Societies. P.P. Vol. iv. 1825.

Number of Parish Churches, and Places of Worship not of the Church of England. County of Lancaster. P.P. Vol. xix. 1830.

Number and Classes of Non-Resident Incumbents, and the Number of Resident Incumbents for 1827. P.P. Vol. xix. 1830.

Return of the Number of Justices of the Peace in each country, City and town, in Wales and England. P.P. Vol. xxxv. 1831–32.

Children in Factories. P.P. Vol. xv. 1831–32.

Observance of the Sabbath Day. P.P. Vol. vii. 1832.

Agriculture. P.P. Vol. v. 1833.

The Sale of Beer. P.P. Vol. xv. 1833.

First Report on Children in Factories. P.P. Vol. xx. 1833.

Second Report on Children in Factories. P.P. Vol. xxi. 1833.

Victualling House Licenses. P.P. Vol. xv. 1833.

Public Walks. P.P. Vol. xv. 1833.

The Petition of Frederick Young and Others. P.P. Vol. xiii. (This is the report on Policeman Popay.) 1833.

Cold Bath Fields Meeting. P.P. Vol. xiii. 1833.

Supplementary Report on Children in Factories. P.P. Vol. xix. Part I. 1834.

[1] P.P. means Parliamentary Papers.

Supplementary Report on Children in Factories. P.P. Vol. xx. Part ii. 1834.
Drunkenness. P.P. Vol. viii. 1834.
The State of Education. P.P. Vol. ix. 1834.
Hand Loom Weavers. P.P. Vol. xiii. 1835.
The State of the Established Church. P.P. Vol. xxxvi. 1836.
Number of Churches and Livings augmented in the Diocese of Durham by the late William Van Mildert, D.D., late Bishop of Durham, during the period of his Episcopacy. P.P. Vol. xl. 1836.
Number of Dissenting Meeting Houses and Roman Catholic Chapels in England and Wales. P.P. Vol. xl. 1836.
Combinations. P.P. Vol. viii. 1837–38.
Health of Towns. P.P. Vol. xi. 1840.
Employment of Children in Mines. P.P. Vol. xv. 1842.
Employment of Children in Mines. Appendix to the First Report. P.P. Vol. xvi. 1842.
Employment of Children in Mines. Appendix to the First Report. P.P. Vol. xvii. Part ii. 1842.
Employment of Women and Children in Agriculture. P.P. Vol. xii. 1843
Employment of Women and Children in Agriculture. P.P. Vol. xiii. 1843.
Employment of Children in Trades and Manufactories. Second Report. P.P. Vol. xiii. 1843.
Employment of Children in Trades and Manufactories. Appendix to Second Report. P.P. Vol. xiv. Part i. 1843.
Employment of Children in Trades and Manufactories. Appendix to Second Report. P.P. Vol. xv. Part ii. 1843.
Sanitary Condition of the Labouring Population of Great Britain. P.P. Vol. xii. 1843.
Midland Mining. First Report. P.P. Vol. xiii. 1843.
Commons Inclosure. P.P. Vol. v. 1844.
State of the Population in the Mining Districts. P.P. Vol. xvi. 1844.
State of Large Towns and Populous Districts. P.P. Vol. xvii. 1844.
State of the Population in Mining Districts. P.P. Vol. xxvii. 1845.
State of Large Towns and Populous Districts. P.P. Vol. xviii. Second Report. 1845.
State of the Population in Mining Districts. P.P. Vol. xxiv. 1846.
Railway Labourers. P.P. Vol. xiii. 1846.
State of the Population in Mining Districts. P.P. Vol. xvi. 1847.
Gases and Explosions in Collieries. P.P. Vol. xvi. 1847.
State of the Population in Mining Districts. P.P. Vol. xxi. 1848. Vol. xxii. 1849.
State of the Population in Mining Districts. P.P. Vol. xxiii. 1850.
Census of 1851. P.P. Vol. xviii. 1851.
Census of Religious Worship. P.P. Vol. lxxxix. 1852–53.
Dissenters Places of Worship. P.P. Vol. lxxviii. 1852–53.

Supplementary Report on Children in Factories. P.P. Vol. xx. Part II. 1834.
Handloom Weavers. P.P. Vol. viii. 1839.
The State of Education. P.P. Vol. ix. 1838.
Hand Loom Weavers. P.P. Vol. xxiii. 1840.
The State of the Established Church. P.P. Vol. xxxvii. 1836.
Number of Churches and Livings augmented in the Diocese of Durham by the late William Van Mildert, D.D., late Bishop of Durham, during the period of his Episcopacy. P.P. Vol. xl. 1836.
Number of Dissenting Meeting Houses and Roman Catholic Chapels in England and Wales. P.P. Vol. xl. 1836.
Combinations. P.P. Vol. viii. 1837-8.
Health of Towns. P.P. Vol. xi. 1840.
Employment of Children in Mines. P.P. Vol. xv. 1842.
Employment of Children in Mines. Appendix to the First Report. P.P. Vol. xvi. 1842.
Employment of Children in Mines. Appendix to the First Report. P.P. Vol. xvii. Part II. 1842.
Employment of Women and Children in Agriculture. P.P. Vol. xii. 1843.
Employment of Women and Children in Agriculture. P.P. Vol. xii. 1843.
Employment of Children in Trades and Manufactures. Second Report. P.P. Vol. xiii. 1843.
Employment of Children in Trades and Manufactures. Appendix to Second Report. P.P. Vol. xiv. Part I. 1843.
Employment of Children in Trades and Manufactures. Appendix to Second Report. P.P. Vol. xv. Part II. 1843.
Sanitary Condition of the Labouring Population of Great Britain. P.P. Vol. xii. 1842.
Midland Mining. First Report. P.P. Vol. xiii. 1843.
Combinations. P.P. Vol. vii. 1842.
State of the Population in the Mining Districts. P.P. Vol. xvi. 1844.
[illegible] and Populous Districts. P.P. Vol. xviii. 1844.
State of the Population in Mining Districts. P.P. Vol. xxvii. 1845.
State of Large Towns and Populous Districts. P.P. Vol. xviii. Second Report. 1845.
State of the Population in Mining Districts. P.P. Vol. xxiv. 1846.
Railway Labourers. P.P. Vol. xiii. 1846.
State of the Population in Mining Districts. P.P. Vol. xvi. 1847.
[illegible] in Collieries. P.P. Vol. xiv. 1849.
State of the Population in Mining Districts. P.P. Vol. xxii. 1848; Vol. xxii. 1849.
State of the Population in Mining Districts. P.P. Vol. xxiii. 1850.
Census. Population. P.P. Vol. xliii. 1852.
Census of Religion. Worship. P.P. Vol. lxxxix. 1852-3.
[illegible] P.P. Vol. lxxxix. [illegible]

INDEX